westermann

FiNALE Prüfungstraining

Zentralabitur 2020

Englisch

Nordrhein-Westfalen

Thomas Lehnen
Miriam Schulz
Claudia Schwarz-Brownbill

FiNALEonline.de

Liebe Abiturientin, lieber Abiturient,

FiNALEonline.de ist die optimale Ergänzung zu diesem Abiturtrainer. Hier finden Sie:
- die Original-Prüfungsaufgaben 2019 nach Eingabe des Codes: **EN2T2P6**
- eine Abi-Checkliste für die effektive Zeitplanung
- allgemeine Tipps zur Prüfungsvorbereitung

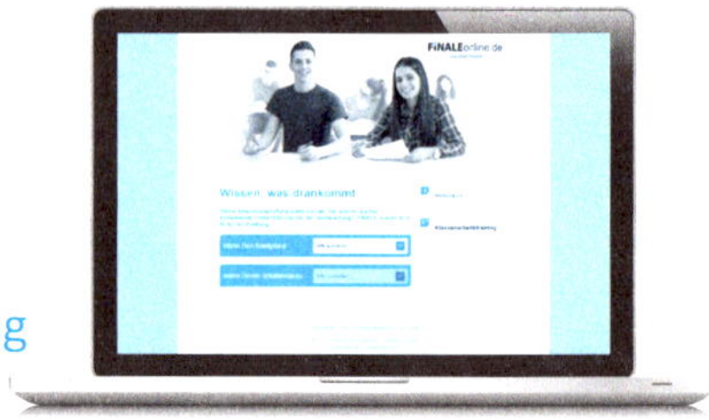

Einfach mal reinschauen: www.finaleonline.de

westermann GRUPPE

Druck A[1] / Jahr 2019
Alle Drucke der Serie A sind im Unterricht parallel verwendbar.

Redaktion: lüra – Klemt & Mues GbR, Wuppertal
Kontakt: finale@westermanngruppe.de
Layout: Druckreif! Sandra Grünberg, Braunschweig
Umschlaggestaltung: Gingco.Net, Braunschweig
Umschlagfoto: Peter Wirtz, Dormagen
Druck und Bindung: westermann druck GmbH, Braunschweig

ISBN 978-3-7426-**2017**-0

Inhaltsverzeichnis

Informationen und Tipps zur Prüfung

Basiswissen

Methoden der Textarbeit

Literarische Texte

Sach- und Gebrauchstexte

Sprachmittlung

Zieltextformate

Letter

Speech Script

Arbeiten mit *Finale*

Finale Prüfungstraining Englisch möchte Ihnen eine praxisnahe Hilfe zur Vorbereitung auf die Abiturprüfung sein. Im Praxis-Teil finden sich zu allen geforderten Themenbereichen authentische Aufgaben, die dem aktuell geltenden neuen Format entsprechen. Daneben finden Sie die Original-Prüfungsaufgaben 2018. Unter unseren Beispielaufgaben sind sowohl Beispiele für Grundkurse als auch für Leistungskurse. Im Abitur unterscheidet sich die Aufgabe für Leistungskurse von denen für Grundkurse einerseits durch den Textumfang, andererseits durch den Schwierigkeitsgrad der Texte, der sich in der Regel aus der Komplexität der Syntax und des Wortschatzes ergibt. Beide Kriterien spielen für Übungstexte keine große Rolle. Auch als Grundkursschülerin oder -schüler sind Sie durch den Englischunterricht mit längeren und komplexeren Texten vertraut. Als Leistungskursschülerin oder -schüler können Sie eine Textanalyse auch an kürzeren, einfacheren Texten üben. Die inhaltlichen Vorgaben sind für beide Kursarten weitgehend gleich.

Je eine Aufgabe zu einem literarischen Text und einem Sach- und Gebrauchstext ergänzt um eine Sprachmittlungs-Aufgabe zu einem deutschen Text wird kleinschrittig erarbeitet und schließt mit einer Musterlösung. Dies soll für Sie eine exemplarische Hilfe sein auf dem Weg von den Ausgangstexten über das Textverständnis, die Methodik der Textanalyse, die Evaluation und die Sprachmittlung hin zur Gliederung und sprachlichen Darstellung der Zieltexte. Den weiteren Aufgabenbeispielen folgen Bewertungskriterien ganz in der Form, wie Ihre Lehrerinnen und Lehrer sie zur Korrektur der Abiturarbeiten an die Hand bekommen. Sie dienen Ihnen zur Selbstkontrolle in Ihrem fortschreitenden Prüfungstraining. Zu Ihrer Orientierung haben wir auch entsprechende Punkte vergeben. „Gummipunkte", Punkte für ein „weiteres aufgabenbezogenes Kriterium", wie es sie im Abitur gibt, erschienen uns für die Beispielaufgaben jedoch wenig sinnvoll.

Geschrieben wurde dieses Buch im Jahr 2019, damit es frühzeitig zur Vorbereitung auf das Abitur 2020 beitragen kann. Die zu diesem Zeitpunkt aktuellen Abituraufgaben 2018 werden jeweils mit einer Musterlösung angeboten. Original-Schülerlösungen unterliegen weiterhin der Geheimhaltung und können nicht veröffentlicht werden. Dennoch versuchen wir, unsere Musterlösung auf der Grundlage unserer Korrekturarbeit der Abiturarbeiten 2018 zu erstellen. Sie greifen die tatsächlich gegebenen Probleme und Fehlerschwerpunkte der Abiturientinnen und Abiturienten auf.

Der eindringliche Wunsch unserer Abiturienten nach einer kompakten inhaltlichen Übersicht über die verbindlich vorgegebenen Themen des Zentralabiturs hat uns bewogen, diese relevanten Inhalte im Kapitel „Basiswissen" zusammenzustellen. Natürlich kann dieses weder den Englischunterricht der Qualifikationsphase noch dessen Vor- und Nachbereitung ersetzen. Es hilft Ihnen jedoch, das im Unterricht erworbene Wissen zu strukturieren und in seinen Grundzügen abzurufen. Um den Umgang mit dem thematischen Vokabular zu vertiefen, ist dieser Teil in englischer

Sprache geschrieben und wird durch Glossare zum thematischen Vokabular ergänzt. Bei den amerikanischen Texten wird auch in den Erläuterungen dazu amerikanisches Englisch verwendet, ansonsten wird die britische Schreibweise benutzt.

Die sprachliche Leistung spielt in der Fremdsprache trotz aller inhaltlich-thematischer Kompetenz immer noch die herausragende Rolle. Während man in der Abiturklausur für den Inhalt maximal 60 Punkte erreichen kann, erhält man für eine perfekte sprachliche Leistung 90 Punkte. Ein sicherer Umgang mit den Strukturen und Wörtern der englischen Sprache ist also unabdingbar. Deshalb haben wir in *Finale* ein Kapitel zur sprachlichen Leistung aufgenommen, in dem es vor allem um kommunikative Textgestaltung und Ausdrucksvermögen geht, die im Zentralabitur – wie die sprachliche Richtigkeit – mit jeweils 30 Punkten bewertet werden.

Wir wünschen Ihnen viel Erfolg!

Informationen und Tipps zur Prüfung

Inhalte des Faches Englisch in der gymnasialen Oberstufe

Gelegentlich beklagen sich Schülerinnen und Schüler und auch Eltern über die Anforderungen und Inhalte des Englischunterrichts, insbesondere der Klausuren und der schriftlichen Abiturprüfung. Textanalyse und kreative Textproduktion erscheinen ihnen nicht als Fertigkeiten, die man im Leben braucht. Auf Unverständnis trifft gelegentlich auch die Bewertung – hat man doch gerade mit einem Australier gechattet, der sich anerkennend zu den Englischkenntnissen äußerte, oder im Urlaub einen Engländer getroffen, mit dem man sich prima bei einer Cola unterhalten konnte. Die Fähigkeit, sich mit anderen unterhalten zu können, ist also offensichtlich nicht der alleinige Aspekt, der in der Oberstufe und im Abitur bewertet wird.
Natürlich ist es primäres Ziel des Englischunterrichts, **kommunikative Kompetenz** zu vermitteln, also Schülerinnen und Schüler in die Lage zu versetzen, im englischsprachigen Ausland oder auch mit dem Englischen als *lingua franca* angemessen zu kommunizieren. Sieht man sich den Kernlehrplan für die Sekundarstufe I an, so wird man schnell erkennen, dass selbst die geforderten Kompetenzen für das Ende der Sekundarstufe I weit über die Kommunikation in Alltagssituationen hinausgehen. Zur Vorbereitung der Schülerinnen und Schüler auf ein Studium an der Hochschule, auf einen beruflichen Weg in Großunternehmen oder international tätigen mittelständischen Unternehmen orientiert sich der Kernlehrplan Englisch am Leitziel der interkulturellen Handlungsfähigkeit. Deshalb behandelt der Englischunterricht soziokulturell und global bedeutsame Themen, die in Texten und Medien dargestellt werden.

In diesem Zusammenhang spricht der Kernlehrplan von verschiedenen **Kompetenzbereichen:**
- funktionale kommunikative Kompetenz
- interkulturelle kommunikative Kompetenz
- Text- und Medienkompetenz
- Sprachlernkompetenz
- Sprachbewusstheit

Funktional kommunikative Kompetenzen sind Leseverstehen, Schreiben, Hör-/Hörsehverstehen, Sprechen und Sprachmittlung. Außerdem zählt man die Verfügbarkeit sprachlicher Mittel dazu, d. h. Wortschatz, Grammatik, Rechtschreibung und Aussprache.
Interkulturelle kommunikative Kompetenz ist das Zusammenspiel von Wissen, Einstellung und Bewusstheit. Vor dem Hintergrund ihrer eigenen Kultur sollen Schülerinnen und Schüler in der Lage sein, sowohl Empathie als auch kritische Distanz gegenüber kulturellen Besonderheiten zu entwickeln.
Für den Erwerb von **Text- und Medienkompetenz** vermittelt der Englischunterricht eine Fülle von Teilkompetenzen. Der Begriff Text umfasst hier – wie immer –

Sachtexte sowie literarische Texte, Filme, Bilder, Diagramme, Statistiken, Grafiken etc. Das Kapitel „Methoden der Textarbeit“ wird sich eingehend damit befassen.

Für den **Umgang mit Texten** in der Q1 und der Q2 gibt der Kernlehrplan folgendes vor:

Sach- und Gebrauchstexte

Texte der privaten und öffentlichen Kommunikation
- Brief, Kommentar, Leitartikel, politische Rede, Leserbrief, Werbeanzeige

Texte in wissenschaftsorientierter Dimension
- Lexikonauszüge, ein längerer Sachbuchauszug

Texte in berufsorientierter Dimension
- Stellenanzeigen, PR-Materialien, Exposé, Protokoll

literarische Texte

lyrische Texte
- zeitgenössische Gedichte, Gedichte in historischer Dimension

narrative Texte
- ein zeitgenössischer Roman, *short stories*

dramatische Texte
- Auszüge aus einem oder aus verschiedenen Shakespeare-Dramen, ein zeitgenössisches Drama, Auszüge aus einem Drehbuch

diskontinuierlicher Texte

Text-Bild-Kombinationen
- Bilder, Cartoons

Grafiken
- Tabellen, Karten, Diagramme

medial vermittelte Texte

auditive Formate
- *radio features/podcasts,* Auszüge aus einem Hörbuch

audiovisuelle Formate
- ein Spielfilm, *documentary/feature, news*

digitale Texte
- *blogs/video blogs,* Beiträge in Internetforen

Sprachlernkompetenz beinhaltet das selbstständige Gestalten des Lernens durch das Entwickeln von Strategien aber auch durch den sicheren Umgang mit Hilfsmitteln, z. B. mit dem Wörterbuch.

Sprachbewusstheit beinhaltet Einsichten zum Beispiel in Varianten des Sprachgebrauchs, in verschiedene Register und Stilebenen, in Beziehungen zwischen Sprache und Kultur, aber auch die Bewusstheit von sprachlicher Manipulation.

Obligatorische Themen und Inhalte für das Zentralabitur

Das Ministerium gibt auf der Grundlage der Kernlehrpläne Vorgaben für eine Schwerpunktsetzung im Hinblick auf das Zentralabitur. Konkret gelten für das Abitur 2020 die folgenden Fokussierungen zu der im Kernlehrplan festgelegten Obligatorik. (Die vollständige Übersicht ist zu finden auf der Website des Ministeriums: https://www.standardsicherung.schulministerium.nrw.de/cms/zentralabitur-gost/faecher/getfile.php?file=4586)

Inhaltliche Schwerpunkte

Amerikanischer Traum – Visionen und Lebenswirklichkeiten in den USA

- Freedom and success (Grundkurs)
- Freedom ans equality (Leistungskurs)

Das Vereinigte Königreich im 21. Jahrhundert – Selbstverständnis zwischen Tradition und Wandel

- Tradition and change in politics and society
  - monarchy and modern democracy (Leistungskurs)
  - multicultural society

Postkolonialismus – Lebenswirklichkeiten in einem weiteren anglophonen Kulturraum

- India – faces of a rising nation (Grundkurs)
- India – from postcolonial experience to rising nation (Leistungskurs)

Chancen und Risiken der Globalisierung

- Globalization and global challenges
  - The role of the United States in international politics at the beginning of the 21st century (Leistungskurs)
- Economic and ecological issues (Leistungskurs)
- The impact of globalization on culture and communication (Grundkurs)

Literatur und Medien in ihrer Bedeutung für den Einzelnen und die Gesellschaft

- The impact of Shakespearean drama on young audiences today:
  - Study of extracts and film scenes (comedy or tragedy) (Leistungskurs)
  - Study of film scenes (Grundkurs)
- Visions of the future – utopia and dystopia (Grundkurs)

Fortschritt und Ethik in der modernen Gesellschaft (Leistungskurs)

- Visions of the future – Utopia and dystopia
- Ethical issues of scientific and technological progress

Lebensentwürfe, Studium, Ausbildung, Beruf international – Englisch als *lingua franca*

- Studying and working in a globalized world

Zieltextformate

In der dritten Teilaufgabe des Klausurteils A haben die Schülerinnen und Schüler die Wahl zwischen einer Stellungnahme und einer kreativen Aufgabe. Dazu wird Vertrautheit mit folgenden Textformaten vorausgesetzt:

- letter (formal letter, letter to the editor, personal letter)
- speech script (talk, public/formal speech, [debate] statement)
- newspaper article (report, comment)

im Leistungskurs zusätzlich:

- (written) interview
- Ausgestaltung, Fortführung oder Ergänzung eines literarischen Ausgangstextes (narrative Texte, zusätzlich im Leistungskurs: dramatische Texte, film scripts)

Die Fachkonferenzen jeder einzelnen Schule gestalten ihre Unterrichtssequenzen auf der Grundlage der geforderten Inhalte und der vom Lehrplan geforderten Obligatorik.

Grundsätze der Abiturprüfung

Aufgabenarten

Aus der Oberstufe sind Ihnen verschiedene Klausurvarianten bekannt. Von den fünf Kompetenzen Leseverstehen, Schreiben, Sprechen, Hör-/Hörsehverstehen und Sprachmittlung werden immer drei geprüft. So kennen Sie etwa die Textanalyse mit zusätzlicher Sprachmittlungsaufgabe oder die Filmanalyse mit zusätzlichem Multiple-Choice-Test zum Leseverstehen oder gar drei verschiedene Einzelaufgaben zu Leseverstehen, Schreiben und Sprachmittlung.

Für das Abitur 2020 ist vom Ministerium nur eine Aufgabenart vorgesehen, nämlich Schreiben und Leseverstehen in Klausurteil A, Sprachmittlung in Klausurteil B. Sie haben die Wahl zwischen zwei Aufgaben, die Ihnen im Klausurteil A entweder einen literarischen Text oder einen Sach- und Gebrauchstext vorlegen. Der Text kann in beiden Fällen durch eine Grafik, einen Cartoon o. Ä. ergänzt werden. Klausurteil B ist in beiden Fällen ein deutschsprachiger Sachtext.

Die Aufgabe des **Klausurteils A** besteht aus einem Text mit den Ihnen bekannten drei Teilaufgaben *(comprehension – analysis – evaluation/re-creation of text).* In der dritten Teilaufgabe *(evaluation/re-creation of text)* wird Ihnen eine Wahlmöglichkeit zwischen einer kreativen Aufgabe und einer Stellungnahme gegeben. Die Übungsklausuren im Kapitel „Beispiele für Prüfungsaufgaben“ bieten beide Aufgabentypen, meist geben sie eine Wahlmöglichkeit.

Die Sprachmittlung, **Teilaufgabe B,** kann durchaus der erste Teil der Klausur sein, denn die Teilaufgaben der Schreibaufgabe (in der Regel die Stellungnahme) können sich auch zusätzlich auf die deutsche Textvorlage beziehen. Wir haben solche Fälle auch in unseren Beispielaufgaben.

Der englische Text hat im Leistungskurs einen Umfang von maximal 560 Wörtern, im Grundkurs maximal 420 Wörter. Der deutsche Text umfasst im Leistungskurs maximal 440 Wörter, im Grundkurs 330 Wörter. Als Ausgangstexte eignen sich nur authentische Texte, d. h. sie dürfen nicht adaptiert oder stark gekürzt sein.

Anforderungsbereiche

Die Teilaufgaben der Prüfungsklausuren entsprechen den folgenden Anforderungsbereichen, die Sie bereits aus der Qualifikationsphase kennen.

Anforderungsbereich I: *comprehension/orientation/context*
- Wiedergabe der zentralen Aussagen eines Textes (meist Inhaltsangabe),
- Einordnung des Textes in einen Kontext unter Verwendung von Hintergrundwissen,
- Einleitung eines komplexen Textes.

Anforderungsbereich II: *analysis*
- Anwendung von Fachmethoden: textanalytische Verfahren, Einsatz von Lesetechniken,
- gezielte Anwendung von Kenntnissen und Wissen – z. B. soziokulturelles oder metasprachliches Wissen (= Wissen über Sprache),
- exakte Arbeit am sprachlichen Detail, Belegen und Zitieren, problemlösende Argumentation.

Anforderungsbereich III: *evaluation*
für die analytisch-interpretierende Aufgabenstellung:
- Bewertung der Problemlösung, Einordnen der Ergebnisse in einen größeren Zusammenhang,
- persönliche Stellungnahme, eigene Meinung (erst hier und nicht etwa in AFB II oder I).

Anforderungsbereich III: *evaluation/re-creation of text*
für die anwendungs-/produktionsorientierte Aufgabenstellung:
- Umsetzung, Bewertung, Reflexion der Problematik des Ausgangstextes bzw. der Analyse im Aufgabenbereich II in Form einer kreativen Aufgabe: Perspektivwechsel (Sicht einer anderen Figur),
- Füllen von Leerstellen (Weitererzählen, neues Ende),
- Textsortenwechsel (Brief an Protagonisten, Leserbrief, Brief an *agony aunt,* Tagebucheintrag, Dialog, etc.).

Die einzelnen Anforderungsbereiche sollen nicht in drei voneinander unabhängigen Texten behandelt werden. Der Zieltext ist ein geschlossener, kohärenter Text, der sich als Essay in seinen drei Teilen etwa in eine Hinführung zum Thema, einen Hauptteil und eine Schlussbetrachtung gliedert. Eine kreative Teilaufgabe wird sich naheliegenderweise nicht in den geschlossenen Zieltext eingliedern, da sie in der Regel ein völlig anderes Textformat hat.

Operatoren

Für die Formulierung der Aufgaben gibt es klare Vorgaben. Verben für die Arbeitsanweisungen (= Operatoren) müssen in ihrer exakten Bedeutung verstanden werden. Eine ungefähre Ahnung, was gefordert ist, reicht keinesfalls aus!
Die folgende Operatorenübersicht ist der Website des Ministeriums entnommen. Die mittlere Spalte definiert die genaue Wortbedeutung des Verbs, die dritte Spalte gibt jeweils ein Beispiel für eine Aufgabenstellung.
Beachten Sie, dass die Operatoren im Anforderungsbereich I vor allem deutlich machen, welcher Umfang der inhaltlichen Wiedergabe von Ihnen verlangt wird. „Outline", „summarize" oder „write a summary" verlangen eine knappe Wiedergabe des Textes oder auch nur einer relevanten Textpassage. „Describe" oder „point out" hingegen erwarten eine ausführliche Beschreibung bzw. Erläuterung des im Text dargestellten Sachverhalts. Letzteres kommt vor allem infrage, wenn der Ausgangstext sehr komplex ist, wie z. B. eine Erörterung, oder sehr dicht, wie beispielsweise ein Gedicht. Ihr Textverständnis weisen Sie dann nicht durch eine knappe Zusammenfassung, sondern durch eine Beschreibung oder Erläuterung in Ihren eigenen Worten nach.

TIPP

Achten Sie darauf, dass Sie, auch wenn Sie zu einer Skizzierung *(outline)* oder Zusammenfassung *(summary)* des Inhalts aufgefordert werden, stets die wesentlichen Inhaltspunkte benennen. Eine abstraktere, allgemeiner gehaltene Zusammenfassung kann durchaus eleganter sein, wird aber durch den Punktekatalog der Bewertungskriterien möglicherweise nicht erfasst.

Die Übersicht enthält Operatoren, die für das im Abitur vorgesehene Klausurformat Schreiben mit integriertem Leseverstehen in Klausurteil A und Sprachmittlung in Klausurteil B infrage kommen.
Weitere Operatoren für weitere Kompetenzbereiche sind auf der Website des Ministeriums zu finden („Konstruktionshinweise – Neue Aufgabenformate in den modernen Fremdsprachen", https://www.standardsicherung.schulministerium.nrw.de/abitur-gost/fach.php?fach=3).
Die Operatoren können unterschiedlichen Anforderungsbereichen zugeordnet werden.

Klausurteil A (Schreiben, Leseverstehen integriert)

Operator	Erläuterung	Illustrierendes Aufgabenbeispiel	AFB
analyse	describe and explain in detail	Analyze the opposing views on class held by the two protagonists. Examine the author's use of language.	II
assess	express a well-founded opinion on the nature or quality of sb./sth.	Assess the importance of standards in education.	III
evaluate	express a well-founded opinion on the nature or quality of sb./sth.	Evaluate the author's view of the present impact of the American Dream …	III
examine	describe and explain in detail	Examine the opposing views on social class held by the two protagonists.	II
give/write a characterization of	provide a thorough analysis of a character	Characterize/Write a characterization of the principal figures in the play.	II
comment (on)	state one's opinion clearly and support one's view with evidence or reasons	Comment on the writer's view of gender roles.	III
compare	show similarities and differences	Compare the attitude of the two characters towards war.	II
describe	give a detailed account of what sb./sth. is like	Describe the way the playwright creates an atmosphere of suspense.	I II
discuss	give arguments or reasons for and against, especially to come to a well-founded conclusion	Discuss the message of the cartoon, referring to work done on the British monarchy.	III
explain	make sth. clear by giving reasons for and details, aspects of sth.	Explain the protagonist's obsession with money.	II
illustrate	use examples to explain or make clear	Illustrate the way in which according to the author school life in Britain differs from that in Germany.	II

interpret	explain the meaning, purpose or message of sth.	Interpret the sonnet, focusing on the way structure and imagery are used to express the speaker's insight into the nature of time.	II
outline	give the main features, structure or general principles of sth.	Outline the author's views on love, marriage and divorce.	I
point out	find and explain certain aspects	Point out the author's main ideas on ...	I
state	present the main aspects of sth. briefly and clearly	State the author's key reasons for taking a gap year.	I
summarize, sum up	give a concise account of the main points or ideas of a text, issue or topic	Summarize/Sum up the information about green energy given in the text.	I
write (+ text type)	produce a text with specific features	Write the ending of the story/a letter to the editor/a dialogue, etc. Write an interior monologue that reflects the character's view of the situation and her/his feelings.	III

Klausurteil B Sprachmittlung isoliert

Die Aufgabenstellung für die Sprachmittlung enthält einen situativen Kontext mit Hinweisen zu Adressat und Zieltextformat.

Operator	**Erläuterung**	**Illustrierendes Aufgabenbeispiel**
explain	make sth. clear taking into account culture-related differences if necessary	Based on the text on environmental policy explain the principle of waste separation in Germany in an email to your British friend.
outline	give a concise account of the main points or ideas of a text, clarifying culture-related aspects if necessary	Outline Mr. Liu's career in Germany in an article for your international school project's website on Successful Immigrants.
present	give a concise account of the main points or ideas of a text, clarifying culture-related aspects if necessary	For an international school project in the EU, present the relevant information on the image of migrants in German media in a formal email to your partner school in Spain.

summarize, sum up	give a concise account of the main points or ideas of a text, clarifying culture-related aspects if necessary	Sum up Manuel's views on working and living as a gap year student in India for your blog. Where necessary add information which might help to avoid possible misunderstandings.
write (+ text type)	produce a text with specific features	Using the information in the German text write an article in English for your project website in which you inform your Polish partners how to get a sports scholarship at a German university.

Bewertung

Für die Bewertung wird den Lehrerinnen und Lehrern ein Raster mit Bewertungskriterien an die Hand gegeben, sowohl für die sprachliche als auch für die inhaltliche Leistung. Es können bei einer Abiturklausur insgesamt 150 Punkte erreicht werden, davon 90 für die Darstellungsleistung (Sprache) und 60 für den Inhalt. Dabei ist die Verteilung der Punkte auf die verschiedenen Anforderungsbereiche immer gleich.

Klausurteil A (Schreiben/Leseverstehen)

Anforderungsbereich I :	12 Punkte
Anforderungsbereich II:	16 Punkte
Anforderungsbereich III:	14 Punkte
Klausurteil B (Sprachmittlung):	18 Punkte
Für die Gesamtbewertung der Abiturklausur gibt das Ministerium die folgende Tabelle vor.	
Gesamtpunkte Inhalt:	**60 Punkte**

Grundsätze für die Bewertung (Notenfindung)

Für die Zuordnung der Notenstufen zu den Punktzahlen ist folgende Tabelle zu verwenden:

Note	Punkte	Erreichte Punktzahl
sehr gut plus	15	150 – 143
sehr gut	14	142 – 135
sehr gut minus	13	134 – 128
gut plus	12	127 – 120
gut	11	119 – 113
gut minus	10	112 – 105
befriedigend plus	9	104 – 98
befriedigend	8	97 – 90
befriedigend minus	7	89 – 83
ausreichend plus	6	82 – 75
ausreichend	5	74 – 68
ausreichend minus	4	67 – 58
mangelhaft plus	3	57 – 49
mangelhaft	2	48 – 40
mangelhaft minus	1	39 – 30
ungenügend	0	29 – 0

TIPP zum Punktesammeln

Die Wertigkeit des Anforderungsbereiches III darf man nicht unterschätzen. Mit 14 Punkten ist er fast so gewichtig wie Anforderungsbereich II. Halten Sie sich mit der Analyse nicht so lange auf, dass Ihnen für eine Stellungnahme nur noch wenige Minuten bleiben. Das würde Sie viele Punkte kosten.
Überdies: Wenn Ihre Stärken nicht in der Textanalyse liegen, Sie aber aus anderen Fächern wie Erdkunde oder Biologie so viel Sachkenntnis haben, dass Sie qualitativ hochwertig zu Sachthemen Position beziehen können, dann setzen Sie dort Ihren persönlichen Schwerpunkt!

Die mündliche Abiturprüfung im Fach Englisch

Während einige von Ihnen Englisch als schriftliches Abiturfach gewählt haben, werden andere sich für Englisch als 4. Abiturfach entschieden haben und damit eine mündliche Abiturprüfung ablegen müssen.
Für den Fall, dass Sie Englisch als 1. bis 3. Abiturfach gewählt haben und Ihre Leistungen in der schriftlichen Abiturprüfung mehr als 3,75 Punkte von Ihrer Vornote abweichen, werden Sie ebenfalls an einer zusätzlich mündlichen Prüfung teilnehmen müssen.
In bestimmten Fällen besteht auch die Möglichkeit, die Abiturnote durch die Teilnahme an einer freiwilligen mündlichen Prüfung zu verbessern.
Ganz egal, welcher Fall für Sie von Bedeutung ist: Die Vorbereitung und der Ablauf der mündlichen Prüfung im Fach Englisch ist immer gleich.

Die mündliche Prüfung im Fach Englisch dauert insgesamt **mindestens 20,** aber **höchstens 30 Minuten** und ist in zwei Prüfungsteile aufgeteilt, deren Dauer ungefähr gleich lang ist.
Vor Beginn der Prüfung haben Sie **30 Minuten Zeit,** das Ihnen von Ihrem Fachlehrer oder Ihrer –lehrerin für den ersten Prüfungsteil vorgelegte **Material vorzubereiten.** Als Hilfsmittel stehen Ihnen hier ein **ein- und zweisprachiges Wörterbuch** und **gegebenenfalls ein herkunftssprachliches Wörterbuch** zur Verfügung. Die Notizen, die Sie hier anfertigen, dürfen Sie mit in die Prüfung nehmen und als Grundlage für Ihren Vortrag nutzen.

Anders als im schriftlichen Abitur können Sie hier **nicht** zwischen verschiedenen Materialien auswählen.
Das Material, dass Ihnen von Ihrem Fachlehrer oder Ihrer –lehrerin vorgelegt wird, stellt einen **Bezug zu den Themenfeldern der Qualifikationsphase** her. Zur häuslichen Vorbereitung verweisen wir hier auf die Kapitel zum Basiswissen auf den Seiten 20 bis 78.

Im **ersten Prüfungsteil** sollen Sie – auf Basis des Ihnen zur Vorbereitung vorgelegten Materials – **einen zusammenhängenden und weitgehend freien Vortrag halten, selbstständig** eine **nachvollziehbare Argumentation** entwickeln und **eine Einordnung in den entsprechenden Themenkomplex** vornehmen.
Grundsätzlich ist der erste Prüfungsteil nichts anderes als eine „mündliche Version" einer Klausur. Daher empfehlen wir Ihnen, die in diesem Buch enthaltenen Klausuren zur Vorbereitung auf die mündliche Prüfung durchzuarbeiten.
Im Grunde bestehen **zwei Möglichkeiten, wie das** von Ihnen vorzubereitende **Material aussehen kann.**
Es können Ihnen **ein oder mehrere Texte beziehungsweise ein längeres Zitat** mit einem Wortumfang von **ca. 200 bis 300 Wörtern** vorgelegt werden. Bei den Texten kann es sich um **literarische Texte oder** um **Sach- und Gebrauchstexte** handeln.
Ihr Fachlehrer oder Ihre –lehrerin kann Ihnen aber auch **eine oder mehrere visu-**

elle Darstellungen (Diagramm, Grafik, Cartoon, Statistik, Bild) vorlegen, die er/sie **gegebenenfalls um** einen **Text ergänzt.**

Im **zweiten Prüfungsteil** wird Ihnen **kein weiteres Material** vorgelegt. Gegenstand dieses Prüfungsteils sind **ein weiterer bzw. mehrere weitere Themenkomplexe zu den Themenfeldern der Qualifikationsphase.**
Hier sollen Sie zeigen, dass Sie **größere Zusammenhänge erkennen und herstellen** können.

Da neben Ihrer inhaltlichen Leistung auch Ihre sprachliche Leistung bewertet wird, sei an dieser Stelle nochmals auf die Listen mit nützlichen Wörtern und Wendungen im Buch (ab S. 207) verwiesen.
Beachten Sie auch die Strategien zur Wortschatzarbeit und Vermeidung „gängiger" Fehler.
Achten Sie in beiden Prüfungsteilen darauf, dass Ihre Ausführungen für die Prüfungskommission verständlich und nachvollziehbar sind.
Bemühen Sie sich darum, im ersten Prüfungsteil Ihre Gedanken und Anmerkungen möglichst strukturiert und frei vorzutragen.
Nutzen Sie die Vorbereitungszeit dazu, Ihre Notizen zu strukturieren. Selbstverständlich dürfen und sollen Sie auf diese zurückgreifen, aber lesen Sie bitte nicht einfach nur alles von Ihrem Notizzettel ab.

Basiswissen

Freedom and Justice – Myths and Realities

Concepts of the American Dream

The USA

The USA was – and still is – a country of unlimited opportunities, where people can work their way "from rags to riches". It has attracted millions of both legal and illegal immigrants over the centuries, who hoped to find a better life there without the kind of persecution or obstacles they had to face in their home countries.

Keyword:

The American Dream: There is no single definition of what the American Dream actually is, as it varies for each and every American.
The term was first used by James Truslow Adams, an American historian, in his book *The Epic of America,* in 1931: "[The] American Dream [is] the dream of a land in which life should be better and richer and fuller for every man with opportunity for each according to his ability or achievement."

In the following pages we are going to take a look at some of the key concepts generally associated with the American Dream, many of which are often touched upon in political speeches.
Please note that these key concepts often overlap and are closely related.

Freedom

The first thing many immigrants saw when they came by ship to New York City during the 19th and the first half of the 20th century, was the Statue of Liberty, which is located on Liberty Island.

The Statue of Liberty

- given to the USA as a gift from France in 1886, to celebrate the first 100 years of American independence from Britain (the centennial)
- a robed woman, holding a lit torch in her right and a tablet in her left hand, showing the date of the Declaration of Independence (July 4, 1776)
- underneath her right foot the remains of broken shackles can be seen
- one of the most famous American icons, symbolizing enlightenment, independence, liberty and freedom
- the theme of Emma Lazarus' famous poem "The New Colossus" (1883), which can be seen on a bronze plaque inside the statue
- located in Upper New York Bay, just like Ellis Island

Ellis Island

- the place where most immigrants first set foot on American s
- an island of hopes but also an island of tears for a number of i
  of them were detained there for legal or medical reasons or eve
  home countries
- the gateway to a new – better – life for the majority of immigra ts
- a federal immigration station from 1892 to 1954

The Puritans

The Puritans' beliefs and values had a lasting impact on New England society:
- towards the end of the 16th century some English Protestants felt that Protestantism in England was not much different from Catholicism
- decided to leave England, seeking their luck elsewhere
- first settled in Holland (1608), but moved back to England
- wished to remain English subjects but free to worship God the way they wanted to
- intention: to purify the Church of England, not to leave it
- September 1620: a group of 102 people left England for America, sailed on a ship called the Mayflower, arrived in America 65 days later, in a bay they called Plymouth Bay.

The New Canaan

In the Bible Canaan was the land God promised to the Israelites. God ordered Moses to lead the people from captivity in Egypt to Canaan – "a land of milk and honey". America sees itself in this tradition. The idea of America as the "New Canaan", the land of milk and honey, is closely linked to the idea of "manifest destiny".

Manifest Destiny/The Frontier

Manifest Destiny

The term "Manifest Destiny" was coined by the American journalist John L. O'Sullivan in 1839:
- stands for the belief that America is the one nation ordered by God to expand across the North American continent
- *The Great Nation of Futurity* by John L. O'Sullivan: "[America is] the nation of progress, of individual freedom, of universal enfranchisement." According to him the American people have been chosen "... to establish on earth the moral dignity and salvation of man – the immutable truth and beneficence of God."[1]
- America = a country that is superior to all other countries
- stresses virtue of the American people, as they are the ones to establish moral rules and values across the globe.

1 aus: "The Great Nation of Futurity," *The United States Democratic Review*, Volume 6, Issue 23, pp. 426 – 430.

American patriotism is deeply rooted in the concept of "Manifest Destiny".
The concept of "Manifest Destiny" is closely linked to the concept of the frontier.

The frontier

- the expansion of the American nation from coast to coast, pushing the borderline between civilization and wilderness further and further back
- Pacific coast was reached in the 2nd half of the 19th century
- after this mission new challenges – new frontiers – were needed, e.g. space exploration (in particular the moon landing in 1969), scientific and technological progress

Life, liberty and the pursuit of happiness

Declaration of Independence

- written in 1776 by Thomas Jefferson
- all American citizens are created equal: "We hold these truths to be self-evident, that all men are created equal, that they are endowed by their Creator with certain unalienable rights, that among these are life, liberty and the pursuit of happiness."
- possibility for every American (at first, women were excluded from this definition) to lead his/her life the way he/she wants to, making his/her own personal dreams come true
- stresses the rights of the individual, while at the same time taking the rights of others into consideration
- 1776: the thirteen colonies declared their independence from England, and were, therefore, at war with England
- Declaration of Independence questioned the rights of the British king, George III, in that it stated that everyone was created equal (quite revolutionary at the time)
- The fact that the new American government was to be radically different from that of the British king was pointed out in the preamble to the American constitution.

American Constitution

- written in 1787
- new ideas of a democratic state stated in the **preamble** of the constitution: "We the People of the United States, in Order to form a more perfect Union[2], establish Justice, ensure domestic Tranquility, provide for the common defense, promote the general Welfare, and secure the Blessings of Liberty to ourselves and our Posterity, do ordain and establish this Constitution for the United States of America."

Bill of Rights

- first ten amendments to the American Constitution
- written because some delegates feared that the new American government would

2 Barack Obama took up the idea of "a more perfect union" in a speech he delivered on May 28, 2008, in which he elaborated on the issues of race and inequality in the USA.

threaten everyone's ability to achieve personal freedom and the pursuit of happiness
- First Congress of the United States originally proposed twelve amendments in 1789, ten of which were added to the constitution as a preamble
- amendments known as the Bill of Rights
- guarantee America's citizens certain inalienable rights, e.g. freedom of religion, freedom of speech and the press as well as the right to bear arms

The American Dream today

Keywords:

Multicultural society: a society where various ethnic groups and their cultural heritage are accepted in their own right

Salad bowl: the various ethnicities living in the United States adding their own traditions, cultural values, etc. to the American people; the various heritages do not merge into one, but stay distinct ("unity in diversity")

Melting pot: the various ethnic groups do not retain their cultural heritage but amalgamate into one new nation
The term first appeared in an essay by Jean de Crèvecoeur entitled "Letters from an American farmer" in 1782.
The term "salad bowl" is now considered to be more politically correct.

- The American Dream itself has come to be seen more critically.
- A considerable number of critics regard the American Dream as an illusion, as not everyone has access to the possibilities usually associated with it.
- Examples of American nightmares are the Vietnam War, September 11, 2001, and the financial crisis starting in 2008.

In order to prevent an influx of illegal immigrants from Southern American countries, the Trump administration established a "zero tolerance" policy which allowed Border Patrol officials to separate children from their parents and to place them in foster families or orphanages. Their parents were transported to adult detention centres. This "zero tolerance" policy, which was traumatic for both parents and children, was heavily criticized by human rights activists and child welfare advocates, as well as by politicians and the public. Reacting to intense criticism and pressure, President Trump signed an executive order ending this policy on June 21, 2018.

The Present Economic Situation in the US

The question whether the American Dream is still alive today is one which cannot be answered with either "yes" or "no", as the concept of the American Dream is not static. It depends on several aspects, e.g. a person's individual definition of and belief in the concept of the American Dream and the point of view one takes.
With regard to the present economic situation in the US, it is often said that the Amer-

ican Dream has been shattered for many people. The financial crisis that began in 2008 made the aim of achieving financial security a distant prospect.
In the following you will find a very short and simplified version of why for many Americans the quest for financial security has become difficult over the last few years.
For many people, owning a house is the goal of a lifetime. This is also true for US citizens, and for many years getting a loan necessary to build or buy a house was not difficult, even for people without a steady or with a low income. This resulted in people taking bigger loans than they could actually afford. They hoped that in the worst case of not being able to pay back the loan, they could still sell their houses, thereby making a profit. In most cases paying back the loan was not a problem as long as the mortgage rates were low.
When the base rate *(Leitzinsen)* increased, many house owners had difficulties paying back their loans. As a consequence, a huge number of houses suddenly had to be sold, which lowered the price, as there was also a decline in demand. In some cases that actually meant that the price for which a house could be sold was lower than the house owner's loan. So instead of making a profit, selling a house in many cases meant incurring a loss.
In the meantime, the banks had started to speculate with their customers' loans. Loans of good, average and bad credit rating were combined into so-called "Mortgage Backed Securities" (MBS). By combining loans of different credit ranking, banks hoped to limit the risk if someone failed to pay back a loan. These "Mortgage Backed Securities" were then sold to other banks worldwide, which meant profit for the seller. This practice went well for several years, but when more and more house owners could not pay back their loans, their banks started to lose large sums of money.
On 15th September 2008, one of America's biggest banks, Lehman Brothers, crashed. This marked the beginning of a series of bank crashes.
Unemployment increased and as many Americans had less money to spend, this led to a drop in consumption as well.
The burst of the housing bubble did not remain an American problem for long. It soon affected the economy of other countries, among them Germany, the Benelux countries and Iceland. Government bailouts for banks and economic stimulus plans were decided and put into action. Nevertheless, many countries were hit by recession.

In 2019, the US economy is in parts still recovering from the economic crisis of 2008, but unemployment has dropped from its highest level of 10% in October 2009 to just under 4.0% (March 2019).[3]
For both major parties in the US, economic growth and an increase in the number of jobs are top issues, although their approaches are quite different. Whereas getting a loan was relatively easy in the past, Americans intending to buy or build a house today face great difficulties, as banks are reluctant to grant loans to private persons.

3 http://data.bls.gov/timeseries/LNS14000000

On November 8, 2016 entrepreneur and TV personality Donald John Trump, candidate for the Republican Party won the U.S. presidential elections against Hillary Clinton, the wife of former US president Bill Clinton. Trump's victory came as something of a surprise.

Born on June 14, 1946 into a family successful in real estate and construction, Trump made a fortune in real estate and the entertainment business. On January 20, 2017 he was inaugurated as the 45th president of the USA; he is the first American president who has never held any political or military office.

Prior to his election Trump had been criticized as a populist, nationalist and misogynist. He promised his voters to put "America first". One of his aims was building a wall along America's southern borders to keep illegal Mexican immigrants from entering the country. According to Trump, Mexico should pay for this wall. He also promised his voters to create 25 million new jobs in the next ten years.

His inauguration was followed by massive protests worldwide, e.g. the Women's March on Washington to promote equal rights and counter discrimination, as well as to address racial inequities.

Donald Trump is known for his obsession with social micro-blogging platform Twitter. There he frequently utters his opinion on various issues. His tweets often tend to be rather impulsive and emotional.

As his sometimes controversial statements and decisions are frequently criticized by the media, he considers himself to be "at war with the media", which he accuses of being biased to his disadvantage.

In the days after his inauguration, Trump signed several important executive orders, attempting to end Obamacare, a healthcare reform law that aimed to improve health insurance and make it affordable for everyone, and another seeking to withdraw the USA from the Trans Pacific Partnership (TPP) trade deal.

However, he could not keep his campaign promise to put a stop to Obamacare. Instead he was advised to withdraw the bill, as there were not enough votes in Congress in favour of it.

In addition to that, he signed an executive order preventing Muslims from Iraq, Iran, Libya, Somalia, Sudan, Syria, and Yemen from entering the United States. This caused a storm of protest and Trump's immigration ban was partly quashed by the courts.

Political leaders in countries worldwide view his presidency with mixed emotions, especially since Trump at the beginning regarded NATO as obsolete (he has already changed opinion) and has praised the United Kingdom for leaving the European Union.

On June 1, 2017, Trump announced that the USA would withdraw from the Paris Agreement on climate change in 2020.

His reasons for doing so were what he saw as a disadvantage for the American coal industry and the consequential loss of millions of jobs.

The USA's withdrawal from the Paris Agreement sparked international criticism and made the country the only one not to be part of the agreement.
As an answer to Trump's announcement, a number of US states formed the US climate alliance, aiming to uphold the aims of the Paris climate agreement.
On April 23, 2018, Michael Bloomberg, the former mayor of New York promised to pay $4.5 million to cover some of the USA's debt to the Paris climate agreement. On TV network CBS Bloomberg explained the reasons for his donation by pointing out that "America made a commitment and, as an American, if the government's not going to do it then we all have a responsibility".

Glossary – Freedom and Justice

assimilation	Assimilation; Angleichung an Bestehendes
base rate	Leitzinsen
civil disobedience	bürgerlicher Ungehorsam
Civil Rights Movement	die Bürgerrechtsbewegung
credit rating	Beurteilung der Kreditwürdigkeit, Bonitätsbeurteilung
cultural heritage	Kulturerbe; kulturelles Erbe
Declaration of Independence	Unabhängigkeitserklärung
discrimination; deprivation	Benachteiligung; Diskriminierung
drop in consumption	Konsumrückgang
E pluribus unum	lat.: aus vielen Eines; ursprünglich bezogen auf die verschiedenen Staaten, aus denen die USA bestehen; heute vielmehr bezogen auf die vielen ethnischen Gruppen und Volksgruppen, aus denen sich die Bevölkerung der USA zusammensetzt
economic stimulus plan	Konjunkturprogramm
entrepreneur	Unternehmer
equality; equal opportunities	Gleichheit; gleiche Chancen
fame	Ruhm
freedom; ~ of speech; ~ of the press; religious ~	Freiheit; Redefreiheit; Pressefreiheit; Religionsfreiheit
frontier	Grenze (zwischen Zivilisation und Wildnis)
gold rush	Goldrausch
government bailouts	Rettungsaktion durch die Regierung

identity	Identität
Immigration Act	Einwanderungsgesetz
"In God we trust"	Wir vertrauen auf Gott; offizieller Wahlspruch der USA
inauguration; inaugural speech	Amtseinführung; Amtsantrittsrede
liberation	Befreiung
loan	Darlehen
melting pot vs. salad bowl	„Schmelztiegel" vs. „Salatschüssel" (unterschiedliche Konzepte, die die Vielfalt unterschiedlicher Kulturen in den USA charakterisieren)
mortgage	Hypothek
multiculturalism	Multikulturalität
naturalisation	Einbürgerung
pioneer; pioneer spirit	Pionier; Pioniergeist
Promised Land; the land of milk and honey; God's own country; the New Canaan	das gelobte Land
recession	Rezession
refugee; refugee camp	Flüchtling; Flüchtlingslager
segregation; desegregation	Rassentrennung; Aufhebung der Rassentrennung
success	Erfolg
supply and demand	Angebot und Nachfrage
the housing bubble	die Immobilienblase
the pursuit of happiness	das Streben nach Glück
to achieve financial security	finanzielle Sicherheit erlangen
to attain self-fulfillment	sich selbst verwirklichen
to be persecuted; religious/political persecution	verfolgt werden; religiöse/politische Verfolgung
to go from rags to riches; from dishwasher to millionaire	vom Tellerwäscher zum Millionär
to immigrate; immigrant; immigration; an influx of immigrants	einwandern; Einwanderer; Einwanderung; Zustrom von Einwanderern
to incur a loss	(einen) Verlust machen
to pledge allegiance to the flag	den Fahneneid leisten
to prosper	Erfolg haben; in Wohlstand leben
to settle; settler; settlement	besiedeln; Siedler; Siedlung
unalienable/inalienable rights	unveräußerliche Rechte

Tradition and Change in Politics and Society

Monarchy and Modern Democracy (in Britain)

Keyword:

British constitution: is not set out in a single document.
It is founded on conventions that are universally accepted, but which have never been formally defined. It is also founded on numerous acts and resolutions of Parliament, as each individual act of Parliament contributes to the constitution. Thus it is adaptable to changing political conditions.

Separation of Powers

The following three branches represent the powers and areas of responsibility:
Legislature: Parliament
Executive:
- government
- government departments responsible for national administration
- local authorities
- public corporations responsible for particular nationalized industries (controlled by Government; most of these have now been privatized)

Judiciary: the Courts
There are **two kinds of law:**
- common law: historic body of conventions ("it has always been like that")
- statute law: parliamentary and EU legislation

Parliament

Elements of Parliament

Queen – House of Lords – House of Commons
- Agreement of all three elements is required to pass legislation.
- Parliament is directly responsible to the electorate – no written constitution.
- An Act of Parliament cannot be disputed by the law courts.

Functions of Parliament

- pass laws
- scrutinize government policy and administration
- debate the major issues of the day

The House of Lords (House of Peers, Upper House, Second Chamber)

The House of Lords consists of hereditary peers, who inherit their peerage, and life peers, whose peerages are granted to them personally for their lifetime.

The political power of the Peers has been gradually reduced over the years, and they have recognized the supremacy of the elected chamber, the House of Commons.

Functions of the House of Lords are

- to discuss, examine or delay Bills
- to introduce Bills.

It used to be the highest court of appeal (since October 2009 this function has been served by the Supreme Court of the United Kingdom).

The House of Commons (Lower House)

646 members are directly elected by voters in the constituencies.
The House of Commons is the actual legislative body of the United Kingdom.

The Queen

The Queen has no overt power but is formally part of the government system.
The Queen is the

- head of State
- symbol of national unity
- head of the executive
- head of the judiciary
- commander-in-chief of the armed forces
- "supreme governor" of the Church of England.

Important functions

The Queen

- appoints the Prime Minister – by inviting the leader of the majority in the House of Commons to form a Government
- summons and dissolves Parliament
- gives Royal Assent to legislation (given as a matter of course)
- formally appoints ministers, judges, officers, diplomats, bishops
- can pardon people
- confers peerages (see below) and knighthoods
- represents the country at home and abroad.

General elections

The election period extends over a maximum of 5 years. Elections are ordered by the Queen on the advice of the Prime Minister.
The Prime Minister calls a new election at any time before the end of the 5-year election period. The United Kingdom is divided into 646 constituencies. Voters from each constituency elect their Member of Parliament (MP) by simple majority vote. The system is also called "first-past-the-post system". The candidate who gains the most votes in each

constituency gets a seat in Parliament. The political party that gains most seats forms the government. This system is preferred by the big parties, because it secures clear majorities. Smaller parties, which may have the support of a considerable proportion of the population, are never represented according to the proportion of the votes cast for them.
By-elections: elections in a single constituency when an MP has to be replaced during the legislative period.

Political parties

The Conservative Party (Tories)

Right-wing party, associated with
- nationalism
- law and order
- private enterprise
- minimal interference of the state in the economy.

The Labour Party

Traditional party of the "working class", formerly associated with
- state control and planning
- nationalization of key industries
- welfare
- affiliation to the trade unions.

However, with Tony Blair the party now known as New Labour changed direction away from socialist ideals towards an acceptance of the free market economy, opening itself to voters from the middle classes.

Governments since 1979

1979	Margaret Thatcher	Conservative	"Thatcherism": ruthless application of free market principles ("Iron Lady")
1983	Margaret Thatcher		
1987	Margaret Thatcher		
1991	John Major	Conservative	
1997	Tony Blair	Labour	"New Labour": more social democratic than socialist
2005	Tony Blair		
2007	Gordon Brown	Labour	
2010	David Cameron	Conservative	
2015	David Cameron	Conservative	
2016	Theresa May	Conservative	

Her Majesty's Government

The Prime Minister is appointed by the Queen and the ministers are appointed by the Queen on the recommendation of the Prime Minister.
The Prime Minister is always a member of the House of Commons. He or she presides over the cabinet, allocates functions to the ministers, and informs the Queen regularly at private meetings. He or she lives at Number 10 Downing Street.

Important members of the present cabinet (April 2019)

Prime Minister	Theresa May
Chancellor of the Exchequer	Philip Hammond
Secretary of State for the Home Department	Sajid Javid
Secretary of State for Foreign and Commonwealth Affairs	Jeremy Hunt
Secretary of State for Exiting the European Union	Stephen Barclay
Secretary of State for Defence	Gavin Williamson

Ministers are traditionally referred to as "The Right Honourable" (The Rt. Hon.), e.g. "The Rt. Hon. Theresa May MP"

Her Majesty's Opposition

The leader of the opposition forms a "shadow cabinet", which can take over at any time if the government loses the support of the majority in parliament.

The Privy Council

The main function of Her Majesty's Most Honourable Privy Council is to advise the Queen on the approval of legislation. Its members are senior politicians who were or are members of either the House of Commons or the House of Lords.

Local government

The system of local government differs in the four countries of the UK. The systems are much too complex to be presented here. You should keep in mind though, that political decisions have to be taken at different levels. There are county councils, district councils and parish councils, which are responsible for all kinds of local affairs, e.g. waste management, transport, traffic, housing, education, licensing, cemeteries, etc.

Devolution

Devolution is the granting of powers to the parliaments of Scotland, Wales and Northern Ireland. At the end of the 1990s the National Assembly of Wales and the Scottish Parliament were inaugurated, with competence to rule on issues like agriculture, fisheries and forestry, education, health, and tourism, whereas Westminster (the UK government) retained power in fields such as foreign affairs, defence, taxation,

fiscal policy, and labour market policy. Because of the Troubles, devolution in Northern Ireland was only implemented in 2007. In the 2014 referendum on full independence held in Scotland there was a narrow majority for the country to remain in the UK.
After the Brexit decision the Scottish Parliament has decided to ask the British Government to be allowed to hold a second referendum on independence in order to give Scotland the chance to stay in the EU.

Society

Class

The British are very class-conscious. Class distinctions are recognizable in speech, habits, style, tastes, and values. The Office of National Statistics produced the following socio-economic classification in 2008[1]. Although many top-ranking people may earn a lot of money, the classification is not based on income alone but on the distinctions mentioned above. In the last two decades class distinctions have become less obvious. The country has become more of a meritocracy, i.e. a society where achievement counts most. But traditional everyday terms are still used to refer to social classes: *upper class, upper-middle class, lower-middle class, working class.*

Ethnicity

Britain has become a multinational society in the last half century (see chapter "Multicultural society", p. 35)

Britain and the EU

Traditionally Britain has preferred to stay out of Europe. The terms "Europe" and "the Continent" have always referred to the European mainland.
Britain has been a member of the EU since 1973 (then the EC). Britain has not joined the monetary union (i.e. they do not have the euro). Britain has not signed the Schengen Agreement, which permits travelling without border controls between 25 European countries.
On June 23, 2016 a referendum about Britain's membership in the EU was held (cf. p. 33). There is a continuing debate on Brexit in Britain between those in favour of the EU and the "Eurosceptics". Eurosceptics are to be found among the supporters of the nationalist right and the Conservative party, but also among Labour Party members. Anti-European propaganda is to be found particularly in the tabloid papers like the *Sun* or the *Daily Mail*.

1 http://www.ons.gov.uk/about-statistics/classifications/current/ns-sec/cats-and-classes/ns-sec-classes-and-collapses/index.html

Main arguments of the Eurosceptics

The EU is

- expensive to run
- dominated by big countries at the expense of the smaller members
- too powerful
- trying to impose regulation in policy areas that should be the responsibility of national governments (e. g. health, education, law, tax)
- corrupt and money-wasting
- a security risk with its open borders
- host to millions of immigrants, some of them hostile and violent
- undemocratic.

Arguments in favour of the European Union

- The EU has created the world's largest international trade market.
- People have the choice to live and work anywhere in the EU.
- Many formerly poor countries have prospered in the EU, and poor regions receive special grants.
- Consumers have more rights.
- Europol provides cooperation on crime.
- The EU has passed many laws to ensure better environmental, consumer and health standards.
- Tourists receive free medical aid.
- Travel in the EU has become easier and cheaper.
- Human rights legislation has helped individuals in all EU countries.

Brexit

Keyword:

Brexit: shorthand way of saying the UK is leaving the EU – merging the words **Br**itain and **exit**

Cause: A referendum on 23 June 2016 → Leave won by 52% to 48%.
The referendum turnout was 71.8%, with more than 30 million people voting.

UK Breakdown

England voted for Brexit by 53.4% to 46.6%
Wales voted for Brexit by 52.5% to 47.5%.
Scotland and Northern Ireland both backed staying in the EU.
Scotland backed Remain by 62% to 38%,
Northern Ireland voted Remain by 55.8% to 44.2%

After the referendum

Prime Minister David Cameron, who was against Brexit, resigned.
New Prime Minister Theresa May, who was also against Brexit, said she would respect the will of the people ("Brexit means Brexit").

Article 50 of the Lisbon Treaty gives Britain and the EU two years to agree the terms of the split. The EU has offered a transition period up to 31 December 2020.

Britain was supposed to leave the EU on 29 March 2019 but the departure date has been postponed.
Negotiations about Brexit have been taking place since the referendum. Basically, they have been about the 'deal', the conditions under which the UK would leave the EU. The outcome of these negotiations has been the "Withdrawal Agreement", which covers several key points. The most controversial of these is the so-called backstop, which deals with the border between the Republic of Ireland and Northern Ireland. This border, which is invisible today, would, when the UK leaves the EU, become an external border of the EU. Nobody really wants soldiers and border controls there again, as they were in many years of the so-called Troubles between 1968 and 1998. The Troubles were an armed conflict between the opposing sides.
The backstop provision says that as long as there is no long-term trade pact, Britain will remain in the European customs union, and Northern Ireland (which is part of the UK) will also have to stick to many rules of the single market. Brexit hardliners therefore fear that the UK will have to follow EU regulations for an indefinite length of time without having a say in them. Thus, although the Withdrawal Agreement was approved by the EU and UK negotiators, it has not yet been approved by the British Parliament. The departure date has been postponed to 31 October.

The outcome is still absolutely open. There are several options the media foresee:
- no deal Brexit: a hard (and probably chaotic) Brexit without an agreement
- Brexit under the conditions of the Withdrawal Agreement
- renegotiations with the EU
- another referendum (e. g. on the Withdrawal Agreement or no Brexit or the no-deal Brexit)
- no Brexit

You should keep up to date with the events and check e. g bbc.com or theguardian.com for topical information, especially shortly before your English exam, in order to be able to cope with a possible task on Britain leaving the EU.

Scotland

Scotland's First Minister, Nicola Sturgeon, said it is "democratically unacceptable" that Scotland has to leave the EU when it voted overwhelmingly to remain. A second independence referendum for the country is now "highly likely" (see chapter on devolution, p. 31).

Northern Ireland

The Republic of Ireland is part of the EU. Northern Ireland voted to remain. Some politicians see this as a reason for a vote on reunification. We will have to wait and see how this issue develops (see above).

Multicultural Society

Keyword:

Imperial Act (1914): Inhabitants of the colonies were given British citizenship.

- Between the 1960s and 1980s many Indians, Pakistanis and Bangladeshis immigrated to Britain. They now form the largest immigrant communities.
- Many of them settled in the Midlands or in towns in Lancashire, Yorkshire and Strathclyde, where they worked in the textile industry.

Britain today

- Britain consists of three countries (England, Scotland, Wales). Together with Northern Ireland it forms the United Kingdom. 12.4% of the population in the UK were born abroad (2013).[2]
- **Ethnic diversity** enriches Britain, not only when it comes to music, fashion and food.
- Many embrace the possibilities and advantages of ethnic diversity (such as the former Foreign Secretary Robin Cook, who said that Chicken Tikka Masala " ... is now a true British national dish ..."[3]).
- Others fear that "Britishness" will eventually be lost; they interpret multiculturalism as meaning that various cultures coexist peacefully, but without having a common basis of shared values.
- **Second generation immigrants,** i. e. children born to parents who immigrated to Britain prior to (or shortly after) their children's birth, face a variety of problems:
  - They often experience a clash of cultures. Outside their parents' home they adopt a western lifestyle, similar to that of their white friends and classmates. At home, however, they live according to values, beliefs and traditions typical of their parents' home countries, which many of these children and teenagers have never visited. Quite often they do not speak their parents' language any more, either. For some, the transition between these two different lifestyles is not easy.
  - They have difficulties when it comes to living up to the expectations of their parents, friends, teachers, etc.
  - They often have to face discrimination.

2 http://visual.ons.gov.uk/uk-perspectives-a-recent-history-of-international-migration/; see also data from February 2019 on https://www.ons.gov.uk

3 Robin Cook's *Chicken Tikka Masala Speech*, The Guardian, April 19, 2001, http://www.guardian.co.uk/world/2001/apr/19/race.britishidentity

Glossary – Traditions and Change

act / bill / law the law	Gesetz das Gesetz
agreement	Abkommen
asylum seekers	Asylsuchende
blend in	sich einfügen, integrieren
citizenship	Nationalität, Staatsangehörigkeit
clash between/of two cultures	das Aufeinanderprallen zweier Kulturen
citizen	Bürger
conservative Conservative Party a conservative	konservativ die Conservative Party ein Konservativer
constitution	Verfassung
delegate	Delegierter
democracy	Demokratie
discriminate against someone	jemanden benachteiligen/diskriminieren
elect to be elected election electorate election period election campaign	wählen gewählt werden Wahl Wählerschaft Wahlperiode Wahlkampf
ethnic minorities	ethnische Minderheiten
ethnicity	Ethnizität, Volkszugehörigkeit
executive	die Exekutive
federal	Bundes-...
government to govern	Regierung regieren
hold racist attitudes	eine rassistische Haltung/Einstellung haben
house	Kammer des Parlaments
imperialism; imperialistic	Imperialismus; imperialistisch
indefinite leave to remain	unbeschränkte Aufenthaltserlaubnis
judiciary	die Judikative
labour	Arbeit
Labour Party	die Labour Party

legislature legislative	die Legislative gesetzgebend
loss of identity	Identitätsverlust
minister prime minister (the Prime Minister) ministry	Minister Premierminister Ministerium
MP Member of Parliament	Abgeordneter
mutual understanding and respect	gegenseitiges/beidseitiges Verständnis und Respekt
office to hold office Home Office/Foreign Office	Amt, Ministerium ein Amt innehaben Innenministerium, Außenministerium
open-minded vs. narrow-minded	aufgeschlossen vs. engstirnig
outsider	Außenseiter
parliament	Parlament
party	Partei
policy economic policy foreign policy	politisches Ziel, Maßnahmen Wirtschaftspolitik Außenpolitik
pluralistic society	eine pluralistische Gesellschaft
politics political politician	Politik politisch Politiker
poll polling-station	Abstimmung, Umfrage, Wahl, Wahllokal
racial equality	Gleichwertigkeit verschiedener Rassen
receive/be granted citizenship	die Staatsbürgerschaft erhalten
referendum	Volksbefragung, Volksentscheid
representative	(Volks-)Vertreter
secretary foreign secretary	Minister Außenminister
the people	das Volk
to support	unterstützen
vote to vote voter	Stimme stimmen, wählen Wähler
wing right/left wing	Flügel rechter/linker Flügel

India – Faces of a Rising Nation

From Empire to Commonwealth

Keywords:

Post-colonialism: term first used in the middle of the 20th century; refers to the time after the British had left the colonies, i.e. after their formal rule over the colonies had come to an end.
Political independence did not necessarily lead to economic independence. The withdrawal of the British often resulted in problems for the ex-colonies, e.g. in difficulties in setting up a functioning government which guaranteed the people the freedom they dreamed of.

The Commonwealth: a group of 52 states; many former British colonies joined at the end of the decolonization process; aims at racial equality and national sovereignty. The British Queen is the head of the Commonwealth.

- At the **beginning of the 17th century** Britain started to expand its empire across the globe.
- The colonizers had a huge impact on the colonies and their people, bringing new traditions, values and beliefs with them.

- **After the 2nd World War** the British Empire changed rapidly.
- Most British colonies became independent from Britain by 1970, but a large number of them stayed closely connected with their former colonizer by joining the Commonwealth.

- While the British ruled the colonies, their culture, values, traditions and language were regarded as superior to those of the colonized.
- This often caused a feeling of displacement and rootlessness on the part of the colonized, as they had grown up being constantly reminded of their inferiority.
- Now, after independence, they faced the difficult task of recreating their own identity, bridging the gap between their country's native traditions and values and British ones.
- As people from member countries of the Commonwealth were allowed to immigrate to Britain, lots of people did so in the second half of the 20th century.
- First they were welcomed, as workers were needed after the 2nd World War, but in the 1970s, when more and more workers faced unemployment because of the economic crisis, immigration came to be seen more critically.

- Much **post-colonial writing** – written both in in the former colonies and in Britain – deals with the issue of being caught between two cultures or of trying to find one's identity.

The Raj

Keyword:

Raj: (Hindustani) = "reign"
The term refers to the time from 1858 to 1947 when the Indian subcontinent was ruled by the British.

- **British influence** in India started as early as the 16th century with the founding of the British East India Company.
- Because of its spices, cotton and tea, India was used as a trading colony.
- **1858:** The British Crown took over the areas ruled by the British East India Company, and in 1876 Queen Victoria became Empress of India.
- **August 15, 1947:** The Indian Empire was divided into the Union of India, with Jawaharlal Nehru as the Prime Minister, and the Dominion of Pakistan.
- The separate colony of Burma in the Eastern part of the Indian Empire, which had become an independent colony in 1937, gained its independence in 1948.

India and Pakistan

- **1947:** India and Pakistan were founded[1].
- The partition of the Indian Empire led to riots, and mass migration started, as the Union of India was predominantly Hindu, whereas the Dominion of Pakistan was Muslim.
- Many people feared persecution because of their religion and attempted to move to the other state. Millions of people became homeless and about half a million people were killed.
- India and Pakistan quarrelled over two regions in the northwest, Jammu and Kashmir, because both India and Pakistan claimed (and still claim) these areas.
- Up to 1846 both Jammu (predominantly Hindu) and Kashmir (predominantly Muslim) were controlled by Sikhs, but when the British fought them, they installed a Maharajah to control these areas.
- At the time of Independence there were more than 500 states ruled by local princes[2] who owed allegiance to Britain. The rulers of those states were asked to join either India or Pakistan.
- When **partition** came, the Maharajah of Jammu and Kashmir still had not decided which state to join. Although he later decided to join India, Jammu and Kashmir have remained a bone of contention between India and Pakistan.
  - The **Pakistani** position: They should join Pakistan, as the majority is Muslim.
  - The **Indian** position: They rightfully belong to India because the Maharajah finally decided to join India.

1 In 1971 East Pakistan became Bangladesh.
2 A princely state is controlled by an Indian ruler rather than directly by the British, but remains loyal to the British crown.

The still existing tension between India and Pakistan originated in the partition of the Indian Empire.

The role of women in India

"You can tell the condition of a nation by looking at the status of women." (Jawaharlal Nehru)

- The Constitution of India guarantees equal rights for both men and women. On its website the Indian Ministry of Statistics and Programme Implementation states that "(Fundamental) Rights, among others, ensure equality before the law and equal protection of law; prohibit discrimination against any citizen on grounds of religion, race, caste, sex or place of birth, and guarantee equality of opportunity to all citizens in matters relating to employment."[3]
- In the past women have played an active role in various areas of life, e.g. Indira Gandhi (born 1917, assassinated 1984) as the second-longest serving Prime Minister of India (1966–1977 and 1980–1984). To date she has been the only female Prime Minister of India. No other country in the world has a higher number of female politicians.
- Despite the fact that women's rights are granted on paper, the reality often looks different:
  - Traditional views and customs still lead to discrimination and harassment of women. Although child marriage and dowries are prohibited by law, they are still practised in rural areas.
  - Women are often subject to various forms of discrimination and crime, such as rape, acid throwing and dowry deaths, where the bride is continually harassed by her husband and in-laws to ensure a higher dowry, and ultimately murdered or driven to commit suicide.
- As in many other countries all over the world, ultrasound scans are part of pre-natal care for a majority of pregnant women in India. Nevertheless, as a large number of female babies had been aborted in the past, revealing a baby's gender before birth became a punishable offence in India in 1994 under the Pre-natal Diagnostic Techniques (Regulation and Prevention of Misuse) Act, which was amended in 2002.
- On August 4, 2009, the Parliament of India passed The Right of Children to Free and Compulsory Education Act[4]. Under this act, the education of any child between 6 and 14 years of age became a fundamental right. According to UNICEF, the youth (15 to 24 years of age) literacy rate in the years 2008 to 2012 was 88.4% for boys/young men and 74.4% for girls/young women[5].

3 http://mospi.nic.in/Mospi_New/upload/man_and_women/Constitutional%20&%20Legal%20Rights.pdf (retrieved January 1, 2016)
4 http://mhrd.gov.in/sites/upload_files/mhrd/files/document-reports/RTEAct.pdf (retrieved January 1, 2016)
5 http://www.unicef.org/infobycountry/india_statistics.html (retrieved April, 2019)

Economy

- With an economic growth rate of 7.43% (based on data provided by the International Monetary Fund[6]), India is currently the 6th largest economy in the world. It recently outperformed China as the world's fastest-growing economy.
- In 2015, the average annual income was about €1100, and almost 30% of the population lived below the poverty line of $1 a day.
- The main drive for India's economic growth is the service sector, e. g. information technology and related services, telecommunications and financial services.
- Economic growth has detrimental effects on India's environment, as pollution of air and water, as well as the combustion of fossil fuels, has increased dramatically.

Glossary – India

adapt to sth.	sich an etw. anpassen
arranged marriage	eine arrangierte Ehe
be oppressed by someone	von jemandem unterdrückt werden
caste	Kaste
colonialism; colonizer; colonized	Kolonialismus; der Besiedler; kolonisiert
combustion	Verbrennung
compulsory education	Schulpflicht
dowry	Mitgift
empire	das Imperium
excluded (from)	(von) etw. ausgeschlossen
hostile	feindlich, feindselig, ablehnend
imperialism; imperialistic	Imperialismus; imperialistisch
indigenous	Einheimischer eines Landes
literacy rate	Alphabetisierungsrate
poverty line	Armutsgrenze
service sector	Dienstleistungssektor

6 http://www.imf.org/external/pubs/ft/weo/2015/01/weodata/weorept.aspx?pr.x=47&pr.y=7&sy=2015&ey=2020&scsm=1&ssd=1&sort=country&ds=.&br=1&c=534&s=NGDP_RPCH&grp=0&a= (retrieved April, 2019)

Globalization and Global Challenges

Keywords:

Globalization: a worldwide movement, involving the integration of financial, economic and communications systems; often seen as an unstoppable process, affecting people all around the globe, no matter whether they live in industrialized or developing countries, in big cities or rural villages. Transfer of goods, capital and services, as well as communications, made easier, but not everyone profits from the development; smaller economies may suffer.
The world is said to be getting smaller, i.e. it has become a "global village". The term was coined by Marshall McLuhan, a Canadian philosopher and media specialist.

It is not easy to say when globalization actually started:
- Did it start with the discovery of America?
- Does it go even further back in time?
- Is it a phenomenon of the modern era?

Everyone can experience the results of globalization, e.g. when
- travelling
- keeping in touch with friends or business partners in distant countries with the help of new means of communication
- buying goods which come from far away.

Globalization is not always regarded as a positive process:
- Some people fear that individual cultures will finally blend into a single global culture, thereby losing all their characteristic features.
- Thousands of people in developing countries still suffer from malnutrition or die of curable diseases.
- Others work under cruel working conditions, producing goods which will be shipped to and sold in industrialized countries at a low price.
- The latest financial crisis, starting in the USA in 2008, shows that a crisis which starts in one country will ultimately affect other countries as well, as businesses are linked and global trade is the rule.
- Due to increased mobility, diseases like H1N1 ("Swine Flu") can easily spread all around the globe, developing into a pandemic.
- There are always two sides to a coin and there are other advantages, and of course challenges, when it comes to globalization.
- The refugee crisis in Europe can partly be seen as connected with globalization: people from all over the world want to participate in growing economic wealth. Many people from poor countries want to find a better future and leave their homes – just like people have always done over the centuries (e.g. emigration to America in the last two centuries). At the same time, civil and other wars force

people to emigrate. As more and more countries close their borders, problems in many regions are growing. Among these problems are huge refugee camps, and people drowning and starving during dangerous journeys.

Aspects of Globalization

Progress

- The development of planes, fast ships and trains made fast transportation of goods from one country to another possible.
- New means of communication, especially the Internet, make the collaboration between business partners easier.
- Multinational companies have branches all over the world, and cost-effectiveness is a decisive factor when new production sites are set up.

Economic challenges

As today's customers wish to buy products at the best cost/performance ratio, the global market has become very **competitive,** with the following (and related) consequences:

- While global players consider efficiency, speed, flexibility and profits as most important, employees are increasingly unable to defend their rights.
- More and more jobs are being outsourced or off-shored to cut down production costs, thereby severely damaging local labour markets.
- When jobs are outsourced to low-wage countries, the workers often work in so-called **"sweatshops"** for long hours at a stretch, earning only minimum wages and under working conditions that are often inhumane. Safety measures in sweatshops are by no means comparable to western standards. Sadly, the lack of efficient safety measures often results in catastrophes. On April 24, 2013 a building housing several garment factories near Bangladesh's capital Dhaka collapsed, resulting in the death of more than 1.000 workers. Despite the fact that factory owners had previously been warned about deep cracks which appeared in the building's structure and had been ordered to evacuate the building, workers were sent in to work. Two weeks after the tragedy, a fire broke out in another clothing factory, killing several people.
- Critics like the Canadian journalist Naomi Klein accuse multinational companies of exploiting the poor and indirectly supporting child labour by only having their own profit in mind.
- Workers often assemble products which they will never be able to afford or do not know how to use, e.g. computers.
- People in developing countries often live under poor conditions, without a decent education or access to new means of communication. Therefore they can't reap the benefits of globalization.
- Advocates of sweatshops claim that these factories provide work for the poor, enabling them to provide for their families.

- They also say that critics of sweatshops argue from a western point of view without considering the actual situation of people in developing countries.
- In order to reduce the number of sweatshops, fair trade is becoming increasingly important. Its aim is to ensure that workers and small-scale producers in poor countries are paid a fair price for their work and products.
- Despite these attempts, a growing number of experts and laypeople alike fear that the gap between the rich and the poor is widening.
- The close links and collaboration between companies all across the globe is both a blessing and a curse.
- The financial crisis which started in the USA in 2008 shows that a national crisis can quickly develop into a global one, affecting the economies of numerous countries.

Ecological challenges and the role of customers

Environmental pollution is growing rapidly. The following factors in particular create global problems:
- **Exhaust fumes** from factories are one important factor.
- Over the last decades the number of **vehicles** on the roads has steadily increased. Cars are no longer found only in industrialized countries.
- The number of people travelling by **plane** is also greater than ever, due to the fact that plane tickets have become affordable for a larger number of people. Short-haul **flights** have become particularly popular.
- **Food-miles:** Whereas some years ago many people bought fruit and vegetables locally and ate seasonal products, they now want to eat strawberries and cherries in December. So more goods are air-freighted. Ecologically conscious customers ask themselves whether it is better to buy local products than food (even fair trade products) which has been flown across continents.
- Everyone leaves a **carbon footprint** (emission of greenhouse gases from factories, cars, trains, planes, etc) either directly or indirectly.
- **Greenhouse gases** cause chemical damage to the atmosphere (e.g. ozone hole) as well as global warming (see below).

Global warming and its consequences

- As Al Gore explains in his film *An Inconvenient Truth,* greenhouse gases form a layer around the earth trapping heat and thereby causing the temperature on the ground to rise ("global warming").
- There are many consequences of climate change, e.g. floods in coastal areas, heavy rainfall in some regions and drought in others, melting of polar ice-caps.
- Biodiversity is threatened, as many plants, flowers and animals die out. Desertification (see below) is an increasingly frequent phenomenon today.

Environmental sustainability

- Due to overgrazing[1], over-extraction (overdraft) of groundwater, unwise use of water resources, e.g. diverting rivers for industrial use or human consumption, deforestation ("slash-and-burn farming") and rising soil salinity, vast areas of land in relatively dry areas deteriorate and become useless (desertification).
- Environmental sustainability is on the agenda of many governments and has been an important topic at various summits to date.

The Kyoto Protocol (came into effect on February 16, 2005)

- The protocol aimed to reduce the emission of greenhouse gases by an annual 5.2% by the year 2012, taking 1990 levels as a basis.
- National limitations were decided, stating which country had to reduce the emission of greenhouse gases by what amount (e.g. EU 8%, US 7%).
- There are no national limitations for some countries, e.g. India and China, as they were not among the highest greenhouse gas emitters prior to the treaty. However, by August 2008 China had become the world's biggest emitter of greenhouse gases caused by power generation, overtaking the USA.
- While 183 parties had ratified the protocol by January 2009, the USA signed but did not ratify it, because
  - scientific evidence was said not to be convincing enough,
  - the protocol would put a strain on the economy,
  - there were no national limitations for China.
- G8 Summit in Heiligendamm, Germany, 2007: Leaders of developed countries reached the decision to cut global CO_2 emissions by at least 50%.
- Not only politicians, but also ordinary people are becoming more aware of environmental issues and try to help save the environment, e.g. by cycling or using public transport instead of going by car, as well as by recycling waste materials and using energy more economically.
- December 2009: Climate Change Summit in Copenhagen. Environment ministers and officials unsuccessfully tried to work on a successor for the Kyoto Protocol. On December 18, 2009, the USA, Brazil, China, India and South Africa worked out the 'Copenhagen Accord'. This document, which is not binding, states that climate change is one of the greatest global challenges and that efforts should be made to ensure that any rise in temperature stays below 2 °C. Although many countries and NGOs were critical of the 'Copenhagen Accord' at first, 138 nations had signed it (e.g. Germany, France and India) or expressed their will to do so (e.g. Afghanistan, Jamaica and Ukraine) by the end of 2010. In the 'Copenhagen Accord' it was also acknowledged that developing and third world countries will need more time and financial support by western countries to pursue the aims of the document.

1 One speaks of "overgrazing" if the number of cattle on a piece of land is too high to be sustainable (in the long term).

- 2014: negotiations in Paris, but some countries – e.g. the USA – made it clear that they would not sign any agreement which forces them to legally reduce CO_2 emissions
- 2015: Paris, 2015: A global agreement on the slowing of climate change (the Paris Agreement) has been reached and adopted by 195 countries. Among the decisions made was the resolution to limit the long-term increase of global average temperature to well below 2°C above pre-industrial levels. The agreement went into effect on 4 November 2016, as enough countries ratified it. However, it is not clear whether the USA will withdraw its consent to the agreement, as announced by President Trump.

Conflict between economic and ecological aspects of globalization

- Companies face global competition: cost-effectiveness and profits seem more important than ecological issues.
- Some governments refrain from setting up strict laws to protect the environment, as this might drive away multinational companies that offer many employment possibilities.
- As environmental pollution does not stop at borders, international cooperation is crucial – and will become even more so in future.

Fridays for Future

In August 2018, Greta Thunberg, a 16-year-old Swedish climate change activist, started protesting outside the Swedish parliament in Stockholm in order to raise awareness of the dangers of climate change.
According to Thunberg, politicians are not taking enough action against climate change, which is putting our planet's future at risk. Thunberg's solitary school strikes, which she still carries out regularly, soon caught the attention of the media in countries all over the world.
Up to May 2019, an estimated 1.4 million teenagers and young adults worldwide have followed her example by going on strike from school every Friday and protesting against climate change. This movement is known as "Fridays for Future".
Greta Thunberg has delivered several public speeches in which she has put pressure on politicians and world leaders to combat climate change more swiftly and resolutely. She spoke at the United Nations Climate Change Conference in Katowice, Poland in December 2018 and at the World Economic Forum in Davos, Switzerland in January 2019.
In her speech in Katowice, Thunberg summarized her intentions as follows: "I care about climate justice and the living planet. Our civilization is being sacrificed for the opportunity of a very small number of people to continue making enormous amounts of money. Our biosphere is being sacrificed so that rich people in countries like mine can live in luxury. It is the sufferings of the many which pay for the luxuries of the few".

Media and communication

Many people experience the advantages of communication on the Internet on a daily basis. Social networking communities like *Facebook* and *MySpace* enable their users to find long-lost friends and to connect with people all over the world, no matter whether they live next door or on a different continent.

Founded by Harvard students Mark Zuckerberg, Eduardo Saverin, Andrew McCollum, Dustin Moskovitz and Chris Hughes in 2004, *Facebook* has become the biggest social networking community with more than 900 million users worldwide (May 2012).
Its development was also made into a film *(The Social Network,* directed by David Fincher in 2010). *Facebook* CEO Mark Zuckerberg has criticized the film for not being true to the development of Facebook.
On *Facebook,* users are able to set up their own profiles and to customize them according to their wishes, e.g. by uploading pictures and information about themselves or by adjusting the privacy settings of their profiles to restrict others from seeing them. Users can also keep track on what their friends are doing and chat with them. As there are special apps for gadgets like smartphones or tablets, users can access their *Facebook* accounts on the go.
While using *Facebook* itself is free of charge, the network has repeatedly been accused of collecting and exploiting its users' private data.
Despite being confronted with considerable criticism regarding issues like privacy protection, cyber bullying or identity theft, *Facebook* is immensely popular worldwide and made its stock market debut in May 2012.

On his own *Facebook* page, Mark Zuckerberg says that "(he's) trying to make the world a more open place[2]". Nevertheless, countries like China, Iran and Pakistan have banned people's access to Facebook.

On a political level, *Facebook* is also said to have played a role in the "Arab Spring" which started in December 2010. Generally speaking, this can be described as a series of protests and demonstrations in several countries of the Arab World, i.e. Tunisia, Egypt and Libya to force rulers from power. The success of these revolutions has partly been accredited to social media like *Facebook* and *Twitter,* as protests, marches, strikes and other examples of civil resistance were organized and coordinated with the help of social media.
Some have therefore suggested calling these revolutions 'Facebook revolutions', whereas others say that although social media might have helped to organize civil resistance and to make the state of things in Arab countries public to the western world, people's active involvement in a revolution is still the key essential for its success.

Facebook and the companies belonging to it, e.g. Instagram, and WhatsApp have certainly revolutionized our way of communicating and interacting with each other.

2 https://www.facebook.com/zuck (August 8, 2012)

Never before has it been easier to broadcast oneself and to stay in touch with people all over the globe, as well as to access news and information from anywhere around the world in real time.
Despite all these achievements, Facebook has been criticized by both opponents and users for a number of reasons.
One reason is that users who report hate speech, rumours, incitement to violence and offensive posts that violate Facebook's community standards often received only standardized answers or no feedback at all. In addition to that, many users found that Facebook did not remove those posts and/or did nothing to avoid the spread of hate speech etc.
The social network's protection of its users' Internet privacy and the safekeeping and storing of personal data is another point of criticism.
In March 2018 it was revealed that Facebook had mishandled user data, enabling Cambridge Analytica, a political consulting firm, to access and evaluate the data of 87 million users and attempting to influence the presidential elections of 2016 in favour of Donald Trump.
As a consequence, Mark Zuckerberg was called to a US Senate committee hearing where he was questioned on Facebook's use and misuse of user data.
In 2018, the European Union has insisted that Mark Zuckerberg should in person attend an official hearing on the same topic.

The UN and the EU

The UN

- October 24, 1945: A group of 51 countries founded the United Nations (UN) as a replacement/successor for the League of Nations.
- The UN headquarters is located in New York City and the current Secretary General is António Guterres.
- The UN has 193 member states (April 2019).
- It defends human rights and fundamental freedoms.

Five of six **main organs** of the UN (General Assembly, Security Council, Economic and Social Council, Trusteeship Council and Secretariat) are located in New York City, while the International Court of Justice is in The Hague in the Netherlands.
There are **various programs** and funds affiliated to the UN. Two of the best known are UNICEF (United Nations Children's Fund) and the UNHCR (Office of the United Nations High Commissioner for Refugees). The latter deals with the needs of refugees and displaced persons in post-conflict countries, e. g. Djibouti.

Aims of the UN

- to preserve international peace and security
- to promote friendly relations between member countries
- to support international cooperation with regard to economic, social and cultural as well as humanitarian issues

- Apart from **peacekeeping** and **peacemaking** operations, **peace-building** has become more and more important.
- Here the UN and its affiliated organizations work to equip national groups with the necessary skills in conflict management, and to ensure that lasting peace can be established.
- Currently (Spring 2019) the UN is involved in 14 peacekeeping operations, e.g. in Haiti, Mali and Darfur.
- **Humanitarian aid** is also of major importance, e.g. providing relief for people affected by either man-made or natural disasters, and helping refugees and displaced persons.
- Other main concerns of the UN are **international law and development** (e.g. sustainable development, agriculture, international trade).

The EU

- Currently 28 states belong to the European Union (EU). The newest members are Bulgaria and Romania, which both joined the EU on January 1, 2007, and Croatia, which became a member on July 1, 2013.
- After the 2nd World War there was a desire for a united Europe in order to prevent extreme forms of nationalism. The European Coal and Steel Community, the European Economic Community (EEC) and the European Atomic Energy Community (Euratom) were merged into the European Community (EC) in 1967.
- The EU as we know it came into existence in 1993, when the Maastricht Treaty – which among other things initiated the euro as common currency – was ratified. The individual member states came to be regarded as a single global player.
- At present the EU faces the challenge of maintaining its unity – and indeed remaining a union at all – in the face of the refugee crisis. The countries of the EU have very different attitudes to solving the refugee problem.
- In 2016, Great Britain decided in a referendum to leave the EU ("Brexit", cf. p. 33).

Aims of the EU

- to promote prosperity and social progress with European citizenship for its peoples while still keeping their diversity alive
- to promote friendly relations between member countries
- to guarantee freedom and justice for the European peoples
- to internationally represent the member states with a single voice, tackling the various challenges of globalization, as well as respecting human rights

When it comes to defence, the individual member countries are sovereign. However, there is military cooperation in peacekeeping missions.
The three main groups which make up the EU are the **Council of Ministers,** the **European Parliament,** the **European Commission.**
Although the EU has no official capital, the official seat of the European Commission, the Council of the European Union and the second seat of the European Parliament are located in Brussels, Belgium.

International peacekeeping

International peacekeeping is one of the aims of the UN:
- Once peace has been established in a country or region, peacekeepers are sent to the country or region in question to oversee the peace process.
- This can be done by overseeing elections, providing reconstruction aid and supervising the withdrawal of combatants.
- Very often, UN peacekeepers are soldiers, but they can also be police officers or other civilian personnel.
- The UN Security Council authorizes peacekeeping missions, which are then carried out by the international community.
- Many of these missions are organized and led by the UN itself. There is no UN army. While the troops acting as peacekeepers are under the control of the UN, they still belong to the armed forces of their country of origin. The UN itself is controlled by the Security Council and the UN Secretariat.
- This reduces the risk that one peacekeeping party only follows its own interests.
- Regional organizations (e. g. NATO) can be authorized by the UN to lead peacekeeping missions. These regional organizations can also organize peacekeeping missions of their own.

Terrorism

Terrorism as become an ongoing global threat which has led to a growing feeling of insecurity in many societies: "[T]errorism casts its lethal shadow across the globe – yet the world's resolve to defeat is has never been greater ..."[3]
- in some countries (e. g. Israel) terrorist attacks have been a virtually permanent feature of life, going back six or seven decades
- in most Western, as well as Middle Eastern countries, what we know as Islamist terrorism – especially the systematic terrorism of such organizations as "Al Qaeda" and the "Islamic State" (also known as "IS", "ISIS", or "Daesh") – began with the "9/11" attacks on the World Trade Center in New York and the Pentagon in Washington on September 11, 2001
- these attacks provoked a military reaction from the U.S. government under George W. Bush, who with his allies (notably the UK) launched the Second Gulf War (2003) against the regime of Saddam Hussein in Iraq
- the ensuing political, social and economic collapse of Iraq rekindled the enduring conflict between two branches of Islam, the Sunni and the Shia religious traditions, which resulted in many acts of terrorism in Baghdad and other centres that have continued to the present day
- also as a result of that breakdown, and at the same time of the war in Syria between the central government and dissenting (or "rebel") forces, the Sunni Islamist terrorist organization ISIS took over control of large parts of Syria and Northern Iraq, territories from which they have recently for the most part been expelled by

3 From: *Patterns of Global Terrorism Report*, 2001, http://www.state.gov/s/ct/ris/pgtrpt/

Iraqi, Syrian and Kurdish military action supported by the U.S. and its allies
- meanwhile in Afghanistan the Taliban (also a Sunni-Islamist organization), who had governed the country after the Soviet occupation (1979-1989), have organized many terrorist attacks since their expulsion from power by U.S.-led forces in 2001
- driven largely by these same Middle Eastern terrorist groups, a series of attacks has been carried out – largely in European countries but also in the U.S. – the most significant being the Madrid train bombings of March 2004, the London bombings of July 2005, the Boston Marathon bombing of April 2013, the Paris "Charlie Hebdo" attacks of January 2015, the Brussels attacks of March 2016, and the Berlin Christmas Market attack of December 2016
- but not all terrorist actions are motivated by anti-Western or Islamist sentiments: some, like the Oslo and Utøya (Norway) attacks of July 2010 were apparently motivated by right-wing ultra-nationalist convictions, and the occurrence in April 2018 in Münster (Germany), when a car was driven into people gathered in a beer-garden, seems to have been committed by a psychologically disturbed person.
- On March 15, 2019, a 28-year-old Australian, whom the media later described as a white supremacist, carried out two terrorist attacks on mosques in Christchurch, New Zealand. He opened fire on people attending Friday prayers, killing more than 40 people and injuring more than 50. The terrorist streamed the first of the two attacks live on Facebook. He was arrested on the same day and charged with murder.
- Exactly two months after these attacks, New Zealand's Prime Minister, Jacinda Ardern and French president Emmanuel Macron met with other national leaders and with executives from Amazon, Facebook, Google, Microsoft and Twitter to discuss how to prevent live-streaming of incidents like the ones in Christchurch and how to fight online extremism and terrorism. They agreed on a nine-point action plan, dubbed the "Christchurch Call to Action".

Glossary – Globalization

Americanization	Amerikanisierung
anti-globalist	Globalisierungsgegner/-kritiker
backwardness	Rückständigkeit
company philosophy	Geschäfts-/Firmenphilosophie
competition; to be competitive	Konkurrenz(kampf)/Wettbewerb; konkurrenzfähig sein
corporate identity	Firmenimage
crop diseases	Krankheiten von Pflanzen/Saatgut
debt relief	Schuldenerlass, Entschuldung
desertification	die Desertifikation/Wüstenbildung, das Vordringen der Wüste

developing countries	Entwicklungsländer
development aid	Entwicklungshilfe
driving forces of globalization	die Antriebskräfte der Globalisierung
drought	Dürren, Dürreperioden
earth's atmosphere	die Erdatmosphäre
economic growth	Wirtschaftswachstum
economic prosperity	ökonomischer Wohlstand
emerging markets	Schwellenländer
environmental commitment	Umwelteinsatz
environmental damage	Umweltzerstörung
environmentally friendly	umweltfreundlich
expansion of capitalism	Ausbreitung des Kapitalismus
fair trade	fairer Handel
floods	Hochwasser, Überschwemmungen
global interconnection	globale Querverbindungen
global marketplace	globaler Marktplatz
global player	Weltfirma
global super power	eine globale Supermacht
global warming	Erderwärmung
greenhouse gases	Treibhausgase
human rights	Menschenrechte
human-generated carbon dioxide	durch Menschen produziertes Kohlenstoffdioxid
increase profit margins	die Gewinnspanne erhöhen
Industrial Age	das Industriezeitalter
industrial nations	Industrieländer/-nationen
interdependence of economy and ecology	gegenseitige Abhängigkeit/Verflechtung von Ökonomie und Ökologie
international stock markets	internationale Börsenmärkte
investment climate	Investitionsbedingungen
labour laws	Arbeitsgesetze
labour market	Arbeitsmarkt
long-range goals	langfristige Ziele
low-wage countries	Niedriglohnländer
mass communication; mass media	Massenkommunikation; -medien
mass tourism	Massentourismus
melting of glaciers	das Schmelzen von Gletschern
micro-credits	Kleinkredite

NGO (non-governmental organization)	Nichtregierungsorganisation
outsourcing	Produktionsverlagerung
political turmoil	politischer Aufruhr, politische Turbulenzen
pollution	Verschmutzung
population overshoot, overpopulation, excess of population	Überbevölkerung
poverty	Armut
reduce greenhouse gas emissions	den Ausstoß von Treibhausgasen reduzieren
reduce the cost of production	die Produktionskosten senken
rise in global temperature	ein weltweiter Temperaturanstieg
robotized production	computergesteuerte Produktion/Fertigung
short-haul flights	Kurzstreckenflüge
surface transport	Bodentransport
supremacy	Vormachtsstellung, Überlegenheit
sustainability	Nachhaltigkeit, Zukunftsfähigkeit
sweatshop	ausbeuterischer Betrieb
trade	Handel
trademark policy	Markenpolitik
undernutrition, malnutrition	Unterernährung; Mangelernährung
unemployment	Arbeitslosigkeit
working conditions	Arbeitsbedingungen

The Impact of Shakespearean Drama on Young Audiences Today

The Elizabethan Age

Keyword:

The Elizabethan Age: named after Queen Elizabeth I, born 1533, crowned 1558, died 1603 (reign of 45 years)

Politics and economics

- England emerged as a world power
- international trade → rise of capitalism
- strongest naval force (defeat of Spanish Armada in 1588)
- internal problems: constant clash between Catholics and Protestants: firm establishment of Protestant Church with Elizabeth as head of the Church of England

Exploration of the New World

- Sir Francis Drake
- Sir Walter Raleigh

Culture

Keyword:

The Golden Age: term used for the Renaissance in Britain at the time of Elizabeth I

- freedom of spirit → imagination
- Greek and Roman thought
- domestic study of the Bible, widely read and heard
- opened new worlds of history and poetry, stimulated English culture
- cultural flowering: theatre, music, poetry, art, architecture
- Writers: William Shakespeare, Christopher Marlowe, Edmund Spenser
- Architect: Inigo Jones (introduced Italianate architecture to England)
- Composers: Thomas Tallis, William Byrd

The era was dominated by contrast: life for ordinary people could be hard, but economic growth also meant better conditions for many.
negative aspects:

- harsh criminal laws
- whipping and hanging for minor offences
- illiteracy
- short life-expectancy
- no rights for women

positive aspects:
- public provision for the poor (possible because of economic growth)
- few beggars

The Elizabethan World Picture

The Great Chain of Being

- vertical chain, hierarchically ordered → universal order
- every single speck of creation a link in the chain → almost infinite chain
- place in the chain determined by the relative proportion of spirit and matter
- the more spirit the higher the place in the chain

Hierarchy of the chain

God
⇩
Angels
⇩
Man
existence, life, feeling and understanding
→ the microcosm
⇩
higher animals
(having touch, memory, movement and hearing)
⇩
animals like ants
(having touch, memory, movement)
⇩
animals like shellfish
(having touch)

} sensitive class
existence, life, feeling

⇩
plants
existence and life
vegetable class
⇩
elements, liquids, metals
mere existence
inanimate class

The hierarchical order also applies within the classes:
- Water is nobler than earth.
- Gold is nobler than silver.
- The oak is nobler than the bramble.
- The lion is nobler than the dog.

The corresponding planes

Different segments of the chain are reflected in other segments. This means there is universal interdependence, i. e. correspondences.

Corresponding planes

divine and angelic

man or microcosm

universe or macrocosm

lower creation

commonwealth or body politic

The planes were connected by an immense net of correspondences.

Keyword:

Correspondences: They existed everywhere. […] When things were properly ordered, reason ruled the emotions, just as a king ruled his subjects, the parent ruled the child, and the sun governed the planets. But when disorder was present in one realm, it was correspondingly reflected in other realms.[1]

Examples of correspondences

macrocosm/microcosm	storms and earthquakes in the macrocosm ↔ passions of human beings
macrocosm/body politic	hierarchy of sun/moon/rainbow ↔ hierarchy of king/princes/governors
body politic/microcosm	debates of king and council ↔ commotions in a person's mind

Elizabethan thinking in terms of correspondences led to the abundance of images in Elizabethan literature.

1 Quelle: http://academic.brooklyn.cuny.edu/english/melani/cs6/ren.html

Elements and humours

As the human being was seen as a microcosm (literally, a “little world”), it reflected the structure of the world as a whole, the macrocosm. The world was composed of four “elements” (earth, water, air, fire), the qualities of which were founded on the notions of hot and cold, dry and moist.
Correspondingly, the human body was composed of four substances called “humours” with characteristics corresponding to the four elements. Imbalance or “disorder” among the humours, i. e. when they did not exist in proper proportion to each other, caused illness.

element	humour	common quality
earth	melancholy	cold and dry
water	phlegm	cold and moist
air	blood	hot and moist
fire	choler	hot and dry

Elizabethan Theatre

Theatres in Elizabethan London were venues of mass entertainment.

Theatres

- were situated outside the city
- offered performances every day
- presented plays, dances and music
- were also used for bear baiting, cruel killing of bears
- were attended by people from all social ranks.

- All performances were presented during the day.
- There was no lighting or special sound effects.
- Women‘s roles were played by men.
- The audience could smoke, eat, and drink.

→ Imagination depended totally on the language used in the play.

Common complaints about the theatre

- disorderly
- corrupts youth
- leads to evil and immoral (“ungodly”) character and behaviour
- stage stories are morally uncontrolled and primitive, not religiously inspiring
- leads to lewdness
- keep people away from work and prayer
- attracts criminals

Elizabethan Drama

Important playwrights: William Shakespeare, Christopher Marlowe *(Dr. Faustus)*, Ben Jonson *(The Alchemist)*, later John Webster *(The Duchess of Malfi)*.
Before the age of Elizabethan drama, plays were usually based on religious themes. Elizabethan drama focuses on more secular issues.

Types of Elizabethan play

Histories

Playgoers learned about England's 'heroic past', e.g. in *Edward II* (by Christopher Marlowe) or in Shakespeare's *Richard II, Richard III, Henry IV, Henry V*, etc.
Dramas like *Julius Caesar, Antony and Cleopatra* or *Macbeth* are not considered histories, because they do not focus on Britain's 'heroic' past but on the individual tragedies of their protagonists.

Tragedies

- end in a catastrophe (death of the character)
- catastrophe is a result of a character's flaw (Macbeth's ambition, Othello's jealousy)
- tragic hero still arouses interest in his fate, sympathy

Comedies

- happy ending
- often bawdy
- the audience went there for a good laugh
- sexual allusion and undertones very frequent even in tragedy: comic passages with strong sexual allusions often serve as comic relief (porter in *Macbeth*, Mercutio in *Romeo and Juliet)*

Romances

Shakespeare's late comedies (e.g. *The Winter's Tale, The Tempest)* are generally classified as romances. They are distinguished from comedies by certain elements:
- redemption, forgiveness, reuniting of long lost family members
- magic
- pastoral setting (beautiful nature, virgin island)

Elizabethan Poetry

Sonnets

Keyword:

Sonnet form: originally from Italy, 14th century
Sonnets were made popular by Francesco Petrarca (engl.: Petrarch)
The fashion of sonnet writing spread to France and England.

Important Elizabethan sonnet writers
- Thomas Wyatt (introduced sonnets to England, translations from Petrarca)
- Sir Philipp Sidney
- Edmund Spenser
- John Donne
- William Shakespeare

The Italian (Petrarchan) sonnet

	rhyme scheme	
octave/octet	a b b a	quatrain
	a b b a	quatrain
turn		
sestet	c d e	*tercet*
	c d e	*tercet*

Characteristics of the sonnet
- addressed to a beloved person
- 14 lines
- clearly defined rhyme scheme (the most common seen above)
- divided into an octet and a sestet
- turn after the octave

The turn after the octave is a shift of thought or feeling, often indicated by "but" or "yet".
Variations of rhyme scheme within the conventional structure are justified by the function they serve.

The English (Shakespearean) sonnet

	rhyme scheme	
octave	a b a b	quatrain
	c d c d	quatrain
sestet	e f e f	quatrain
turn		
	g g	*couplet*

The turn in the English sonnet occurs after the third quatrain. The couplet is a conclusion or a summary. However, one should still be aware that there can be the traditional turn after the octave. A sonnet may also be structured in terms of the three quatrains. Ideally there should be "three turns of the screw" in the three quatrains, before the point is driven home in the couplet.

Shakespeare's sonnets

- Shakespeare wrote 154 sonnets.
- Sonnets 1 to 126 are addressed to a young man.
- Sonnets 127 to 154 are addressed to a "dark lady".

Main themes: love, beauty, transience, old age, death

The **basic metre** is iambic pentameter but Shakespeare does not use it slavishly. Metre is used functionally, e. g.
- regular metre: harmony, peace, tranquillity, balance, stability, etc.
- irregular metre: disharmony, confusion, parody

Shakespeare's language

Prose

Ordinary speech, no metric pattern

Visual clues

- Printed lines extend from the left to the right margin.
- Lines do not start with a capital letter (unless following a full stop).

Function of prose

- often used by low status characters (murderers, servants, craftsmen, etc.), but not as a dogmatic rule
- low comedy (especially dirty jokes) often written in prose
- suggests a realistic tone
- used for bantering, e.g. Beatrice and Benedick
- sometimes indicates madness (Lady Macbeth, Lear)

Verse

Rhymes

- usually occur as rhymed couplets (aa bb cc)
- rhyme pair in iambic pentameter called "heroic couplet"

Function of rhymes

They often serve the same function as in a sonnet: concluding a scene, hammering the point home ("capping couplet").

Rhymes are used for
- highly lyrical passages
- choruses, prologues, epilogues
- romantic passages which are slightly over the top
- supernatural beings (witches, fairies).

Blank Verse

- an **unrhymed iambic pentameter**
- the standard verse in Shakespeare's plays

Blank verse resembles prose in that the final words of the lines do not rhyme in any regular pattern.
Unlike in prose, there is a recognizable metre: most (not necessarily all) lines are in iambic pentameter, i.e. they consist of ten syllables alternating unstressed and stressed syllables: da**dum** da**dum** da**dum** da**dum** da**dum**.

Example:
Give **me** your **han**d bef**ore** this **ho**ly **fri**ar.
I **am** your **hus**band **if** you l**ike** of **me**.
(from: *Much Ado About Nothing*, Act V, Scene 4, ll. 58-59)

Visual clues

- Printed lines do not extend from left to right margin.
- Lines start with capital letters.

Function of blank verse

Unlike rhyme, which sounds artificial, blank verse comes close to the natural speaking rhythms of English. Yet it makes it sound more elevated, less ordinary.

Other types of metre

Dimeter

A ***drum*** *a* ***drum***
*Mac**beth** doth **come.** (Macbeth,* Act I, Scene 3)
→ echoing the drum

Tetrameter

Double, double toil *and* ***trouble,***
Fire burn *and* ***caul**dron* ***bubble.*** *(Macbeth,* Act IV, Scene 1)

Fair *is* ***foul*** *and* ***foul*** *is* ***fair.*** *(Macbeth,* Act I, Scene 1)

The tetrameter here is used for spells (from the witches' speeches in *Macbeth).*

Shakespeare's Relevance to Modern Audiences

Pros	Cons
timeless themes – love – hate – rejection – jealousy – envy – greed – ambition – revenge – equivocation – appearance and reality etc.	outdated world picture
authentic characters, human and understandable modern adaptation in all literary genres – opera – musical – drama – novel – film – poetry – pop song Hollywood blockbusters	outdated attitudes and values regarding – gender roles – loyalty – generations – science – religion – superstition – social hierarchies etc.
aesthetics of language ubiquitous language in – idioms – proverbs – quotations – titles – allusions	outdated language partly incomprehensible imagery allusions and jokes

Glossary – Shakespeare and the Elizabethan Age

actor actress (not in Elizabethan times)	Schauspieler Schauspielerin
aside	beiseite gesprochener Text
blank verse	Blankvers
play drama tragedy comedy history romance	Schauspiel, Drama Drama Tragödie Komödie Historiendrama Romanze
Elizabethan age/era	elisabethanisches Zeitalter
enter exit; exeunt	tritt auf (Regieanweisung) geht ab; gehen ab
fatal flaw	verhängnisvolle Schwäche (des Tragödienhelden)
groundlings	stehende Zuschauer im elisabethanischen Theater
hero heroine	Held Heldin
Jacobean	aus der Zeit James I.
Master of the Revels	für Theater zuständiger Beamter
medieval the Middle Ages	mittelalterlich Mittelalter
performance to perform	Vorstellung vorführen
playhouse	Theater
playing company troupe The Lord Chamberlain's Men The Admiral's Men	Theatertruppe (berühmte Truppen der Shakespeare-Zeit)
playwright dramatist	Bühnenautor
Renaissance	Renaissance
scenery	Kulisse
soliloquy	Monolog/Selbstgespräch
stage stage props	Bühne Requisiten
wit	Geist, Witz

Visions of the Future

Utopia and Dystopia

Keywords:

Utopian literature: a fictional text dealing with an ideal (future) society.

Dystopian literature: a fictional text dealing with a future society in which human freedom is severely limited. A dystopia often criticizes our present-day society by exposing trends and tendencies towards totalitarian control.

Extrapolation: here: fictitious description of elements of a future society on the basis of present day phenomena and developments. The writer criticizes his or her own society by demonstrating what certain trends may lead to or what point society has already reached.

School Classics – Background Knowledge

The three novels presented here are so well known (not only) in English-speaking countries that you may encounter references to any one of these works in numerous texts. They will be presented here in the order of their first publication.

Aldous Huxley: *Brave New World*

Written in 1931, set in the distant future (26th century)

Generally known elements

- total control of society by in-vitro fertilization, artificial laboratory breeding, "cloning" of work force, and conditioning
- society strictly divided into Alpha, Beta, Gamma, Delta and Epsilon people with Alphas constituting the ruling class and Epsilons constituting a slave-like work force
- natural reproduction outlawed, sex as pure entertainment, monogamy regarded as unnatural and immoral
- people kept happy by means of a drug called "soma"
- religion replaced by a strong belief in technology and science

Extrapolation of developments of 20th century society in *Brave New World*

- belief in science, technology and progress
- misuse of science
- political and economic control and manipulation
- mass production and mass consumption
- decline of religion and values
- decline of educational standards
- drugs

- mass entertainment
- sensationalism

George Orwell: *1984*

Written in 1948, hence about a future society

Generally known elements

- **Big Brother:** constant surveillance, “Big Brother is watching you.” (Orwell's Big Brother: origin of the name of the popular present-day TV show)
- **Newspeak:** invention of a new, simplified form of the English language to manipulate thought, complex (i. e. critical) thinking cannot be put into words anymore Examples:
  - words like *goodthink, oldthink, crimethink:* simplify expressions of thought, make them imprecise, one-dimensional, eventually devoid of meaning
  - euphemisms like *Miniluv, Minipax, Minitrue:* sound positive, conceal their true meaning (Ministry of Love = police, Ministry of Peace = war, Ministry of Truth = propaganda)
  - **rewriting of history:** books and newspapers are manipulated

Extrapolation of elements of 20th century society in *1984*

- intrusion in people's privacy, spying on people: (Nazi Germany, Soviet Union)
- propaganda, misuse of mass media (Nazi Germany, Soviet Union)
- psychological torture

Ray Bradbury: *Fahrenheit 451*

Written in 1953, set in the future

Generally known elements

- **451 degrees Fahrenheit:** the temperature at which paper starts to burn
- society marked by entertainment, speed, restlessness and superficiality: extremely fast driving, multi-screen television at high volume with very shallow programmes, constant exposure to sound and advertising (individually by the wearing of ear-plugs or collectively by loudspeaker announcements)
- critical thought impeded as books are forbidden
- the firemen's job: to burn books

Extrapolation of elements of 20th century society in *Fahrenheit 451*

- burning of books (Nazi Germany)
- atomic bomb (Hiroshima)
- rise of television and audio media, effect on reading
- speeding-up in all areas of life: transport, communications, work, production, consumption
- dominance of entertainment
- decline of education

Science Fiction

Science fiction is a genre of fiction dealing with imaginary content such as future settings and futuristic science and technology.
As opposed to fantasy, its imaginary elements are largely possible within scientifically postulated laws of nature.
The settings for science fiction are often contrary to known reality, but most science fiction relies on potential scientific explanations or solutions to various fictional elements. There is no magic involved.

Elements of Science Fiction

- a setting in the future
- a setting in outer space (e.g. spaceflight), in other worlds, or in remote regions of the earth (underground, bottom of the sea)
- characters that include aliens, mutants, androids, or humanoid robots
- technology that is futuristic (e.g. ray guns, teleportation machines, humanoid computers, space ships, artificial planets)
- scientific principles that are new and have overcome known laws of nature, for example time travel, wormholes, or faster-than-light travel
- new and different societies, especially post-apocalyptic worlds
- paranormal abilities such as mind control, telepathy, telekinesis, and teleportation

There is considerable overlap between utopia/dystopia and science fiction.
However, one may say that science fiction is a lot more concerned with futuristic science and technology, which is central to the story, whereas utopian/dystopian narratives rather put their focus on society. Thus the element of extrapolation plays a central role in dystopian films and novels.
As an example, the films *Star Wars* or *Alien* do not really draw on extrapolation from today's society. The novels *Fahrenheit 451* and *Brave New World* or the film *Gattaca* do so extensively.

Classic Science Fiction Narratives

These classics are so well known (not only) in English-speaking countries that you may encounter references to any one of these works in numerous texts.

Mary Shelley, *Frankenstein* (1818)

Dr. Frankenstein brings to life a creature made of dead body parts and is then repulsed by what he has done. The creature becomes lonely and violent after being rejected by its creator, and turns against him.

H. G. Wells, *The Time Machine* (1895)

This story has popularized the concept of time travel, using a machine that allows an operator to travel to whatever period of history he wants. It has inspired countless science fiction stories, the most popular probably being the Hollywood production *Back to the Future*. The term “time machine”, coined by Wells, is now universally used.

H. G. Wells, *The War of the Worlds* (1898)

The story of an invasion of late Victorian England by Martians. The story has become particularly famous because of its adaptation in the 1938 radio broadcast that was narrated and directed by Orson Welles. It led to widespread panic by listeners who thought the invasion was real.

20th and 21st century science fiction novels and films are so abundant that there is no use listing any of them here. For your final exam, make sure you are familiar with the texts you studied.

Glossary – Utopia and Dystopia

anti-individualist	anti-individualistisch
anti-utopian	anti-utopisch
authoritarian	autoritär
brainwashing to brainwash	Gehirnwäsche (durchführen)
dissent	abweichende Meinung haben
dissenter	Andersdenkender
dystopia	Anti-Utopie, Dystopie
extrapolation	Übertragung, Ableitung
fiction fictitious fictional	Dichtung, erzählende Literatur fiktiv, erfunden literarisch
future	Zukunft, zukünftig
futuristic	futuristisch
hierarchy	Hierarchie
imaginary	erfunden
individualist	Individualist, individualistisch
indoctrination	Indoktrination/Indoktrinierung
oppression	Unterdrückung
restriction	Einschränkung
surveillance	Überwachung
totalitarian	totalitär
utopia	Utopie

Ethical Issues of Scientific and Technological Progress

Science

Keyword:

Genetics: field of study dealing with the way living organisms inherit features from their ancestors. These features are called traits. Traits are e. g. a person's eye-colour or height.

- Genetic information is carried by a molecule called DNA which is copied and inherited across generations.
- DNA is widely known as the "double helix" and looks like a twisted ladder. It is made up of nucleotides which are the rungs of the ladder. There are four types of nucleotides (A, T, G and C). The order of the nucleotides determines the genetic code of an organism.
- Genes are segments of DNA which provide information that an organism needs so that it can build or do something. They are like sentences spelled out by means of the "letters" of the nucleotide alphabet.
- The complete set of genes in a particular organism is known as a genome.
- Genes are copied each time a cell divides into two new cells. It is through a similar process that a child inherits genes from its parents, when a copy from the mother is mixed with a copy from the father.

Genetic engineering

Putting a new piece of DNA into a cell can produce a new trait. For example, crop plants can be given a gene from an Arctic fish, so they produce an antifreeze protein in their leaves. This may prevent frost damage. Other crops can be given genes including a natural insecticide, which will protect the plant.
People with genetic disorders can be treated by means of gene therapy. The idea is to replace a malfunctioning gene with one that functions properly.

Important steps in genetic engineering

- 1953: discovery of double helix by Watson and Crick, Cambridge, UK
- 1973: blend of unrelated organisms
- 1973: production of human protein insulin
- 1981: blend of species
- 1980s: work with human genes
- 1986: open-air experimentation with plants
- 1996: commercial cultivation of genetically modified plants
- 1996: cloning of mammals (Dolly)
- 2003: sequencing of the human genome
- 2009: first transgenic primates
- 2013: use of cloning to create human embryonic stem cells

Applications of GMOs (genetically modified organisms)

- biological and medical research
- production of pharmaceutical drugs
- experimental medicine (e. g. gene therapy)
- agriculture (e. g. golden rice)
- The **widest application** exists for crops resistant to herbicides or for producing pesticides from within.
- In 2014 1,815,000 sq km throughout the world were cultivated with GMO crops.The largest share of GMO crops planted globally is owned by Monsanto Inc.
- 18 million farmers planted biotech crops in 2015, 54% of them are small farmers from developing countries.[1]

Transgenic microbes

Bacteria were the first organisms to be modified in the laboratory. These organisms are now used for several purposes, and are particularly important in producing human proteins for use in medicine.

Genetically modified bacteria are used

- to produce insulin to treat diabetes,
- to produce clotting factors to treat haemophilia,
- to produce human growth hormone to treat various forms of dwarfism,
- to facilitate crop growth in some soils or prevent crop pests.

Transgenic animals

Transgenic animals are used

- as experimental models to test genes whose function is unknown,
- for the production of human hormones such as insulin.

Transgenic mice are used to study diseases and test treatments. Mice can be grown with the same genetic disorders that occur in human beings.

First genetically modified pet: the GloFish is a patented brand of genetically modified (GM) fluorescent zebra-fish with bright red, green and orange fluorescent colours.

Transgenic plants

Transgenic plants have been engineered to

- resist pests, herbicides or harsh environmental conditions,
- improve product shelf life,
- increase their nutritional value,
- produce bigger yields, thus making farmland more efficient.

"Terminator" Technology: GM plants do not yield seeds. This means that farmers have to buy new seeds every time.

1 https://isaaa.org/resources/publications/pocketk/16/default.asp

Designer Babies (Reprogenetics)

The colloquial term “designer baby” refers to a baby whose genetic makeup has been artificially selected to ensure the presence or absence of certain characteristics, especially with regard to the sex of the child.

Cloning

Cloning is the creation of an organism that is an exact genetic copy of another. This means that every single bit of DNA is the same between the two.
Dolly: (July 5, 1996 – February 14, 2003) a female sheep (ewe), was the first mammal to be cloned from an adult body cell. She lived until the age of six, when she developed severe diseases, which has led to speculation that a clone may be born with the genetic age of the organism from which it was cloned.

Ethics

Biotechnology in agriculture

Pros	**Cons**
higher productivity	genes can end up in unexpected places
more efficient land use	genes can mutate with harmful effect
more ecological farming (no ploughing, no fertilizing, no insecticides, no pesticides)	“sleeper” genes could be accidentally switched on, active genes could become “silent”
solution to problem of famine in the world	interaction with wild and native populations: negative impact on birds, insects and soil
higher quality of food	transfer of allergenic genes
longer shelf life	GM products in the food chain
rehabilitation of damaged land	transfer of antibiotic resistance
	loss of farmers’ control over material; “terminator” technology prevents sustainable farming → dependence on big corporations

Reprogenetics

Pros (once it is safe)	**Cons**
parents have a right to choose	technology is not safe yet
moral obligation to give children the best life possible	bioethical codes condemn experiments with human beings
will lead to improvement of the whole species	“super humans” may look down on normal people

	"imperfect" human beings would be discriminated against
	rich people would be at an advantage
	the human gene pool may be damaged
	"New Eugenics": people are designed to suit the needs of society
	people may be thought of as products
	human beings should not play God

Sex selection

Pros (once it is safe)	**Cons**
parents have a right to choose	preferences in patriarchal cultures lead to demographic imbalance
in some cultures male offspring are important to provide support for old age	members of the unwanted sex may be discriminated against
theory that having sisters (as opposed to brothers) enhances adults' quality of life	the child may not be loved if sth. goes wrong and it is not of the desired sex
	parents fulfil their own wishes, disregarding the rights of the child
	human beings are not allowed to play God

Human Cloning

Pros	**Cons**
medical reasons: resource of bone marrow or replaceable organs	cloning is inherently evil, an intrusion into human life
infertile couples may have children	a person who wants to clone himself/herself is self-centred
	cloning in order to produce superior beings is eugenics and eugenics is discriminatory
	using a human being as a resource for "spare parts" is unethical
	reproduction by means of cloning might have long-term consequences for human relationships
	children may be thought of as products
	Hinduism: What about the person's karma?
	dictators may become immortal

Glossary – Ethical Issues

achievement of scientists	Errungenschaft/Leistung der Wissenschaftler
artificial insemination	künstliche Befruchtung
development	Entwicklung
DNA (deoxyribonucleic acid)	DNA/DNS
double helix (DNA)	Doppelhelix, DNA
error rate	Fehlerrate
genetic disorders	genetische Funktionsstörung
genetic engineering	Gentechnik, Genmanipulation
genetic fingerprint	genetischer Fingerabdruck
genetic make-up, genetic constitution	Erbgut
genetic modification (GM)	genetische Veränderung
heredity, inheritance	Vererbung
inherit	erben
insecticide	Insektizid
in-vitro fertilization	In-vitro-Befruchtung
laboratory	Labor
to modify modification	modifizieren, verändern Modifizierung
molecule	Molekül
to mutate mutation	mutieren Mutation
non-polluting	umweltfreundlich
organ donor	Organspender
to pass on	vererben
pesticide	Unkrautvernichtungsmittel, Pestizid
progress (no article, no plural)	Fortschritt
reproductive cloning	Klonen von Menschen
research (into)	Forschung
research facility	Forschungseinrichtung
resistance	Resistenz
stem cell	Stammzelle
technology	Technologie, Technik
test-tube baby	Retortenbaby
therapeutic cloning	therapeutisches Klonen
transgenic	transgen (genetisch verändert)

Studying and Working in a Globalized World

With the world constantly becoming smaller due to globalization, it has become much easier to spend some time in a foreign country for educational reasons, both during one's time at school and/or as part of studies at a university or vocational training. Some future employers consider it an essential aspect of a prospective employee's CV (résumé) to have spent some time abroad, very often in an English-speaking country.

Benefits for oneself

- getting a personal insight into other cultures
- improving one's foreign language skills
- experiencing different educational systems
- contributing to one's personal development, e.g. to become more independent, self-confident, adaptable to different situations
- making new friends
- improving one's career opportunities
- broadening one's horizon on various levels

Studying and working abroad also has benefits for employers. A growing number of companies tend to employ people who have studied abroad, as these prospective employees are said to possess key job skills, e.g. cultural empathy, excellent foreign language skills, self-organization, adaptability, open-mindedness and flexibility.

Volunteerism and voluntourism

In the last couple of years **volunteerism** has become more popular. It means that a person volunteers to use his/her time and skills to contribute to a community without receiving any payment. An increasing number of people combine being a volunteer with spending some time abroad. There are various ways in which one can contribute to a community, e.g. humanitarian aid or teaching at a local school in a rural village. Volunteerism should not be confused with **voluntourism,** which can generally be defined as a combination of volunteering and sightseeing.
Voluntourism is a neologism based on the words "volunteer" and "tourism" and has been criticized as counterfeiting the original idea of volunteering.
Some of the arguments critics put forward against voluntourism are that it is not truly beneficial for communities, since "voluntourists" only spend a relatively short time in the communities in question and therefore often do not truly immerse. In addition to that, they are said to enjoy all the benefits of an ordinary tourist, e.g. staying in hotels far above the living-standard of the community they are helping, while not being really prepared for their placements. Whereas in the past charities and NGOs were mostly in charge of matching volunteers with the right projects, some major travel agencies now also specialize in offering placements for "voluntourists" against payment.

English as a *lingua franca*

English can be regarded as a *lingua franca,* which means that it is a language spoken by such a vast number of people all over the world that it enables speakers of different first languages to successfully communicate with each other.
These non-native speakers of English have a huge impact on the English language, e.g. when it comes to grammar or pronunciation, for when non-native speakers of English communicate with each other it is their main intention to communicate a message. As a consequence, grammatical constructions regarded as incorrect by native speakers of English are accepted by both speakers and do not impede the flow of their conversation.
Code mixing and code switching also occur.
Code mixing means that a speaker uses words, syntax etc. from his mother tongue and English words in the same sentence. In contrast to that, the term code switching is used to refer to a speaker who switches between the vocabulary, syntax etc. of his or her mother tongue and English, often in the same sentence.
Nowadays English language skills are not considered a special feature but are taken for granted in many areas of life.

The changing world of work

Past generations often spent their entire working life with one employer, retiring from the same company with which they started. But, due to globalization, the world of work has changed rapidly over the last half century. Advances in information technology have made it possible for a company's employees in different countries to work on the same project and to exchange information on the spot. Due to new technological and economic developments, new types of jobs have been created which were unheard of only half a century ago.
Still, finding one's dream job has not become easier, and employees are often expected to show a high level of flexibility and adaptability. Changing jobs and places of residence frequently is not uncommon, as there is high competition in certain jobs. Nor do the realities of the job market always match one's expectations and wishes. Despite the fact that there is employment growth in the United Kingdom, Germany and the USA, not everyone profits from it. The number of jobs for people with no or low work skills is decreasing and the gap between the rich and the poor is widening all over the world.

Minimum wage and living wage

22 countries of the European Union, and the USA, have a statutory minimum wage. In 2015 Germany introduced a minimum wage, calculated either on the basis of an hourly rate or as a monthly payment. The minimum wage varies in different fields of work. Being paid a minimum wage means that an employee receives the lowest wage his/her employer is legally allowed to pay. Some of the arguments put forward in favour of the minimum wage are that it prevents people from being exploited by

employers and from having to rely on social benefits in order to make ends meet.
In the UK some companies and institutions voluntarily pay their employees a "living wage" instead of the legal minimum wage. While a "minimum wage" is calculated in accordance with the development of the job market, a "living wage" is an hourly rate calculated on the basis of the cost of living index (e.g. accommodation, travel, food and drink, costs for heating, water and electricity), which in the UK is adjusted annually. In 2019 the voluntarily paid living wage in the UK was £9.00 an hour, with the exception of London where it is £10.55 an hour, due to higher costs of living.
In April 2019 the compulsory "national living wage" for people aged 25 or older was £8.21 per hour; lower than the living wage calculated by the Living Wage Foundation.

Living Wage Foundation

On its website, the London-based Living Wage Foundation says that it developed from a citizens' movement in 2001 when the charity "Citizens UK" brought parents together to exchange views on the ups and downs of family life: "It emerged that too many parents were working two jobs just to make ends meet and so had no time to spend with their children. They worked hard but couldn't earn enough to afford a decent standard of living."[1] The Living Wage Foundation is supported by the UK's political parties, and both Houses of Parliament are among those who pay their employees a living wage.

In January 2017, Finland launched a social experiment in which the Finnish government granted 2000 unemployed people an unconditional basic income (UBI) of €560 for 24 months, without urging them to look for employment or to accept job offers. Those who took a job during this period still received UBI.
The intention behind this social experiment was to find out whether UBI motivates unemployed people to find jobs or enter job training. UBI provides a "safety net" so that they will not feel too much financial pressure.
It is not easy to say whether this experiment has been a success or not. The number of unemployed participants in the experiment has not decreased as much as was hoped, but those who participated said that they felt more contented for the duration of the experiment.

Glossary – Studying and Working in a Globalized World

adaptability	Anpassungsfähigkeit
apprenticeship, vocational training	Berufsausbildung, Lehre
charity	Wohlfahrtsorganisation
community service	ehrenamtliche Tätigkeit
compulsory education/schooling	Schulpflicht
CV (curriculum vitae) (BE)/résumé (AE)	Lebenslauf
exchange student	Austauschschüler(in)/-student(in)

1 http://www.livingwage.org.uk (retrieved April 2019)

flexibility	Flexibilität
gap year	freiwilliges (soziales, ökologisches etc.) Jahr/Auszeit
job advertisement/job offer	Stellenanzeige/-angebot
job interview	Bewerbungsgespräch
key qualifications	Schlüsselqulifikationen
minimum wage	Mindestlohn
open-mindedness	Aufgeschlossenheit
placement/internship	Praktikum
scholarship	Stipendium
school exchange	Schüleraustausch
social commitment	soziales Engagement
social skills	soziale Kompetenz
study abroad	Auslandsstudium
to apply for (a job)	sich (für eine Stelle) bewerben
to broaden one's horizon	seinen Horizont erweitern
to climb the social ladder	Karriere machen
to donate/give sth. to charity	etw. an eine Wohltätigkeitsorganisation spenden/weiterleiten
to gain experience	Erfahrungen sammeln
to get an insight into foreign cultures	einen Einblick in fremde Kulturen erhal-ten
to speak from one's own experience	aus eigener Erfahrung sprechen
volunteer	Freiwillige(r)

Methoden der Textarbeit

Literarische Texte

Narration

Keyword:

narrative texts: narrative texts can have many forms, among them short story, novel, fairytale, satire, parable, legend, etc.
Most relevant for your final exam are the short story and the novel.

When asked to analyze a narrative text, you will have to focus on particular elements that are characteristic of short stories or novels.

Elements of narration

Structure

Plot

INFO Elements of a complete plot

exposition → rising action → climax/turning point → falling action → ending

A **plot** need not necessarily be complete (e. g. open ending).

The **sequence** need not necessarily be in chronological order.
There may be foreshadowing or flashbacks or there may be reverse narration (umgestelltes Erzählen).
In particular, an excerpt from a longer text, which is the most common sort of text in the final exam, may not contain all the elements of plot.
Certain **key events** within the action of a story will raise the tension; they will create suspense, rising to a climax or turning point. After that there will be falling tension or relief.

INFO Tension curve

rising tension → climax or turning point → falling tension or relief

Theme

The **theme** of a story is always abstract. Themes are *e.g.* love, poverty, racism, childhood, *etc.*
The **subject matter** of a story is the concrete realization of the theme.

Example
Two stories may have the same theme: racism. The subject matter of the one may be the murder of an African-American, of the other the bullying of a black schoolgirl.

Character

When asked to characterize a figure from a narrative text, you will have to be aware of different aspects. There are key questions that can guide you.

Direct characterization
- What does the narrator say about the character?
- What do other characters say about the character?
- What does the character say about himself/herself?
- How objective is what they say? Be aware of words with negative or positive connotations.

Indirect characterization
- How does the character act?
- What does the character say?
- What kind of language does he/she use?

It might help to fill in a table with the following headings:

Character's outward appearance	Character's language	Character's actions	What the character says	Other characters' statements (or actions)
...	...	...	...	...

Narrator/point of view

INFO Narrator

The narrator is either a first-person or a third-person narrator.
The first-person narrator is NOT the author!

limited point of view	unlimited/omniscient point of view
first-person narrator	third-person narrator (neutral omniscience, God-like knowledge about all facts)
third-person narrator (one character's point of view)	third-person narrator (several characters' points of view)

The narrator always works like a camera, taking a point-of-view shot through a character's eyes or looking at the characters from the outside.

Example:
In Alan Sillitoe's novel *Saturday Night and Sunday Morning* (1975), the reader is presented with an episode in a pub (p. 10). When the narrator says, "Brenda and two other women sitting at Arthur's table saw him push back his chair and stand up with a clatter, [...]", he takes Brenda's and the women's point of view: Arthur is clearly seen from outside, not by a neutral narrator but through the women's eyes: The women sitting at Arthur's table saw him push back his chair, NOT Arthur pushed back his chair.
→ limited point of view

A few lines later the point of view changes: "He felt electric light bulbs shining and burning into the back of his head."
The narrator takes Arthur's point of view, knows what Arthur feels.
→ limited point of view

Mode of presentation

Panoramic presentation (telling) vs. scenic presentation (showing)

There are two modes of presentation to be found in narratives: the **panoramic** and the **scenic** mode:

The **panoramic** mode is employed when the narrator summarizes several events, whereas **scenic** mode is used when the narrator describes scenes in great detail.

Interior monologue is a particular kind of scenic presentation, in which the thoughts and feelings passing through a character's mind are depicted. In **reported thought** the thoughts are presented as reported speech.

This is closely connected with the concepts of *narrated time and narrating* (or *acting) time:*

narrated time longer than narrating time	usually summary of events
narrated time identical with narrating time	e.g. direct speech
narrated time shorter than narrating time	e.g. stream of consciousness, interior monologue, detailed description of a scene, comparable to slow motion in film

INFO Function of mode of presentation and point of view

A neutral, omniscient narrator, who observes the action and the characters from above and who uses a panoramic mode of presentation, is more detached and thus creates a distance between the reader and the action. On the other hand, a narrator who takes a character's point of view creates immediacy, directly involves the reader in what happens.

Setting

The place and time where the action is set is called the setting. It is especially important for *atmosphere* and *symbolism.*

Atmosphere

Atmosphere is created by means of setting, objects, colours, light and darkness, but also by reference to a character's mood or the use of language.

Example:
In Kate Chopin's short story "Desirée's Baby" a "yellow stuccoed house" is described with a roof that comes down "steep and black like a cowl." (Mönchskutte). It is surrounded by "big, solemn oaks", the "thick-leaved, far-reaching branches" shadowing "it like a pall" (Leichentuch).

colour	black, dirty yellow
light/darkness	shadow of the oaks
language: similes, "like a pall", "like a cowl"	→ connotations of death, darkness, mystery.

The atmosphere created here is gloomy, sombre, sinister, threatening, eerie.

Symbolism

Symbols are part of the setting of the narrative.

INFO Established symbols

These are conventional symbols which have long been used and have a certain, traditional significance which everybody knows. Examples of established symbols: rose, cross, the colour white.

INFO Created symbols

Something becomes symbolic within a certain context, because it is closely connected to an event, a situation or a character.

Example:
In the novel *Angela's Ashes* (1996), Angela, the family's mother, vomits over the side of the ship when they leave New York harbour for Ireland and the wind from the Atlantic blows it all over the family. (p. 53)
In the course of the novel the reader will learn how unfortunate the family's decision to leave America will turn out to be and how disastrous the wind from the Atlantic will be for the family. Thus this passage from the first chapter of the book is symbolic.

INFO Symbols and metaphors

Symbols are NOT metaphors!
Symbols are really there, are part of the story. Metaphors or similes are figures of speech.

Examples:
She was a rose, so beautiful. → metaphor
She was like a rose, so beautiful. → simile/comparison
They fell in love when they first met in her father's rose garden. → symbol

Language and style

In order to determine the style of a text it is necessary to examine aspects such as register, diction (choice of words), tone, and also sentence structure.

Register is the level of language used in a particular situation. It may be formal, neutral, informal, or vulgar. There may be a lot of slang words, even taboo words, or technical terms, or jargon.

The **tone** may be ironic, sarcastic, sad, humorous, serious, playful, angry, etc., depending on the emotional attitude it expresses. This depends on the choice of words, level of speech, rhythm, sentence length, etc.

Stylistic devices will be considered at length in the chapters on poetry and non-fictional texts (pp. 88, 94)

Poetry

Poetry focuses on the **aesthetic function** of language.
Poetry appeals to the senses. It is to be enjoyed for its beauty, its cleverness, its wit, its impact. This is achieved by

- the sound of words
- the rhythm of the words and phrases
- the choice of words
- the structure of the sentences
- the composition of the poem
- the visual arrangement of words and lines
- and, above all, by means of imagery.

In your final exams, however, you will be asked not so much to enjoy the poem but to examine its meaning and the effect of the language the speaker uses.

How to proceed

Questions to be asked

- Who is the speaker of the poem?
- Where is the speaker?
- Does the speaker address somebody?
- Does the speaker contemplate something?
- Does the speaker describe something or somebody?
- Does the speaker tell a story?
- Does the speaker explain something?
- Does the speaker argue against or in favour of something?
- What is the speaker's attitude? What is he/she saying?
- How is the poem composed? Is it structured by rhyme scheme, or by division into stanzas, or by some other device?
- Is there a correspondence between the structure of the poem and the structure of the speaker's thoughts?
- What is the significance of the title?
- What words does the speaker use? What do they mean?
- What is the structure of the sentences? Simple? Complex?
- What poetic devices does the speaker use?
- And what is the effect of all this? What is the experience of reading?

In order to understand and describe poetry you need to be familiar with its most important elements.

Elements of poetry

INFO Speaker and author

The speaker of the poem is NOT the author. Poems may be autobiographical, but you must still refer to the "speaker of the poem".

Poems are composed of **stanzas** and **lines**.
Stanzas may have a certain **rhyme scheme.**

Rhyme

Rhyme schemes

rhyme pair	a a b b
alternate rhyme	a b a b
embracing rhyme	a b b a

Types of rhymes

masculine rhyme (on one syllable)	kiss/this
feminine rhyme (on two syllables)	dreary/weary
true rhyme	kiss/this, dreary/weary
slant rhyme assonance (same vowel) consonance (same consonant)	 comb/coat hope/heap

Lines may be marked by a certain rhythm. The smallest unit that determines rhythm is the foot, consisting of at least one stressed and one or two unstressed syllables. The pattern of stressed and unstressed syllables is called **metre.**

A sequence of stressed and unstressed syllables is nothing artificial. It is the natural rhythm of the English language. It is the poet's skill to choose words in a way that this pattern will constitute a regular metre.

Types of foot

foot	stresses	example
iamb/iambic	– / (da-**dum**)	compare
trochee/trochaic	/ – (**dum**-da)	lovely
spondee/spondaic	/ / (**dum dum**)	drop dead
anapest/anapestic	– – / (da-da-**dum**)	lemonade
dactyl/dactylic	/ – – (**dum**-da-da)	whispering

The number of feet or stressed syllables in a line determines its metre. The most common types are shown here:

number of feet	metre	example
1	monometer	"And find / What wind ..." (John Donne, "Song", ll. 7 – 8)
2	dimeter	"Why dost thou thus ..." (John Donne, "The Sun Rising", l. 2)
3	trimeter	"Go, Soul, the body's guest Upon a thankless errant;" (Sir Walter Raleigh, "The Lie")
4	tetrameter	"Busy old fool, unruly sun ..." (John Donne, "The Sun Rising", l. 1)
5	pentameter	"Love, all alike, no season knows, nor clime ..." (John Donne, "The Sun Rising", l. 9)
6	hexameter	"A needless alexandrine ends the song That, like a wounded snake, drags its slow length along" (Alexander Pope, "An Essay on Criticism", ll. 356 – 357)

INFO Most important metre in English poetry

Iambic pentameter:
"But thy eternal summer shall not fade" (Shakespeare, Sonnet 18).

Lines

end-stop lines	natural pause for the end of a thought at the end of a line	"Shall I compare thee to a summer's day?" (Shakespeare, Sonnet 18)
run-on lines (enjambement)	The meaning requires no pause between the lines.	"When yellow leaves, or none, or few, do hang Upon those boughs which shake against the cold ..." (Shakespeare, Sonnet 73)
caesura	The meaning requires a pause in mid-line.	"Let me not to the marriage of true minds Admit impediments; love is not love ..." (Shakespeare, Sonnet 116)

Imagery

A writer or speaker using language beyond its dictionary meaning makes use of **imagery.** All figurative use of language is imagery. Imagery appeals to all the senses, it is meant to stimulate the reader's or listener's imagination.

TIPP Watch out!

The word *imagery* is an abstract noun. There is no plural. You can only talk about single *images*.

Types of imagery

metaphor	A metaphor compares two basically dissimilar things without using the words 'like' or 'as'. Some characteristics of the one are thus transferred to the other in order to illustrate its qualities. Example: Eve Merriam's poem at the head of this chapter.
simile/ comparison	Like a metaphor, a simile draws a comparison, but it explicitly uses the words 'like' or 'as' to do so. "My love is like a red red rose" (Robert Burns)
personification	It is a kind of metaphor in which animals, plants, inanimate objects or abstract ideas are represented as if they were human beings and possessed human qualities: "Busy old fool, unruly sun, / Why dost thou thus, / Through windows, and through curtains call on us?" (John Donne, "The Sun Rising")
symbol	see examples in previous chapter, p. 83

Other poetic devices

stylistic device	definition	example
alliteration	repetition of a sound (usually a consonant) at the beginning of adjacent words	"From forth the fatal loins of these two foes A pair of star-crossed lovers take their life." *(Romeo and Juliet,* Prologue)
onomatopoeia adj. onomatopoeic	the use of words which imitate the sound they refer to	"the stuttering rifles' rapid rattle" (Wilfred Owen, "Anthem for doomed youth")
anaphora (use: "example of anaphora/ examples of anaphora")	One or more words are repeated at the beginning of adjacent sentences or lines.	"In every cry of every man In every infant's cry of fear In every voice, in every ban" (W. Blake, "London")
chiasm	reversal of order of the words in the two parts of a sentence	"Fair is foul, and foul is fair" (Shakespeare, *Macbeth)*
oxymoron	a combination of contradictory words and meanings.	"O heavy lightness, serious vanity, Misshapen chaos of well-seeming forms," (Shakespeare, *Romeo and Juliet)*

Drama

When asked to analyze a dramatic text, you will have to focus on particular elements that are characteristic of plays or film scripts.

Elements of drama

Structure

Plot

The audience is confronted with the action on stage or on the screen directly. There is no narrator. Yet one can identify the same elements of plot as are found in narration.

INFO Elements of a dramatic plot

exposition → rising action → climax or crisis → falling action → dénouement or catastrophe

In tragedy, the opponents of the hero gain the upper hand in the falling action, which ends in the catastrophe.
Comedy has a happy ending, in which conflicts are resolved (dénouement).

Stage directions

The dramatic text consist of **two kinds of text:** the more important kind of text is the dialogue spoken by the characters (i. e. dialogue, monologue, and asides).
The stage directions are the second kind of text. They give the instructions concerning the stage design, about sounds to be heard, visual effects, the characters and also the way some of the dialogue has to be spoken.
The following visual and acoustic elements will have to be considered in your analysis of stage directions. They will help to characterize a character, create atmosphere or function as symbols. (cf. p. 83)

concerning the actors		**concerning the stage**	
visual	**acoustic**	**visual**	**acoustic**
size	voice	scenery	music
facial expression	intonation	stage design	noise
gestures	language of the play	lighting	sound
costumes	non-verbal noises	properties *(Requisiten)*	

Characters

The audience is confronted with the characters on stage directly, there is no narrator. A character is presented through action, interaction and dialogue and, of course, his outward appearance on stage (see above).
There are **flat** characters, types that act in a predictable way, and **round**, lifelike characters that are fully developed.

Language/Dialogue/Communication

When analysing the language of a play you have to keep in mind that it works on two levels:
1. The inner system of communication, i. e. the communication among the characters.
2. The outer system of communication between the playwright and the audience.

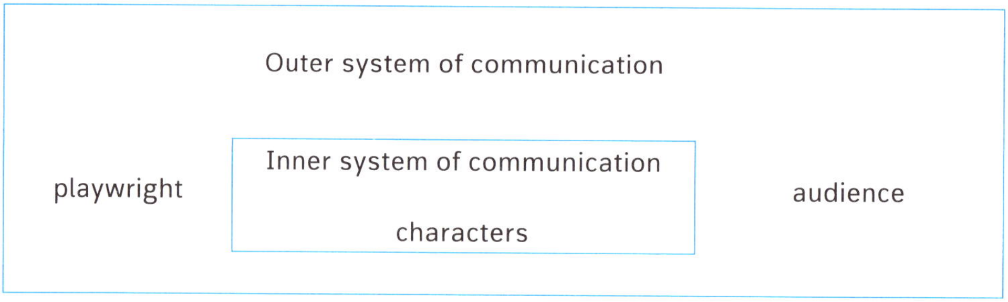

<u>Dramatic irony</u>
Dramatic irony is an important effect that is created by these two levels of communication. If the audience knows more than a character, an utterance will be perceived as ironic when it sharply contrasts with reality.

<u>Example</u>
In Shakespeare's Macbeth, King Duncan praises the peaceful atmosphere at Macbeth's castle, whereas the audience knows that Duncan will be murdered.

<u>Comedy</u>
On the level of communication between playwright and audience, dramatic irony, the audience's awareness of facts the characters do not know, may serve a comic effect, too.

<u>Aside</u>
In an aside an actor speaks to the audience in order to provide information on his thoughts and feelings or intentions. The other characters on stage supposedly do not hear what he says.

TIPP

As many of Shakespeare's plays are written in verse, you may approach their language the same way as poetry.

Glossary – Vocabulary for analysing literary texts

the narrator tells of/shows/relates/reveals
the narrator takes xy's point of view
the narrator is omniscient
the story is told in the first person/third person
the story is told from the first-person-singular point of view
the narrator uses/employs/makes use of metaphors, similes, comparisons
a metaphor shows/stands for/suggests
the narrator speaks in an ironic/satirical/detached/matter-of-fact/serious tone
the story deals with/treats of/concentrates on/focuses on ...
atmosphere is created
tension/ suspense is created/built up
a poem is written/composed
a poem is read, spoken, recited
a recital of a poem
the poem is by Shakespeare
it is a song by Genesis
the speaker of the poem/the poetic I/the poetic persona
the poem consists of/is composed of/is arranged in stanzas
the comedy ridicules/mocks/satirizes
the exposition sets the action in motion
the action moves towards and culminates in a turning-point
the play/film has a simple/complex/tight plot
it has a happy/unhappy ending
there are main/major/minor characters
the protagonist is in conflict with an opponent
the antagonist fights the protagonist
the spectator/audience follows the play
the play is performed/produced/staged
scenery is shifted
actors perform/play/enact
an actor enters/makes an entrance
an actor exits/makes his exit

Sach- und Gebrauchstexte

Argumentative Texte: *How to deal with (political) speeches*

Keyword:

(Political) speeches: aim at convincing *(überzeugen)* the audience of the speaker's position, winning them over to his/her side. Very often, the speaker tries to persuade (überreden) the listener by appealing to his/her feelings. In some cases, the orator may even attempt to manipulate *(manipulieren)* his audience. You should always keep in mind that the speaker wants to present his/her opinion/conviction/point of view as positively as possible.

When asked to analyse a political speech, you will have to focus on the topic and characteristic features.

How to proceed

Reading of the text

1. Read the (political) speech (or, more likely, an extract from it) as a whole, trying to identify the main topic of the speech (reading for gist).
2. Re-read the (political) speech (the extract) several times, paying special attention to certain characteristic features of such speeches. Mark words or phrases in the text and take notes (intensive reading).

Pay special attention to

- key words and phrases
- references to historical events
- use of symbols, key words, slogans
- references to famous people
- references to works of literature
- stylistic devices (see below)

Questions to be asked

When it comes to analysing a (political) speech, you should always ask yourself the following questions:
- What is the main topic of the speech?
- What is its political, historical and social context?
- What do I know about the speaker (biography, political orientation)?

Elements of a (political) speech

Structure

(Political) speeches can usually be divided into **introduction, main part** and **conclusion.** These parts serve different purposes:

INFO Introduction to a speech

In the introduction the orator announces the topic/purpose of the speech and explains why it is of major importance. He/she also wants to attract the audience's attention so that they will follow the speech closely and accept his/her opinion.

There are several ways to make listeners interested:

- The speaker can open by telling the audience **something about their personal history/recent experiences,** thereby underlining the fact that the topic of the speech is of personal importance to them. By relating a **little story** to the audience, the speaker will also appear more human and less flawless.
- Another common way of starting a speech is to **open it with a question** that refers to the main topic and which will be answered later in the speech. By asking the audience a question, the speaker actively involves them, indirectly asking them to think more deeply about the question.
- A speaker may also **present visuals to the audience,** e.g. pictures, concrete objects or a short extract from a film. This also helps to attract the audience's attention: listeners will become curious about how the object or visual is related to the content of the speech.

INFO Main part of a speech

In the main part of the speech the orator needs to keep the audience interested and to make sure that they can follow the train of thought.

Again, there are several ways to do this. The following techniques are particularly effective:

- **using short and simple sentences,** developing the argumentation step by step and ensuring that the audience can follow
- **quoting reliable sources/experts, referring to statistics and providing the audience with facts and necessary background information,** which shows that the speaker is well-informed and has researched the subject
- **pointing out problems, but also providing solutions** for them, thus showing that the speaker is competent
- **including personal experiences** and vivid, concrete events, again aiming for a personal relationship to the audience, **often using personal pronouns like "we", "us", "our".**

Towards the end of a speech the speaker might
- take up a question posed at the beginning of the speech;
- appeal once more to both the audience's head and heart;
- ask for support, giving the listeners the feeling that their support is important;
- develop a vision for the future.

Argumentative comments use the same stylistic means as political speeches.

Language and style

There are certain stylistic devices, which are often used in (political) speeches. They aim at making the speech more lively and interesting.

Important stylistic devices

analogy	A resemblance is established between things which are unlike.
simile	This is a direct comparison using the words "like" or "as", e.g. *He fought like a lion in the battle.*
metaphor	This is an indirect comparison without using the words "like" or "as", e.g. *He was a lion in battle.*
alliteration	A consonantal sound of two or more adjacent words is repeated, e.g. *We will win … "We must understand that ties of trade bind nations in closest intimacy …"* (Warren G. Harding: Inaugural address, March 4, 1921).
repetition	Repeating certain words or phrases puts emphasis on the meaning of the words and phrases in question, e.g. *"The answer to the slavery question was already embedded within our Constitution – a Constitution that had at its very core the ideal of equal citizenship under the law; a Constitution that promised its people liberty, and justice (…)."* (Barack Obama: *A More Perfect Union)*
parallelism	Two or more parts of a sentence (or two or more sentences) have the same (or similar) syntactical structure. Like repetition, parallelism puts stress on the parts of the sentence in question, intensifying the force of the statement and encouraging the audience to think about its meaning, e.g. *"Let us be our sister's keeper. Let us find that common stake we all have in one another, and let our politics reflect that spirit as well."* (Barack Obama: *A More Perfect Union)*
antithesis	Two ideas are opposed to one another, using a parallel syntactical structure to reach the desired effect, i.e. establishing a contrast, e.g. *"It's a story that hasn't made me the most conventional can-didate. But it is a story that has seared into my genetic makeup the idea that this nation is more than the sum of its parts – that out of many, we are truly one."* (Barack Obama: *A More Perfect Union)*

rhetorical question	A rhetorical question is one to which no answer is expected; instead the listener is asked to think about the question and its relevance, e.g. *"How long should this suffering continue?"*
irony	Words or phrases are used to mean something different, often the opposite of their literal meaning. This is often done for rhetorical or humorous effect.

Glossary – Vocabulary for analysing speeches

By telling the listeners something about his personal history he attempts to establish a personal relationship with his audience.	Er bemüht sich, eine persönliche Beziehung zu seinen Zuhörern aufzubauen, indem er seinem Publikum etwas über seine persönliche Geschichte erzählt.
She attempts to win her listeners over to her side.	Sie versucht, das Publikum auf ihre Seite zu ziehen.
He draws a comparison between … and …	Er zieht einen Vergleich zwischen … und …
He puts emphasis on the meaning of his words by using a parallelism/repetition in l. X (line …).	Durch den in Zeile X verwendeten Parallelismus/die in Zeile X verwendete Wiederholung verleiht er seinen Worten Nachdruck.
He refers to well-known historical events such as …	Er bezieht sich auf allgemein bekannte historische Ereignisse wie z. B. …
He wants to call/draw the audience's attention to the fact that …	Er möchte die Aufmerksamkeit des Publikums auf die Tatsache lenken, dass …
His frequent use of rhetorical questions is intended to show that …	Sein häufiger Gebrauch rhetorischer Fragen soll verdeutlichen, dass …
His metaphorical use of language is intended to make his speech more lively and interesting.	Sein metaphorischer Sprachgebrauch soll seine Rede interessanter und lebendiger machen.
In l. X (line …) he directly criticizes his political opponents.	In Zeile … kritisiert er offen seine politischen Gegner.
The frequent use of personal pronouns such as "we", "us" and "our" gives the audience the impression that he does not regard himself as superior to them, but as one of them.	Der häufige Gebrauch der Personalpronomen „wir", „uns" und „unser" soll dem Publikum das Gefühl geben, dass er sich als einer von ihnen und nicht als eine höher gestellte Person sieht.
The speaker appeals to the audience's emotions by …	Der Redner/die Rednerin spricht die Gefühle des Publikums an, indem er/sie …

The speaker begins by ...	Der Redner/die Rednerin beginnt mit ...
The speaker makes frequent use of metaphors/similes/symbols/examples to point out/to underline that ...	Der Redner/die Rednerin macht regen Gebrauch von Metaphern/Vergleichen/Symbolen/Beispielen, um herauszustellen/zu unterstreichen, dass ...
The speaker tries to convince his audience of his point of view by ...	Der Redner/die Rednerin versucht sein/ihr Publikum von seinem/ihrem Standpunkt zu überzeugen, indem er/sie ...
The speaker aims to convince/persuade/manipulate the audience.	Es ist das Anliegen des Redners/der Rednerin, das Publikum zu überzeugen/überreden/manipulieren.

Expositorische Texte: *How to deal with essays*

Keyword:

Essays: There are various kinds.

a) essays which reflect the author's opinion on a certain topic (**comment**)
b) essays in which the author weighs the pros and cons of a particular subject (**argumentative essay**)
c) essays in which a topic is presented in a clear and logical way and which do not contain the author's opinion (**expository essay**)

How to proceed

First you have to find out which kind of essay you are asked to analyse.

TIPP Argumentative comments

Argumentative comments use the same stylistic means as political speeches.

For details on how to analyse **comments** you can refer to the section on **political speeches** above.
Here we will focus on the **argumentative essay.**

Structure

- In the **introduction** the author expresses the main idea of the essay. Instead of giving a personal opinion, she/he might choose to provide the reader with some background information, or start with a question which will serve as a guideline and be answered in the course of the essay.

- For the **main part** of the essay the author can decide on a dialectical or an enumerative approach.
- In an **enumerative approach** the author will enumerate all the aspects of the subject in a neutral way. A **dialectical approach** can either present all the arguments in favour of a position before focusing on the counterarguments (or vice versa), or it can present the pros and cons alternately. The latter is usually considered more skilful.
- Each **new aspect** is usually presented in a new paragraph. The various **arguments** can be backed with examples from real life, established facts, an expert opinion, or other reliable sources. These pieces of evidence are very important, as they enable the author to make his argument convincing and thus to persuade the reader.
- In the **conclusion** the author sums up the arguments, frequently also restating his/her own opinion and giving an outlook on the future.

Glossary – Vocabulary for analysing essays

The author discusses the pros and cons of …	Der Verfasser/Die Verfasserin diskutiert die Vor- und Nachteile von …
The author gives his/her personal opinion on the problem of …	Der Verfasser/Die Verfasserin äußert seine/ihre eigene Meinung zum Thema …
He/she believes/is convinced/presumes that …	Er/sie glaubt/ist überzeugt/nimmt an, dass …
She/he wants to persuade the reader …	Sie/er möchte die Leser überreden …
One can easily follow his train of thought.	Man kann seinen Gedankengang leicht nachvollziehen.
At the end of her essay she draws/comes to the conclusion …	Am Ende ihres Berichts kommt sie zu dem Schluss …
His/her arguments are (not) convincing/well-chosen.	Seine/ihre Argumente sind nicht überzeugend/gut gewählt.
The main topic of the essay is …	Das Thema des Berichts ist …
The tone of this essay is humorous/neutral/ironical/serious.	Der Ton des Berichts ist humorvoll/neutral/ironisch/ernst.
The author uses real examples to convince her readers.	Die Verfasserin verwendet reale Beispiele, um ihre Leser zu überzeugen.
The author's choice of words shows/underlines that he is for …/against …	Die Wortwahl des Verfassers/der Verfasserin zeigt/unterstreicht, dass er für …/gegen … ist.

In the introductory paragraph of her essay she asks a rhetorical question which serves as a thread.	Im einleitenden Abschnitt ihres Berichts stellt sie den Lesern eine rhetorische Frage, die sich wie ein roter Faden durch den Bericht zieht.
The author uses adjectives with a positive/negative connotation to support his/her point of view.	Der Verfasser/Die Verfasserin verwendet Adjektive mit einer positiven/negativen Konnotation, um seinen/ihren Standpunkt zu verdeutlichen.
Her attempt to persuade the readers backfires/works very well.	Ihr Versuch, die Leser zu überreden, misslingt/gelingt.

Narrative Texte: *How to deal with reports*

Keyword:

Report: This is a special kind of newspaper article.
It provides answers to the five "W" questions *(Who? What? Where? When? Why?)*, as well as the *How* question (how something happened). Its aim is to inform its readers and NOT to manipulate or influence them.
A report deals with current events and only contains facts.

Sometimes students have problems when it comes to differentiating between a *report* and an *article*, which might also deal with current events but which is usually a mixture of both fact and opinion.
The style of an **article** is usually more personal and its main aim is to entertain the reader. This is ensured by using many adverbs and adjectives to make the article lively and by addressing its readers directly, often by asking them a hypothetical question, e. g. *How would you feel if you discovered that someone had stolen your brand-new car?*
The main characteristics of a **report** are outlined below.

Elements of a report

Structure

- To arouse the reader's curiosity, reports have **headlines** containing basic information without providing too much detail.
- The basic information is generally provided in the first paragraph, which serves as an **introduction.**
- The **main body** of a report consists of different paragraphs, which contain one piece of information each.
- The last paragraph serves as a kind of **conclusion.**

Language and style

- A report is written in a factual style and neither reflects the author's personal opinion nor contains any kind of speculation.
- Individual paragraphs are relatively short and consist of short sentences, which aim to ensure that the reader understands the information presented.
- Experts – or people who have first-hand experience of the topic in question – are often quoted, but no authorial comment is given about what they say.

Glossary – Vocabulary for analysing reports

The report [title] written by [author] deals with/is about/relates/ describes …	Der Bericht [Titel] von [Verfasser] beschäftigt sich mit/handelt von/berichtet von/ beschreibt …
The theme(s) of the report is (are) …	Das Thema/Die Themen des Berichts ist/sind …
In the introduction the reader learns about/gets to know …	In der Einleitung erfährt der Leser/die Leserin …
The report can be divided into … paragraphs.	Der Bericht kann in … Absätze gegliedert werden.
The report consists of … paragraphs.	Der Bericht besteht aus … Absätzen.
It's the author's aim to inform the reader about …	Es ist das Anliegen des Autors/der Autorin, den Leser/die Leserin über … zu informieren.
The 2nd/3rd paragraph contains information on …	Der 2./3. Absatz enthält Informationen über …
The author quotes an eye-witness/ expert who says that …	Der Autor/die Autorin zitiert einen Augenzeugen/Experten, der sagt, dass …
The author describes how …	Der Verfasser/Die Verfasserin beschreibt, wie …
The author does not give his/her personal opinion on the subject/problem/ question but merely relates facts.	Der Verfasser/Die Verfasserin äußert nicht seine/ihre eigene Meinung zum Sachverhalt/Problem/zu der Frage, sondern gibt Fakten wieder.
The factual style of writing shows that it is the author's aim to inform the reader and not to entertain him/her.	Der sachliche Sprachgebrauch verdeutlicht, dass es das Anliegen des Autors/ der Autorin ist, den Leser/die Leserin zu informieren und nicht, ihn zu unterhalten.

How to deal with cartoons, diagrams and statistics

Keyword:

Cartoons: visual images aiming at criticizing, ridiculing or commenting on current events or ideas.
Diagrams and statistics: intend to present information by comparing different items and their relations to each other. Diagram types include pie charts, bar charts, tables and line graphs.
In written exams, cartoons, diagrams and statistics will always be accompanied by a text.

Dealing with cartoons

Taking a closer look: What is shown?

Describe all the important elements of the cartoon in detail and point out the relation between them,

- start with the foreground and end with the background; of course, you can also proceed from top to bottom, or from left to right, but make sure that your reader can easily follow your train of thought,
- indicate the key features of each object or character, including captions and speech bubbles.

Analysing the message: What is the cartoonist's intention?

Explain what the artist wants to express by

- examining the use of colours if the cartoon comes in colours,
- focusing on the relation of the objects and characters presented in the cartoon (e.g. size, situation and role within the cartoon),
- interpreting the meaning of the caption or speech bubble (if the cartoon has these features).

In written exams cartoons will not have to be analysed alone, but always in combination with a text. Therefore, one should always pay close attention to the respective task.
It might also be necessary to consider the political, historical or social context and to refer to one's background knowledge.
Here it is also important to look at the task once more (What is the connection between cartoon and text?)

Evaluating the cartoon: Does the cartoonist get his message across? Is the cartoon effective?

After having described and analysed the cartoon, you should evaluate whether it is effective or not. You are free to give your own opinion, but do not forget to give reasons for it.

Dealing with diagrams and statistics

Taking a closer look:
What is the diagram/What are the statistics about?

First say what kind of diagram (table, pie chart ...) you are describing and state what it is about.
Diagrams or statistics usually come with a heading, which includes necessary information about what is being described, referred to or compared, as well as the source the information is taken from. Do not forget to mention this.

Analysing the diagram/statistics:
What can be concluded from the diagram/statistics?

Describe the relation between the different items (e.g. in bar charts and pie charts) or the development shown (e.g. in line graphs).
Then it is time to draw your conclusions from what is shown. In written exams you should also point out the connections between the diagram/statistics and the text.

Glossary – Vocabulary for analysing cartoons, diagrams and statistics

pie chart	Tortendiagramm
bar chart	Säulendiagramm
table	Tabelle
line graph	Kurvendiagramm
per cent/percentage	Prozent/prozentualer Anteil
The cartoon/pie chart etc. shows/depicts/presents/is about ...	Der Cartoon/das Tortendiagramm etc. zeigt/stellt ... dar/zeigt ...auf/handelt von ...
The cartoon/diagram etc. is taken from ...	Der Cartoon/das Diagramm stammt von/aus ...
The artist mainly uses light/bright/dark colours to achieve the desired effect.	Der Künstler verwendet überwiegend helle/strahlende/dunkle Farben um den gewünschten Effekt zu erzielen.
The cartoonist wants the spectator to ...	Der Karikaturist möchte, dass der Betrachter ...
The artist intends to ...	Der Künstler beabsichtigt ...
The message of the cartoon is that ...	Die Botschaft des Cartoons ist, dass ...
In the foreground/background of the cartoon one can see ...	Im Vorder-/Hintergrund des Cartoons kann man ... sehen.
In the top left-hand corner/in the bottom right-hand corner ... is shown.	In der linken oberen/der rechten unteren Ecke wird ... gezeigt/dargestellt.

The bar chart compares the development of ... and ...	Das Säulendiagramm vergleicht die Entwicklung von ... und ...
The pie chart is divided into ... slices, each slice representing ...	Das Tortendiagramm ist in ... Stücke aufgeteilt, von denen jedes ... darstellt.
Looking at the size of the different slices of the pie chart/at the height of the different bars of the bar chart one can conclude that ...	Wenn man die Größe der verschiedenen Stücke des Tortendiagramms/die Höhe der verschiedenen Balken des Balkendiagramms betrachtet, kann man darauf schließen/erkennen, dass ...
The bar chart describes the relation between ... and ...	Das Säulendiagramm beschreibt die Beziehung zwischen ... und ...
The line graph shows the population development in ... from (month/year) to (month/year).	Das Kurvendiagramm stellt die Bevölkerungsentwicklung in ... von (Monat/Jahr) bis (Monat/Jahr) dar.
Over the period of time covered by the line graph the number of inhabitants/the population in... increased/decreased/remained constant from ... to ...	In dem Zeitraum, der durch das Kurvendiagramm abgedeckt wird, hat sich/ist die Zahl der Einwohner/die Bevölkerung in ... vergrößert/verkleinert/gleich geblieben.
The horizontal axis of the line chart shows..., while the vertical axis represents ...	Die horizontale Achse (x-Achse) des Kurvendiagramms zeigt ..., während die vertikale Achse (y-Achse) ... abbildet.
The number of ... in ... is compared in the pie chart/bar chart.	Das Tortendiagramm/Balkendiagramm vergleicht die Anzahl von ... in...
All figures are given in per cent.	Alle Zahlen werden in Prozent angegeben.

Sprachmittlung

Im Klausurteil B, der Aufgabe zur Sprachmittlung, werden Sie dazu angehalten, die wesentlichen Inhalte von authentischen deutschen Texten sinngemäß für einen bestimmten Zweck adressatengerecht und situationsangemessen zusammenfassend in englischer Sprache wiederzugeben.

Eine Sprachmittlungsaufgabe gibt immer eine fiktive Situation vor, die eine Mittlung des deutschen Ausgangstextes verlangt. Im Gegensatz zu einer Übersetzung, die die wörtliche Übertragung eines Textes in die andere Sprache mitsamt aller möglicherweise vorhandenen Untertöne, Bildhaftigkeit, Ironie etc. erfordert, geht es bei der Sprachmittlung nur um die sinngemäße Übertragung in die Fremdsprache. In jedem Fall wird sich daher die Textform ändern.

Je nach Aufgabenstellung geht es entweder um eine Zusammenfassung des Textes, häufiger jedoch um das „Herauspicken" relevanter Informationen. Die Methodik für die inhaltliche Bearbeitung der Aufgabe gleicht also der Methodik für die Erstellung von Inhaltsangaben.

Beim Schreiben des englischen Textes berücksichtigt man die verschiedenen Aspekte der Sprachmittlung, wie sie hier in einer Übersicht dargestellt werden:

sinngemäß	– keine wortwörtliche Übersetzung – keine Übernahme von Stilmitteln oder Ton – ggf. implizierte Inhalte – nur die Inhalte des Textes, kein eigenes Wissen
situationsange- messen	– angemessener Stil – Beachtung der vorgegebenen Textform
adressatengerecht	– passendes Register (Freund? Professor? Gastmutter?) – Erläuterung von sprachlichen und kulturellen Eigenheiten[1]
zusammenfassend	– wesentliche Inhalte – ggf. wesentliche Details – nicht detailliert – nicht kommentiert (d. h. keine eigene Meinung)

TIPP zum Punktesammeln

Beachten Sie – wie immer – genau die Aufgabenstellung! Anders als bei der kreativen Teilaufgabe in Klausurteil A müssen Sie möglicherweise nicht den kompletten Zieltext erstellen, sondern nur den Teil, den die Sprachmittlung ausmacht. So kann die Aufgabenstellung z. B. lauten: "Write the part of your e-mail that is based on ..." oder "Write the part of your speech that deals with ...".

1 Viele Eigennamen oder Konnotationen werden sich dem fremdsprachlichen Adressaten nicht erschließen. Sie bedürfen daher einer Erklärung oder Umschreibung (z. B. *Rosenmontag, Abigag, Bildzeitung*).

Zieltextformate

Die in diesem Kapitel behandelten Textformate beziehen sich auf die anwendungs/produktionsorientierte Teilaufgabe *re-creation of text* des Klausurenteils A.
Folgende Textformate sehen die Vorgaben vor:
- *letter (formal letter, letter to the editor, personal letter)*
- *speech script (talk, public/formal speech, [debate] statement)*
- *newspaper article (report, comment)*
- *(written) interview*

Im Leistungskurs zusätzlich:
Ausgestaltung, Fortführung oder Ergänzung eines literarischen Ausgangstextes (narrative Texte, dramatische Texte, *film scripts)*

Die Formate werden weitgehend in unseren Beispielen für Prüfungsaufgaben berücksichtigt.

Letter

Formal Letter (förmlicher Brief)

Äußere Form
Adresse:

- eigene Adresse: anders als in Deutschland oben rechts, üblicherweise ohne Namen
- Empfänger: darunter auf der linken Seite

Datum:

unter der Anschrift entweder rechts oder links, Monat als Wort

persönlich bekannter Empfänger
Anrede:
Dear Mr/Mrs/Miss/Ms/Dr/Professor/ ...
(*Ms* ist die neutrale Form, um *Mrs* bzw. *Miss* zu umgehen)

Schlussformel:

Yours sincerely/Kind regards

unbekannter Empfänger
Anrede:

Dear Sir/Dear Madam/Dear Sir or Madam,

Schlussformel:

Yours faithfully

Unterschrift:

persönliche Unterschrift
darunter Name in Druckschrift

Inhaltliche Gliederung
Einleitung:

Bezug und Zweck des Briefes

Hauptteil:

relevante Informationen, klar und logisch dargelegt, keine Schnörkel und Abschweifungen

Ende:

Erwartung an den Empfänger, z. B. als Bitte oder Aufforderung

Sprache

förmlich, **keine** *informal language,* d. h. **vermeiden** Sie

- *short forms*
- Interjektionen und Füllwörter wie *well, alright, okay, I see, you know*
- *question tags (isn't it, don't you, etc.)*

Benutzen Sie Wendungen wie

- *With reference to your letter of May 13th ...*
- *Thank you for your letter of ...*

- *I am writing to apply/to enquire about/to inform you/to complain about ...*
- *I should be delighted if ...*
- *I would be very glad if ...*
- *It would be very convenient if ...*
- *Please find enclosed ...* (In der Anlage finden Sie ...)

- *I should very much appreciate it if ...*
- *Please note that ...*

- *Thank you very much in advance.*

Letter to the Editor (Leserbrief)

Ein Leserbrief ist eher ein Zeitungsartikel als ein förmlicher Brief.
Zur sprachlichen und inhaltlichen Gestaltung siehe *Comment* (S. 110).

Äußere Form
Anrede:
Sir (bzw. *Madam)* – kein *Dear,* (gilt nicht bei einer Schülerzeitung)

Unterschrift:
Name, Stadt, ggf. Land/US-Staat

Personal Letter (persönlicher Brief)

Äußere Form
Adresse und Datum:
- eigene Adresse: anders als in Deutschland oben rechts, üblicherweise ohne Namen
- Datum darunter

Anrede:
Dear ...

Schlussformel:
Yours (nicht: *your)/Best wishes/All the best/(Lots of) Love* (nicht: *in love)/Your friend ...*

Unterschrift:
Vorname

Inhaltliche Gliederung
Einleitung:
Bezug zum Ausgangstext, Grund des Schreibens

Hauptteil:
z. B. Erzählung, Erklärung, Erläuterung, relevante Informationen

Ende:
z. B. Fragen, Vorschläge, Ausblick

Sprache
freundlicher Ton
informal language, d. h.:
- *short forms*
- Interjektionen und Füllwörter wie *well, alright, okay, I see, you know*

- *question tags (isn't it, don't you, etc.)*
- weitgehend einfache Satzgefüge

Alltagsvokabular, thematisches Vokabular

Speech Script (Rede)

Denkbar – und in den vergangenen Jahren im Abitur als kreative Teilaufgabe vorgekommen – sind verschiedene Formen der Rede, wie *talk* (Vortrag), *public/formal speech* (öffentliche/formelle Rede) oder *statement* (Statement, Erklärung).

Talk (Vortrag)

Einleitung:

- Begrüßung der Zuhörerschaft
- ggf. Vorstellung der eigenen Person
- Anknüpfung an den Ausgangstext
- Zusammenfassung von Inhalt und Zielen des Vortrags
- ggf. vorgesehene Gliederung

Hauptteil:
richtet sich nach dem Zweck des Vortrages:

- etwas mitteilen
- Interesse für ein Thema wecken
- für Publikation, Produkt, Dienstleistung werben
- einen Standpunkt verteidigen
- Zuhörer überzeugen
- Diskussion anregen

Strukturieren Sie ihren Hauptteil inhaltlich stringent! Ein inhaltlicher Aspekt folgt dem anderen, Argumente und Beispiele unterstreichen die einzelnen Aspekte.

Ende:

- Zusammenfassung
- Appell
- Ausblick
- Dank an die Zuhörer

Public/Formal Speech

Öffentliche Rede ist meist politische Rede und dient der Überzeugung der Zuhörerschaft.

Einleitung:

weniger sachlich als der Vortrag, d. h.:
- keine Zusammenfassung von Inhalt und Zielen
- keine Vorstellung der Gliederung
- keine persönliche Vorstellung

Begrüßung der Zuhörer

Anknüpfung an den Ausgangstext
provokative oder plakative Hinführung zum Thema
Problemstellung (und evtl. Lösung in Aussicht stellen)

Hauptteil:

klare Argumentation
Kausalketten beachten
Belege durch logische Argumente, Beispiele, Expertenmeinungen, Verweis auf Autoritäten (Regierung, Kirche, Wissenschaft)

Ende:

Zusammenfassung
Appell

Statement

Ein Statement wird gewöhnlich im Vorfeld einer Debatte abgegeben, um die Fronten zu klären. Ziel eines Statements ist es, einen Standpunkt zu verteidigen oder gar die Zuhörer zu überzeugen. So wird es den objektiven Ton eines Vortrages mit den Zielen der öffentlichen Rede verbinden.

Sprache
Anrede:

Unbedingt der vorgebenen Situation anpassen, z. B.
- *Dear Students, Dear Listeners, Dear Members of ...., (talk)*
- *Fellow Citizens, Friends, Dear Citizens of ... (public speech)*
- *Ladies and Gentlemen*
- bei Anwesenheit hochrangiger Personen oder auch nur Gastgebern: *Mr President, Your Majesty, Prime Minister, Mr Chairman, Mr Jones*

Hinführung:

plakative Aussagesätze
weitgehend einfache Satzgefüge
Fragen

public speech:
rhetorische Fragen
Anspielungen
Ironie

Hauptteil:

talk/statement:
klare, weitgehend einfache Aussagesätze
sachlicher, objektiver Stil

public speech:
emphatische Mittel: Parallelismen, Aufzählungen, Wiederholungen
(s. „Methoden der Textarbeit“, S. 92)

Ende:

appellative Strukturen:
- *We must, we have to, we should*
- *It is imperative that ...*
- *Let us ...*

Tipp zum Punktesammeln

Überfrachten Sie Ihre Rede nicht mit Metaphern und emphatischen Mitteln! Das kann albern wirken.

Dank:
- *Thank you.*
- *Thank you for your attention.*

Newspaper Article

Report

Ein *report* ist ein Bericht, ein objektiver, sachlicher Artikel, dem eine Begebenheit oder eine Geschichte zugrunde liegt. Damit handelt es sich um einen narrativen Text. Sie können einen *report* in einer kreativen Aufgabe erwarten, wann immer eine Geschichte zu erzählen ist, insbesondere wenn der Ausgangstext gerade kein Zeitungsartikel ist.
Dramen oder Gedichte bieten häufig Stoff als Grundlage für einen Bericht.

Beachten Sie die Merkmale eines Berichtes, wie sie im Kapitel „Methoden der Textarbeit“ zusammengefasst werden (S. 98).

Comment

Ein *comment* ist die Textform, die Sie besonders häufig als Sachtextvorlage Ihrer Analyseaufgabe finden. Als kreative Aufgabe sind verschiedene *comments* vorstellbar:
- ein Artikel aus Ihrer persönlichen Sicht
- ein Artikel aus der persönlichen Sicht einer Figur des Ausgangstextes
- ein Artikel aus der persönlichen Sicht des lyrischen Ichs eines lyrischen Ausgangstextes
- (ein Artikel aus der persönlichen Sicht einer Figur aus Werken, die Sie im Unterricht behandelt haben)

Immer muss ein Bezug zum Ausgangstext vorhanden sein. Stellen Sie sicher, dass Sie Ihre Erkenntnisse aus den Teilaufgaben 1 und 2 heranziehen, um die Aufgabe optimal zu lösen! Der Schlüssel zu Ihrer persönlichen Stellungnahme, aber auch zur Person eines fiktiven Verfassers und dessen persönlicher Meinung liegt genau darin.

Sprache und Aufbau

Beachten Sie die Merkmale eines Essays, wie sie im Kapitel „Methoden der Textarbeit" (S. 96) zusammengefasst werden! Für den Sprachgebrauch orientieren Sie sich an der Rhetorik der öffentlichen Rede (s. S. 92)!

(Written) Interview

Auch im Interview geht es um eine persönliche Stellungnahme, allerdings nicht um Ihre persönliche Meinung, sondern um die eines fiktiven Gesprächspartners.

> **Achtung, häufiger Fehler:**
> Schreiben Sie nur in Dialogform! Schreiben Sie keinen Erzähltext mit nur Anteilen von wörtlicher Rede!

Struktur

Beginn:

Aufnahme der situativen Vorgabe der Aufgabenstellung
Begrüßung, Vorstellung
Anknüpfung an den Ausgangstext
Hinführung zum Thema, ggf. Vorstellung des Anliegens

Hauptteil:

Frage/Antwort in sinnvoller Verknüpfung
Argumente und Beispiele

Schluss:

zum Beispiel:

- Zusammenfassung
- Witz
- Ausblick

Dank
Verabschiedung

Sprache

freundlicher Ton
informal language, d.h.:

- *short forms*
- Interjektionen und Füllwörter wie *well, alright, okay, I see, you know*
- *question tags (isn't it, don't you, etc.)*
- weitgehend einfache Satzgefüge

Alltagsvokabular, thematisches Vokabular

rhetorische Mittel: Wiederholungen, Aufzählungen, Anaphern, aber keine ausgefeilten Stilfiguren
Grußformel: *Good morning/afternoon/evening Mr/Mrs Jones/ Sir/Ma'am*
Schlussformel: z. B. *Thank you for your time, good bye ..., Thank you very much for the interview. Good bye ...*

Literarische Texte

Narrative Texte

Im Abitur werden Ihnen narrative Ausgangstexte meist als Roman- oder Kurzgeschichtenauszug begegnen. Folgende Varianten einer kreativen Aufgabenstellung sind denkbar:

- Lücken füllen (d. h. Begebenheiten, die im Ausgangstext nur erwähnt werden oder die der Leser nur aus dem Handlungsverlauf erschließen kann, sollen kreativ ausgestaltet werden)
- ein Ende oder eine Fortsetzung schreiben
- ein alternatives Ende schreiben
- Perspektivwechsel

Übernehmen Sie – falls die Aufgabenstellung es nicht ausdrücklich anders verlangt – die Erzählperspektive des Ausgangstextes!
Beachten Sie, dass Figuren sich weiterhin so verhalten, wie es ihrem Charakter entspricht, auch in ihrer Sprache!

Schreiben Sie keine neue Story mit einem vollständigen *plot* und einem neuen Höhepunkt. Es geht nicht um die Erfindung einer spannenden oder besonders originellen Handlung, sondern um eine logisch-konsequente Ausgestaltung des Ausgangstextes.

Sprache

Übernehmen Sie, soweit es geht, den Stil des Ausgangstextes.

Übernehmen Sie das Tempus des Ausgangstextes. In der Regel werden narrative Texte im *past tense* erzählt. Beachten Sie die Tempora der Vergangenheit.

Beispiel:

The ground ***was*** *wet because it* ***had been raining*** *all morning and although the rain* ***had stopped*** *and the sun* ***was shining*** *now, it* ***would be*** *difficult to find the track. On dry ground it* ***would have been*** *easy.*

was wet – Erzähltempus
it had been raining – vorzeitig, andauernd bis hin zum Erzählzeitpunkt
had stopped – vorzeitig
was shining – gerade ablaufende Hintergrundhandlung
it would be difficult – Zukunft aus der Sicht der Vergangenheit
it would have been easy – reine Hypothese in der Vergangenheit

Wechsel der Textform

Sollte die Aufgabenstellung eine vollständige Erzählung z. B. auf der Grundlage eines Gedichtes oder eines Zeitungsartikels verlangen, so achten Sie auf einen plausiblen inhaltlichen Bezug. Für die Ausgestaltung Ihrer Erzählung beachten Sie die Erzählelemente, wie sie im Kapitel „Methoden der Textarbeit“ (S. 79) vorgestellt werden.

Dramatische Texte (Schauspiel/Film)

Folgende Varianten einer kreativen Aufgabenstellung sind denkbar:
Bei einem dramatischen Ausgangstext:

- Lücken füllen (d. h. Begebenheiten, die im Ausgangstext nur erwähnt werden, sollen kreativ ausgestaltet werden)
- ein Ende oder eine Fortsetzung schreiben
- ein alternatives Ende schreiben

Bei anderen Ausgangstexten (z. B. Erzählung, Zeitungsartikel, Gedicht):

- Wechsel der Textform

Beachten Sie, dass Figuren sich so verhalten, wie es ihrem Charakter entspricht, auch in ihrer Sprache.

Sprache
Dialogtext:

gesprochene Sprache, d. h.

- *short forms*
- Interjektionen und Füllwörter wie *well, alright, okay, I see, you know*
- *question tags (isn't it, don't you, etc.)*
- weitgehend einfache Satzgefüge

Alltagsvokabular, thematisches Vokabular

Stage directions:

- in Klammern
- stichpunktartig
- *present tense*

Achtung, häufiger Fehler!
Erzählen Sie keine Geschichte mit wörtlicher Rede! Schreiben Sie ein Bühnenstück mit Dialogen und Regieanweisungen!

Beispiele für Prüfungsaufgaben zu den Fokusthemen

Die Beispielaufgaben sind vom Umfang und vom Schwierigkeitsgrad her teilweise für Leistungskurse, teilweise für Grundkurse konzipiert. Für Grundkurse gilt eine maximale Wortzahl von 420 Wörtern (Sprachmittlung maximal 330 Wörter), für Leistungskurse von 560 Wörtern (Sprachmittlung 440 Wörter). Für ein Prüfungstraining spielt die Zuordnung keine entscheidende Rolle.
Um den verschiedenen Vorgaben für die beiden Kursarten gerecht zu werden, wurden überwiegend Texte ausgewählt, die den Vorgaben beider Kursarten entsprechen (Ausnahme: Shakespeare).

Aufgaben mit Bearbeitungsschritten und Beispiellösungen

Themenfeld *India – Faces of a Rising Nation*

Aufgabenbeispiel Abitur Englisch Grundkurs
Aufgabenart gemäß KLP: 1.1: Schreiben mit Leseverstehen integriert und Sprachmittlung isoliert
Bezug zu den Vorgaben: Postkolonialismus – Lebenswirklichkeiten in einem weiteren anglophonen Kulturraum *India – faces of a rising nation*
Auszug aus einem englischsprachigen literarischen Text (415 W.) (Klausurteil A, Text 2) Auszug aus einem deutschsprachigen Sach- und Gebrauchstext (289 W.) (Klausurteil B, Text 1)
Quellenangaben: Text 1: „Das hässliche Gesicht der Zuwanderung – Slums mitten in deutschen Großstädten“, rtlNEXT.de, 12.02.2014 Text 2: Swarup, Vikas: Q&A: *Slumdog Millionaire,* Random House UK 2005, S. 156–157

Aufgabe

Klausurteil B (Text 1)

1. At an international youth camp you are asked to give a very short talk on slums in Germany. After a quick check of the internet on your smartphone, you provide some information on the basis of this RTL article. Write your talk.

Klausurteil A (Text 2)

2. Describe the slum the narrator lives in. *(Comprehension)*

3. Examine the way the narrator presents Dharavi. Consider his choice of words, the point of view, imagery, and other stylistic devices. *(Analysis)*

4. Choose one of the following tasks.

4.1 Against the backgrounds of both texts and your own experience, compare what poverty means in Germany with what it means in India. *(Evaluation)*

OR

4.2. As a reporter for an internet youth magazine you have managed to arrange an interview with a local Mumbai politician. Write the interview in which you critically question him on the situation in Dharavi. *(Creation of text)*

Text 1 RTL-Reporter Alexander Oetker besucht Elendsviertel

Es gibt Städte in Deutschland, die die Schattenseiten der Einwanderung widerspiegeln. In Dortmund und Duisburg zum Beispiel stößt die Integration von Armutsflüchtlingen aus Bulgarien und Rumänien allmählich an Grenzen. Denn hier leben – anders als in München – vor allem unqualifizierte Zuwanderer, die sich schwertun, Arbeit zu finden. RTL-Reporter Alexander Oetker hat sich auf den Weg gemacht und zeigt das Elend fehlgeschlagener Integration.

In der Dortmunder Nordstadt warten sie auf Arbeit, manche betteln. Sogar die Schilder in Banken sind auf Rumänisch. Es sind mehr geworden seit dem 1. Januar. An diesem Tag fielen die Schranken, der deutsche Arbeitsmarkt hat sich für Rumänen und Bulgaren geöffnet. Die negativen Auswirkungen bekommen nun vor allem arme Städte zu spüren, die selbst tief in den roten Zahlen stecken.

Doch auch, wenn es eine Sperrfrist für Kindergeld, Hartz IV und andere Sozialleistungen gibt – irgendwann müssen die Ämter zahlen. Das ist Teil der europäischen Arbeitnehmerfreizügigkeit. Aktuell gehen 170 Millionen Euro Hartz IV an Rumänen und Bulgaren. 36 Prozent der Leistungsbezieher sind aber Aufstocker. Heißt: Sie werden hier in Deutschland viel zu schlecht bezahlt.

Illegale hausen unter unwürdigen Bedingungen

Was das bedeutet, zeigt sich in einem Slum, nur drei Minuten von Frankfurts Innenstadt entfernt. Hier hausen illegale Zuwanderer in provisorisch zusammengezimmerten Baracken. Leben in Würde sieht anders aus. Kein Job, kein Hartz IV. Urin läuft in die Verschläge, überall liegt Müll. Erklären, warum sich niemand offiziell gemeldet hat, kann keiner.

Calin und seine zehn Landsleute machen alles zu Geld, was sie finden können – auf legalem Wege, so versprechen sie uns. „Wir verkaufen Schuhe auf dem Wochenmarkt, oder sammeln Pfand. Damit kann ich hier mehr verdienen, als in Rumänien als Bauarbeiter." Arm bleibt in den meisten Fällen eben arm, ob in Rumänien oder Deutschland.

Text 12 Slumdog Millionaire

Vikas Swarup

I live in a corner of Mumbai called Dharavi, in a cramped hundred-square-foot shack which has no natural light or ventilation, with a corrugated metal sheet serving as the roof over my head. It vibrates violently whenever a train passes overhead. There is no running water and no sanitation. This is all I can afford. But I am not alone in Dharavi. There are a million people like me, packed in a two-hundred hectare-triangle of swampy urban wasteland, where we live like animals and die like insects. Destitute migrants from all over the country jostle with each other for their own handful of sky in Asia's biggest slum. There are daily squabbles – over inches of space, over a bucket of water – which at times turn deadly. Dharavi's residents come from the dusty backwaters of Bihar and UP and Tamil Nadu and Gujarat. They came to Mumbai, the city of gold, with dreams in their hearts of striking it rich and living upper-middle-class lives. But that gold turned to lead a long time ago, leaving behind rusted hearts and gangrenous minds. Like my own.

Dharavi is not a place for the squeamish. Delhi's Juvenile Home diminished us, but Dharavi's grim landscape of urban squalor deadens and debases us. Its open drains teem with mosquitoes. Its stinking, excrement-lined communal latrines are full of rats, which make you think less about the smell and more about protecting your backside. Mounds of filthy garbage lie on every corner, from which rag-pickers still manage to find something useful. And at times you have to suck in your breath to squeeze through its narrow, claustrophobic alleys. But for the starving residents of Dharavi, this is home.

Amidst the modern skyscrapers and neon-lit shopping complexes of Mumbai, Dharavi sits like a cancerous lump in the heart of the city. And the city refuses to recognize it. So it has outlawed it. All the houses in Dharavi are 'illegal constructions', liable to be demolished at any time. But when the residents are struggling simply to survive, they don't care. So they live in illegal houses and use illegal electricity, drink illegal water and watch illegal cable TV. They work in Dharavi's numerous illegal factories and illegal shops, and even travel illegally – without ticket – on the local trains which pass directly through the colony.

The city may have chosen to ignore the ugly growth of Dharavi, but a cancer cannot be stopped simply by being declared illegal. It still kills with its slow poison.

Bearbeitungsschritte und Musterlösungen

Klausurteil B
Sprachmittlung *(Mediation)*

1. At an international youth camp, you are asked to give a very short talk on slums in Germany. After a quick check of the internet on your smartphone, you provide some information on the basis of this RTL article. Write your talk.

Vergegenwärtigen Sie sich die **Prinzipien der Sprachmittlung,** wie wir sie auf Seite 102 dargestellt haben. Für den vorliegenden Text beachten wir konkret:

Zieltext: *talk* (vgl. Zieltextformate S. 107)

Für eine knappe, sachliche Wiedergabe gehen wir wie bei einer Zusammenfassung vor:
Der Text ist bereits vorstrukturiert, sodass wir nur noch die wesentlichen Merkmale der jeweiligen Slums herausarbeiten müssen:

Armut in einigen Städten als Folge fehlgeschlagener Integration
- Zuwanderung unqualifizierter Migranten
- Problem der Integration

wegen der neuen Freizügigkeit insbesondere Rumänen und Bulgaren
- Betteln
- Problem der armen Städte: nach Sperrfrist müssen Sozialleistungen gezahlt werden
- selbst Menschen mit Arbeit müssen bezahlt werden (Aufstocker)

illegale Einwanderer in Frankfurt hausen in einem Gebiet, das die Merkmale eines Slums aufweist.
- Baracken, keine Arbeit, kein Hartz IV
- Urin, Müll
- Pfand- und Müllsammler

Adressatenorientiertung

In Ihrer fiktiven Situation als Teilnehmer an einem internationalen Camp müssen Sie dafür sorgen, dass Ihr Kurzvortrag adressatengerecht gestaltet wird. Wörter wie Arbeitnehmerfreizügigkeit, Hartz IV oder Aufstocker müssen für die internationalen Teilnehmer erläutert werden. Auch Pfandflaschen sind nicht unbedingt in allen Kulturen geläufig, sodass eine simple Übersetzung möglicherweise nicht reicht. Ganz schlecht ist eine Übernahme eines Wortes in Anführungsstrichen (z. B. „Hartz IV"). Anführungsstriche helfen dem armen des Deutschen unkundigen Menschen gar nicht beim Verständnis.

Beispiellösung

I found an article on the internet which deals with slums in Germany. It shows examples of integration gone wrong. Many immigrants from Romania or Bulgaria have come to Germany after the German labour market opened to them in line with EU law, but most of them are not qualified to find a job in Germany. Some end up as beggars. They present a problem especially to poor cities. According to EU regulations, the authorities have to pay benefits to them after a certain time. Even people with jobs often get benefits as a supplement to their wages, which are not sufficient even to cover basic needs.

In the centre of Frankfurt there is a slum settled by illegal immigrants who have not registered with the authorities, for whatever reasons. They live a life without dignity in provisional shacks. They have no jobs and no unemployment benefit. There is rubbish and urine everywhere. People search the rubbish for things to sell or for plastic bottles, on which there is a deposit in Germany. This way they earn more money than they would on a construction site in their home country.

Klausurteil A
Anforderungsbereich I *(Comprehension)*

2. Describe the slum the narrator lives in. *(Comprehension)*

Der Operator „describe" verlangt eine gewisse Ausführlichkeit etwa im Gegensatz zu „outline" oder „sum up". Eine solche Aufgabe bietet sich an, wenn die Textvorlage selbst sehr deskriptiv ist, wenn es keine wirkliche Handlung gibt.

Das Isolieren von Schlüsselwörtern ist eine unabdingbare Methode, profundes Textverständnis zu erlangen. Dies geschieht normalerweise durch Markierung und Notizen im Text. Hier werden wir sie auflisten. Danach sollten sie in einen Sinnzusammenhang gebracht werden.

paragraph	keywords	→
1	Dharavi, Mumbai	place, location
1	hundred-square-foot shack, no natural light or ventilation, corrugated metal sheet as roof, no running water, no sanitation	narrator's shack

1	train passes, a million people, two-hundred-hectare, swampy urban wasteland, destitute migrants	general description
2	open drains, mosquitoes, communal latrines, rats, smell, garbage, claustrophobic alleys	detailed description
3	amidst the modern skyscrapers	location
3	local trains	detailed description

Vor dem Verfassen des Textes rufen wir uns die **Prinzipien der Inhaltsangabe** ins Gedächtnis:

- eigene Formulierungen
- einleitender Satz
- Antwort auf die geforderten W-Fragen (hier: Wo, Was und Wer)

Gliederung des Textes:

- zum besseren Textverständnis Text in Sinnabschnitte unterteilen. Meist helfen die Absätze des Textes schon dabei.

Bei Ihrer Sammlung von Schlüsselwörtern sollte Ihnen deutlich werden, dass der Text im dritten Abschnitt weitere Elemente zuvor beschriebener Aspekte erwähnt (siehe Spalte 3). Ihren eigenen Text sollten Sie dann nicht anhand der Textchronologie, sondern anhand der Inhaltsaspekte strukturieren.

TIPP zum Punktesammeln

Reduzieren Sie Ihre Inhaltsangabe auf das Wesentliche (keine Ausschmückung durch besondere Adjektive, keine kleinen Details, keine Zitate, keine Metaphorik). Lassen Sie aber auch keine Merkmale, die den Slum ausmachen, weg!
Verweisen Sie nicht auf Abschnitte oder Zeilen im Ausgangstext! Zitieren Sie nicht! Nehmen Sie keine Wertung vor!
Grundtempus ist das *simple present* (Achtung: Die Zuwanderer haben sich in der Vergangenheit angesiedelt, deshalb müssen Sie ggf. ein vorzeitiges Tempus verwenden, also *came* oder *have come.)*

Beispiellösung:

In the excerpt from Vikas Swarup's novel "Slumdog Millionaire" the narrator describes the slum he lives in.
He lives in Dharavi, which is a part of Mumbai, located in the vicinity of the modern business centre. It covers two hundred hectares of swampy wasteland, with the local railway going right through it. It is home to a million migrants from different parts of the country.

The narrator, like all the others, lives in a small shack with a corrugated iron roof. There is no daylight, no fresh air, no running water and no sanitation.
The slum is overcrowded, there is not enough space for all these people. The alleys are narrow, there are open drains which attract mosquitoes, and stinking latrines full of rats. There is rubbish everywhere.

Anforderungsbereich II *(Analysis)*

3. Examine the way the narrator presents Dharavi. Consider his choice of words, the point of view, imagery, and other stylistic devices. *(Analysis)*

Prinzipiell geht es im Anforderungsbereich II immer um Struktur und/oder Sprache des Textes oder um die Analyse von Erzählelementen wie *character* oder *point of view*, nicht mehr um Inhalt, wenn auch dieses Prinzip leider nicht immer gewahrt wird.
Die vorliegende Aufgabe fordert ausdrücklich eine Beschäftigung mit der Sprache des Erzählers. Mit einer Analyse der Textstruktur sollte man sich also auch nicht aufhalten!
Die Aufgabenstellung spezifiziert ausdrücklich *choice of words, point of view, imagery, stylistic devices*. Sie sollten das dann auch ganz genau nehmen und diese Anweisung als Checkliste benutzen.

Besonderheiten der Sprachverwendung sind im Text zu markieren, und zwar alle! Im Zieltext muss dann nicht zwingend jeder einzelne Beleg zitiert werden, Verweise auf die entsprechenden Zeilen sollten jedoch in jedem Fall erfolgen. Wir werden im Folgenden die wesentlichen Elemente benennen.

quotation	**aspects of language**
cramped	choice of words, negative connotation
packed	choice of words, negative connotation
swampy, wasteland	choice of words, negative connotation
destitute, jostle	choice of words, negative connotation
live like animals	comparison, simile
die like insects	comparison, simile, parallelism
squabbles	choice of words, negative connotation
over inches of space, over a bucket of water	parallelism
city of gold	metaphor
gold turned to lead	metaphor
rusted hearts	metaphor
gangrenous minds	metaphor
... diminished us, but ... debases us	antithesis

grim, squalor, deaden, debase	choice of words, negative connotation
drains, teem, mosquitoes, rats, smell	choice of words, negative connotation
filthy, garbage, stinking, excrement-lined, latrines	choice of words, negative connotation
claustrophobic, starving	choice of words, negative connotation
skyscrapers, neon-lit	choice of words, contrasting positive connotation
like a cancerous lump	simile
heart of the city	metaphor
illegal ... illegal ... illegal ...	parallelism, enumeration, repetition
ugly growth, cancer	metaphor
slow poison	metaphor

Es fällt auf, dass sich die sprachlichen Mittel, die der Erzähler einsetzt, wiederholen. Es macht daher wenig Sinn, den Text rein chronologisch zu bearbeiten, wie es Schüler immer wieder gerne tun. Dies braucht viel zu viel wertvolle Arbeitszeit und Energie und führt zu einem unübersichtlichen und viel zu umfangreichen Zieltext. Viel eleganter ist es, den Zieltext inhaltlich anhand der sprachlichen Mittel zu strukturieren und nicht Zeile nach Zeile zu behandeln. Jeder Ihrer Sinnabschnitte erhält dann aussagekräftige Zitate und ergänzende Textverweise. Wichtig sind Aussagen zur **Funktion** der rhetorischen Mittel, selbst wenn diese in der Aufgabenstellung nicht ausdrücklich genannt wird. Es reicht nicht, eine Metapher zu finden und zu benennen, man muss sie auch erläutern.

Passagen, in denen die Erzählperspektive *(point of view)* eine besondere Wirkung erzielt, sind ebenfalls im Text zu markieren. Die Erzählperspektive zu bestimmen, ist in diesem Fall leicht, denn wir finden sofort im ersten Satz das Pronomen „I“. Natürlich bleibt die Perspektive erhalten, selbst wenn der Erzähler in anderen grammatikalischen Personen spricht. Durch den Ich-Erzähler ist die Perspektive in diesem Text eindeutig als *limited point of view* festgelegt. Ein Ich-Erzähler kann die Welt nicht mit anderen Augen sehen und zwischen Charakteren hin- und herspringen.
Vor allem die folgenden Passagen, die Sie im Text markieren sollten, geben dem Leser eine Innensicht des Slums, Einblicke in die persönliche Situation des Erzählers. Der Leser erfährt die Situation des Slums durch die Wahrnehmung des Erzählers:

I live in a corner of Mumbai ... But I am not alone in Dharavi (Z. 1–9)
.. which make you think less of the smell and more about protecting your backside (Z. x)
... you have to suck in your breath to squeeze (Z. 32–34)

Da die Vorgaben einen zusammenhängenden Zieltext fordern, sollte man Teil II elegant an Teil I anbinden. Ein erneuter Einleitungssatz wäre genauso unglücklich wie eine Formulierung wie „Now I am going to analyse ..." gefolgt von einer Paraphrase der Aufgabenstellung. Es wäre ein regelrechter Bruch, keine kohärente Anbindung. Eine solche Formulierung strukturiert einen mündlichen Vortrag, nicht jedoch einen Aufsatz (vgl. Kapitel 5).

Beispiellösung:

The reader gets an insight into these conditions in the slum by means of the narrator's use of the first-person point of view. As one of the slum dwellers, the narrator can convey his own experience to the reader, thus the reader is close to the scene. This becomes particularly obvious when the narrator tells the reader about his own shack (ll. 2-7), which vibrates when a train passes. The reader can sense this perception with the narrator. This is even more the case when the narrator conveys his first-hand experience of the latrines ("... you think less about the smell and more about protecting your backside", ll. 32-34) or when he refers to the claustrophobic alleys in his slum ("You have to suck in your breath to squeeze through ...", ll. 37-38).

The atrocious living conditions are presented by the narrator by means of numerous words with negative connotations.
The lack of space, the overpopulation is described by the use of words like "cramped", "packed" or "claustrophobic" (ll. 2, 10, 38) The comparisons "we live like animals and die like insects" (ll. 11-12), which is additionally underlined by parallelism, illustrates the situation of the crowded masses even more drastically. Living like animals, meaning living in the dirt, living without any comfort, living on very reduced space, responsible only for oneself and constantly having to struggle for survival. And then they die "like insects", in masses, easily, with hardly anybody taking notice. Another parallelism underlines their daily struggle "over inches of space, over a bucket of water" (ll. 16-17), and the metaphor "they jostle ... for their own handful of sky" (ll. 13-15) gives the reader an idea not only of the cramped confines, but also of the lack of fresh air, the lack of room to breathe freely and the lack of a view other than the desolate surroundings of the slum.
The nauseous circumstances in Dahravi are described by numerous words with negative connotations referring to the word-field of dirt and disease. The place is described as a "swampy wasteland" (l. 10) and with words like "grim", "squalor", "deaden", "debase" (ll. 28, 29). Details are described with words which connote extreme disgust (drains, teem, mosquitoes, rats, filthy, garbage, stinking, excrement-lined, latrines, ll. 30-34). All this contrasts starkly with the expressions "modern skyscrapers" and "neon-lit shopping complexes" (ll. 41-42), with which we associate the complete opposite of the situation in Dharavi: glamour, space, wealth, abundance, beauty, cleanliness and success. The idea of disease is taken up in one of the central metaphors of the text. Dharavi is seen as a "cancerous lump" (l. 43) in the "heart of the city", a "cancer" which "still kills with its slow poison" (l. 59). The uncontrolled growth, the social problems it produces, social discontent, illness, pollution, crime, all this will have an impact on the city of Mumbai just as a cancer will slowly destroy the human body.

The other important metaphor in this text describes the dreams and disappointment of the people living in the slum. To them Mumbai seemed a "city of gold" (l. 21). "Gold" signifies wealth, opportunity, success. Very much like the American Dream of golden opportunities, the dream of participating in the economic growth of modern India attracted people to Mumbai. The metal metaphor is continued when the narrator says that the gold "turned to lead" (l. 23). Lead is a contrast to gold, a cheap metal, grey and ugly, even toxic. Lead idiomatically pulls people down under water, it is associated with fatigue and immobility. Moreover he says that this has left behind "rusted hearts" (l. 24). Here the metaphor is carried on to describe a state of decomposition, dysfunction, crumbling or falling apart. People's hearts are broken, people have lost their dreams and hopes. Likewise, their minds are metaphorically described as gangrenous. He uses this term – usually denoting physical illness – to describe people's state of mind, which has to be understood on the same lines as "rusted hearts". People are broken, their souls are suffering, they are sick, perhaps full of depression, despair, grief, anger, hatred and aggression.
Apart from the above-mentioned parallel structures, the narrator also uses emphatic stylistic means in lines 27 to 29. "Delhi's juvenile home diminished us, but Dharavi's ... squalor deadens and debases us" is an antithesis which emphasizes the horrible situation in Dharavi by relating it to something apparently bad enough. The repetition of the word "illegal" puts emphasis on the ridiculousness of the administration declaring Dharavi illegal and subsequently ignoring it.

Anforderungsbereich III (*Evaluation*)

4.1 Against the backgrounds of both texts and your own experience, comment on what poverty means in Germany and what it means in India. *(Evaluation)*

Der Operator „comment" verlangt eine persönliche Stellungnahme zum Ausgangstext, in diesem Fall zusätzlich auf der Grundlage des deutschen Ausgangstextes. Daneben sind Kenntnisse aus dem Unterricht zu Indien hilfreich vor allem aber Allgemeinwissen zum deutschen Sozialstaat.

Ihre Sammlungen zu den Anforderungsbereichen I und II geben hinreichend Hintergrundinformation zur Armutsproblematik in Indien. Sie sollten am Anfang der Stellungnahme unbedingt (ganz knapp) zusammenfassend darauf Bezug nehmen. Wiederholen Sie aber ja nicht alles, was Sie bereits geschrieben haben!

Ggf. könnten Sie diese Aspekte durch weitere Armutsaspekte, die Sie aus dem Unterricht kennen, ergänzen, z. B. Kinderarbeit, Bildungsferne o. Ä. Setzen Sie diese dann in Bezug zu den Ihnen aus den Medien, dem Politikunterricht oder aus der persönlichen Erfahrung bekannten Ausprägungen von Armut in Deutschland. Der Mediationstext beschreibt eine untypische Minderheit von mittellosen Menschen und ihrer Situation. Dies sollte in Ihrer Stellungnahme auch herausgestellt werden.

aspects mentioned in the texts	with regard to Germany
infrastructure	grids: roads, streets, water, sewers, electricity, hardly any wasteland
hygiene	bathrooms, toilets, sewers
housing	stone houses, tower blocks, housing benefits
jobs	minimum wages
health	health care, health insurance
dreams, perspectives	compulsory education, free education
unemployment	unemployment benefit
indifference of government	Basic (Constitutional) Law, constitution: welfare state

Die Stellungnahme schließt sich ebenso nahtlos an die Analyse an, wie diese sich an die Inhaltsangabe anschließt. Wichtig ist, dass ein Bezug hergestellt wird zum bisherigen Zieltext. Da die Formulierung der Aufgabenstellung so nicht im Text erscheint, darf auf sie nicht z. B. mit Pronomen Bezug genommen werden. Ganz schlecht ist auch der sofortige Einstieg mit „I think“ oder „In my opinion“, denn auch die eigene Meinung erfordert eine Hinführung.

Beispiellösung:

Ignoring the misery of a million people living in filth and excrement with hardly a chance to ever escape from it should not be possible in a country like Germany. The Basic Law of the Federal Republic of Germany states that Germany is a "democratic and social federal state". This means that people who cannot work are supported by the state. People without jobs receive unemployment benefits, there is compulsory health insurance and subsequent free health care. Low income families receive housing benefits. Employers have to pay minimum wages.
Nevertheless, poor people often have to live in precarious housing conditions, but these are still very different from Indian slums. Germany's infrastructure is intact. There is a functioning sewer grid, there is electricity and running water and, above all, there are stone and concrete houses or tower blocks where poor people live. Inside bathrooms and toilets are the norm.
Germany has compulsory education, all children have to go to school, so basically and in theory, all people should have a chance to climb the social ladder of success. Unfortunately, there is more to education than just access to schools, so the educational gap between rich and poor is still too wide.
The text from rtlNEXT.de shows that there are slums in Germany which resemble Indian slums. Still this Frankfurt slum cannot be compared to Dharavi or any other slum in India. Talking about Dharavi, we are talking about a million people, the population of Cologne. In Frankfurt it must be a relatively small number of illegal immigrants that squat close to the city centre. You would not even be able to find urban wasteland of the size of Dharavi in a German city.

The immigrants living there are illegal, not outlawed like the people in Dharavi, but in the sense that they have not registered with the authorities. If they had, they would qualify for social benefits, at least after a certain period of time.
To conclude, poverty in India is nothing like poverty in Germany. It is a misery that we Europeans cannot even begin to imagine.

Anforderungsbereich III *(Evaluation/Re-creation of text)*

4.2 As a reporter for an internet youth magazine you have managed to arrange an interview with a local Mumbai politician. Write the interview, in which you question him on the situation in Dharavi. *(Creation of text)*

Für die kreative Aufgabe ist zu beachten:

Perspektivwechsel
- Wer ist der fiktive Schreiber des Textes?
- Wie ist seine Sicht der Dinge?
- Was für eine Art Sprache benutzt er?

Inhaltliche Anknüpfung an Teilaufgaben 1 und 2 durch einleitenden Satz *(topic sentence)*.
- Inhaltlicher Bezug zu den beiden ersten Teilaufgaben zum englischsprachigen Text, z. B. durch
- Vergleich (Ähnlichkeiten/Unterschiede)
- Kritik
- Wertung
- Gegendarstellung

Textkohärente Anknüpfung an Teilaufgabe 3 in diesem Fall **nicht** möglich, denn die Textform ist eine völlig andere.

Die Herausforderung in diesem Interview liegt darin, die unerträglichen Zustände, die der Text beschreibt und die der Reporter ansprechen sollte, in irgendeiner Art und Weise zu rechtfertigen oder schönzufärben.
Auch hier hilft die obige Tabelle. Kenntnisse aus dem Unterricht über Indien sind hier wichtiger als in Aufgabe 4.1.

aspects mentioned in the texts	with regard to Germany
infrastructure	illegal, technical feasibility
hygiene	illegal, money problem
housing	illegal, money problem
jobs	qualification, over-population, free market

health	mentality
dreams, perspectives	education programmes, individual naivety
unemployment	education, individual fault, qualification
indifference of government	money, over-population

Beispiellösung:

Reporter: Hello, Mr. Kapoor, you are a representative of the City of Mumbai and I'm very happy that I have the chance to talk to you. The readers of our internet youth magazine are very interested in how the Indian administration is trying to tackle poverty. Dharavi is said to be the biggest slum in Asia and it is right on your doorstep and part of your responsibility.

Politician: Good afternoon.

Reporter: Would it improve the situation in Dharavi if you provided legal jobs or if you legalized the jobs that people already have there?

Politician: No, I don't think so. There are simply not enough jobs around. There are important jobs and manufacturing industries in Dharavi which help Mumbai's economy, but if we developed them and the quarter itself, we would also have to drive many people away.

Reporter: Most of the residents don't have the qualification to work in a legal job. Would it be possible to give the residents a small amount of money, so they could buy basic stuff like water or food? In Germany it is possible to receive some money from the state.

Politician: No, this is hardly possible either. The people in the slum aren't registered, the slum is getting bigger every day so how would you register all the residents? Also the amount of money the government or the city administration would have to pay is way too big. There are so many people!
The Hindu population would not be happy either, if the slum-dwellers were given the taxpayer's money. According to traditional hierarchical thinking, Dharavi – to their mind – stands for everything that has to be despised, that deserves contempt.

Reporter: So you can't do anything to change the situation in the slum?

Politician: Yes, we can. We have to provide schooling in the area so the children can get better jobs in future, and also to give grown-ups the chance to get basic education so they can work in legal jobs. We would have to create a body that overlooks the food problem and the water problem, as a short-term measure.
We would also have to care about the inhabitants' minds. Most of them are broken and angry about their situation and have given up. We need a programme that offers some quality of life with regard to sports or culture.
Unfortunately, with Indians stereotypically being rather passive or – if you wish – having

a strong consciousness of being mortal and a mere grain of sand on the shore, they are able to accept suffering with a lot of indifference. Against this background, it is also not easy to improve the situation.
In the long run, we do have to develop the slum. There are ambitious plans for tower blocks providing space to live, even for the socially deprived.

Reporter: Would all the people in Dharavi be able to afford a flat in those blocks?

Politician: Unfortunately not.

Reporter: Thank you very much for your time.

Politician: Pleasure.

Themenfeld *Globalization and Global Challenges*

Aufgabenbeispiel Abitur Englisch Leistungskurs
Aufgabenart gemäß KLP: 1.1: Schreiben mit Leseverstehen integriert und Sprachmittlung isoliert
Bezug zu den Vorgaben: Chancen und Risiken der Globalisierung *Globalization and global challenges* – *The role of the United States in international politics at the beginning of the 21st century* – *economic and ecological issues* – *lifestyle and communication* (GK)
englischsprachiger literarischer Text (599 W.) (Klausurteil A, Text 1) Cartoon (Klausurteil A, Text 2) Auszug aus einem deutschsprachigen Sachtext (433 W.) (Klausurteil B, Text 3)
Quellenangaben: Text 1: Neil White: "Trick or treat? The worst example of Americanisation in modern society", *Derby Telegraph*, 3.11.2014 (online) Text 2: Cartoon: Andy Singer, Saint Paul, MN Text 3: Dückers, Tanja: „Von Geburt an Multikulturalist", *Die Zeit Online*, 6.2.2015 http://www.zeit.de/gesellschaft/zeitgeschehen/2015-02/europa-identitaet-migration-einwanderung/komplettansicht (zuletzt abgerufen: 26.4.2019)

Aufgabe

Klausurteil A: Schreiben/Leseverstehen (Texte 1 und 2)

1. Sum up what the cartoon states about the impact of globalization on cultural diversity and sum up Neil White's view on the quality of this impact. *(Comprehension)*

2. Analyse the way the cartoonist and the writer try to convince the reader of their respective views. In doing this, examine the elements of the cartoon in detail and consider the structure and stylistic devices of the text. *(Analysis)*

3.1 Evaluate the view that local culture is "pitted" (l. 7) and "pock-marked" (l. 40) by American culture. Consider the cartoon, the text, and your own experience. *(Evaluation)*

3.2 Write a letter to the editor of the *Derby Telegraph* stating your personal view on the matter of globalization and Americanization with regard to White's article. *(Evaluation/re-creation of text)*

Klausrteil B: Sprachmittlung (Text 3)

4. At your English partner school you participate in a debate on "globalization and identity". You have done research in the German press and would like to present the views proposed in the German media. Write the part of your talk that deals with Tanja Dückers's article. *(Mediation)*

Klausurteil A

Text 1 "Trick or treat? The worst example of Americanisation in modern society" *Neil White*

WHAT sort of strange society encourages children to dress up like the undead and threaten a trick against their neighbours if they refuse to give them a treat.

Halloween has become the very worst example of the Americanisation which has pitted the British psyche.

All Hallows Eve is a religious festival at which the dead are remembered.

In the 12th century, poor children would go door-to-door and receive "soul cakes" in return for praying for the householders.

The origin of the "trick" part of trick or treat is less easy to establish.

A work colleague told me that her refusal to answer the door on Halloween resulted in eggs being thrown at her house.

Yes, that's right. She decided not to participate in this ghastly ritual and her house was attacked as a consequence.

Fortunately, she was of an age where she just cleaned up the mess and got on with life.

But what of those who are more frail and are frightened to answer the door on dark nights?

Why has it become acceptable for October 31 to be the one day a year when it is fair game to scare them out of their wits or even blackmail them by making demands with menaces?

[...]

It strikes me as ironic that we, as a nation, should be preoccupied with trying to repel European influences and yet allow ourselves to be shrouded in Americanisation.

The latter now dominates our lives from fashion to TV, where we drink our coffee or even our government's foreign policy.

Our language is pock-marked with Americanisms and so we should not be surprised that our children aspire to mirror the behaviour of those in the United States.

The latter has been responsible for what I would call the "oh, my God" culture as seen on reality TV programmes, starring families such as the Kardashians or the Osbournes.

Their hallmark is self-obsession and "greed is good" and, in my opinion, this translates into promotion of activities such as trick or treating.

Wouldn't it be nice if role models were less shallow and keener on contributing to the greater good?

I can't see much in American culture which is worth aping and believe that Europeans tend to be a bit more civilised.

Thus, I am delighted by the advent of German and French markets in the UK and the popularity of Italian and, more recently, Spanish restaurants as a counterpoint to

American fast food.

Interestingly, the Germans just use Halloween as an excuse for a "cool" party.

They have it right. A glass of beer, a sausage cob and prancing around in fancy dress seems infinitely better than trick or treating.

Annotations
pitted – indented, pock-marked
to shroud – to cover; note: a shroud is a cloth to cover dead bodies

Text 2

Cartoon: Andy Singer, Saint Paul, MN

Klausurteil B

Text 3 „Von Geburt an Multikulturalist" *Tanja Dückers*

[...]

Was Europa derzeit fehlt, ist ein neuer Identitätsbegriff. Bislang haben wir unsere europäische Identität in erster Linie über Abgrenzung konstruiert: Wir sind nicht wie die Amerikaner, die Russen oder die

Afrikaner. Statt sich zu einer Identität zu bekennen, haben sich Europäer nur gegen andere Nationen, Kulturen und zum Teil auch pauschal gegen nicht-christliche Religionen gerichtet.

[...]

Viele Menschen beklagen zwar, dass die Binnenkräfte, die Europa zusammenhalten, vor allem ökonomischer Natur seien. Sie haben aber, nach ihrem Identitätsverständnis von Europa befragt, selber wenig zu bieten. Dass die Europäer sich schwer damit tun, eine europäische Identität festzulegen, ist verständlich. Zu viele Einflüsse haben historisch den Kontinent geprägt.

Der Kontinent war zwar schon immer geprägt von regem Handel und Austausch – aber auch von vielen Kriegen. Es gibt keine Region in der Welt, in der so viele von der Fläche her kleine Länder eng beieinanderliegen und keine, deren Geographie so kleinteilig und ineinandergreifend ist. Europa müsste sich jetzt auf seinen Platz in der Welt als Drehkreuz zwischen Ost und West berufen.

Denn Europa kann sich eigentlich nur als regen Marktplatz der Welt, als Vielvölkerstaat mit zahllosen kulturellen, linguistischen und ökonomischen Verbindungen zur außereuropäischen Welt verstehen. Der Europäer ist, wenn er diese Offenheit zulässt, qua Geburt ein Multikulturalist. Es war der kürzlich verstorbene deutsche Soziologe Ulrich Beck, der als einer der ersten den Europäer als Kosmopolit gedacht hat. Doch für Beck bedeutete Europa nicht das Ende der alten Nationalstaaten. Das neue Europa könne vielmehr das alte in sich bergen und zugleich sanft verändern.

Das eine – die transnationale Identität – schließt nämlich das andere – die Herkunftsidentität – nicht aus. Mit dieser Einsicht können wir die große Angst vor einem transnationalen Identitätsbegriff besiegen, die in vielen Regionen Europas geschürt wird, erst recht vor einem, der außereuropäische Fremde miteinschließt. Die Angst ist verständlich, denn es scheint zunächst schwer vorstellbar, dass die Erweiterung eines Identitätsbegriffs nicht gleichzeitig einem Verlust an anderer Stelle gleichkommt.

Berlinerin, Atheistin, Europäerin

Unsere Aufgabe ist es deshalb, einen facettenreichen, multidimensionalen Identitätsbegriff zu etablieren. Einer Identität, die sich gleichwertig aus einem nahen Herkunftsbereich („Berlinerin“) speist, einer soziokulturellen und religiösen Zugehörigkeit („atheistische Schriftstellerin“) und einem geographisch weitergefassten Bereich („Zugehörigkeit zu einem sich als heterogenes Staatengebilde verstehenden Europa“). Was bislang eher als exkludierend empfunden wurde, könnte in Zukunft integrierend verstanden werden. Wenn europäische Bürger sagen: Ich stamme aus einem Kontinent, in dem ich nicht nur jeden Tag Deutsch höre, nicht nur Nachbarn mit meiner Hautfarbe habe. Zu meiner Identität gehört es dazu, mehrere Sprachen zu sprechen und viele Sprachen ein wenig zu verstehen.

Ich lebe in einem Kontinent, der sich dem keineswegs toten, sondern von 500 Millionen Menschen täglich gelebten Multikulturalismus verschrieben hat.

Bearbeitungsschritte und Musterlösungen

Klausurteil A: Leseverstehen/Schreiben
Anforderungsbereich I *(Comprehension)*

In dieser Beispielaufgabe haben wir es im Teil A (Schreiben/integriertes Leseverstehen) mit einem Text in Verbindung mit einem Cartoon zu tun. Bei solchen Aufgaben besteht immer ein enger inhaltlicher Zusammenhang zwischen Text und Cartoon. Doch betrachten wir sie zunächst natürlich getrennt voneinander.

1. Sum up what the cartoon states about the impact of globalization on cultural diversity and sum up Neil White's view on the quality of this impact. *(Comprehension)*

Obwohl Sie es gewohnt sind, ein Bild mit einer ausführlichen Bildbeschreibung anzugehen, ist dies in diesen kombinierten Aufgaben häufig nicht sinnvoll. Eine ellenlange Beschreibung dessen, was auf dem Cartoon zu sehen ist, würde zu Doppelungen in Teilaufgabe 2 führen, und wäre deshalb wenig elegant. Vor allem aber würde eine detaillierte Beschreibung des Bildes nicht den Arbeitsauftrag „sum up what the cartoon states about the impact of globalization" erfüllen. Tun Sie also grundsätzlich nur das, was die Aufgabenstellung von Ihnen verlangt, in diesem Fall also die Aussage des Cartoons zusammenfassen.

Was den Text angeht, so verlangt der Operator „sum up" eine kurze Zusammenfassung der Behauptungen und Argumente des Autors. Die entsprechenden Schlüsselbegriffe werden im Text markiert. Hier werden wir sie auflisten:

	Key phrases
claim	worst example of Americanisation let ourselves be shrouded in Americanisation
evidence/example	strange society dress up like the undead and threaten a trick
evidence/example	Our language is pock-marked with Americanisms
evidence/example	"Oh, my God" culture, reality TV programmes, families such as the Kardashians or the Osbournes, self-obsession and "greed is good"
conclusion	I can't see much in American culture which is worth aping and believe that Europeans tend to be a bit more civilised.

Nachdem diese Vorarbeiten abgeschlossen sind, geht es nun darum, Ihre Notizen und Markierungen in einen zusammenhängenden Text zu bringen. Es bietet sich an, eine der allgemein gehaltenen Aussagen Whites als *topic sentence* voranzustellen, dann seine Beispiele und Argumente anzuführen und mit seinem Fazit abzuschließen. Beginnen Sie mit einem Einleitungssatz, der sich auf die jeweilige Textvorlage bezieht (s. S. 206, Kapitel zur sprachlichen Leistung) und vergegenwärtigen Sie sich die Grundsätze für das Verfassen von Zusammenfassungen.

TIPP zum Punktesammeln

Vermeiden Sie Wendungen wie „In the first paragraph“, „from line x to line y“, „then the author says ...“. Dies sind Wendungen, die eine Strukturanalyse charakterisieren, keine Zusammenfassung.

Beispiellösung (Teilaufgabe 1)

Andy Singer's Cartoon presents globalization as Americanization, the spread of American products and American culture throughout the entire world, which amounts to a military invasion and occupation of foreign countries that the indigenous people do not welcome. Also the text "Trick or Treat" from the "Derby Telegraph" of 3 November 2014 harshly criticizes Americanization. The writer, Neil White, sees American culture as shallow and not worth copying. He wonders why British people reject European influences and at the same time let themselves be strongly influenced by American culture. He sees Halloween as the worst example of Americanization in Britain, as the trick-and-treat tradition is pure blackmail and menace.
According to White, the American influence on the English language leads to British children's imitation of American behaviour, which in turn leads to the acceptance of self-obsession and greed as shown in American reality TV programmes. There is nothing the writer sees as worth copying from US culture and he is happy about the increasing influence of central and southern European culture in Britain.

Anforderungsbereich II *(Analysis)*

2. Analyse the way the cartoonist and writer try to convince the reader of their respective views. In doing this, examine the elements of the cartoon in detail and consider the structure and stylistic devices of the text.

Die Aufgabe verlangt eine Analyse des Cartoons, der Textstruktur und der Stilmittel. Diese Analysen sollten Sie getrennt voneinander angehen.
Die Grobstruktur des Textes zeigt sich schon in den Notizen zum Inhalt.

	Key phrases	**function**
introductory statement, ll. 1–3	WHAT sort of strange society encourages children to dress up like the undead and threaten a trick against their neighbours if they refuse to give them a treat.	get reader interested, set topic

author's claim ll. 5–7	Halloween has become the very worst example of the Americanisation which has pitted the British psyche.	
reference to peaceful religious origin, ll. 8–12	All Hallows Eve is a religious festival at which the dead are remembered. In the 12th century, poor children would go door-to-door and receive "soul cakes" in return for praying for the householders.	establish a contrast
present day example ll. 15–23	A work colleague told me that her refusal to answer the door on Halloween resulted in eggs being thrown at her house.	show contrast
evaluation ll. 24–36	Why has it become acceptable for October 31 to be the one day a year when it is fair game to scare them out of their wits or even blackmail them by making demands with menaces?	show dubious nature of the tradition
general claim ll. 37–39	The latter now dominates our lives from fashion to TV, where we drink our coffee or even our government's foreign policy.	
arguments ll. 40–51	– language is pock-marked with Americanisms – our children aspire to mirror the behaviour of those in the United States. – responsible for what I would call the "oh, my God" culture as seen on reality TV programmes, starring families such as the Kardashians or the Osbournes – self-obesession – "greed is good" → translates into promotion of activities such as trick or treating	support
conclusion ll. 52–62	Wouldn't it be nice if role models were less shallow and keener on contributing to the greater good? I can't see much in American culture which is worth aping and believe that Europeans tend to be a bit more civilised.	

example of alternative, ll. 63–end	Halloween in Germany	confirm his opinion, show resistance, contrasting light note

Bei der Umwandlung Ihrer Notizen in einen zusammenhängenden Text müssen Sie darauf achten, nicht den Inhalt, sondern die Funktion der einzelnen Abschnitte wiederzugeben. Mit dem Inhalt haben Sie sich hinreichend in Teilaufgabe 1 befasst. Inhaltliches wird hier auf ein Mindestmaß reduziert.
Überdies wird verlangt, dass Ihre Klausur aus einem zusammenhängenden Gesamttext besteht. Fangen Sie also nicht mit einem neuen Einleitungssatz an, sondern schließen Sie nahtlos an Teilaufgabe 1 an. Da Sie in Aufgabe 1 mit dem Inhalt der Textbearbeitung aufgehört haben, bietet es sich an, mit dem Text fortzufahren und den Cartoon danach zu analysieren.

TIPP zum Punktesammeln

Denken Sie daran, dass eine Analyse Belege in Form von Verweisen oder Zitaten verlangt.

Der Teil Ihrer zweiten Teilaufgabe, der sich mit der Analyse der Struktur befasst, könnte wie folgt aussehen:

White begins his text with a statement on the nature of Halloween, which arouses the reader's interest and immediately introduces the author's view of American culture as being "strange" (l. 1), a view which is explicitly confirmed in the lines that follow (ll. 3, 4). He goes on to contrast the harmless religious origin of Halloween with what it has become in modern times, by giving an example from his own experience in order to show the absurdity of this festival.

In lines 27 to 51 White expands on the extent of Americanization in Britain, which, to his mind, has led to the promotion of Halloween. In order to support his view, he enumerates different fields strongly subject to Americanization: he refers to what he sees as the bad influence of American usage on the English language, and to the Kardashians and Osbournes as negative examples of American culture that influence British TV viewers.
He concludes with a rhetorical question (l. 52) stressing the superiority of European cultures. This cultural superiority is supported in his last lines (58–68), when he praises examples of Spanish, French and German culture.

Es handelt sich hier um einen persuasiven Text, einen Text, der den Leser überzeugen möchte. Ein solcher Text bedient sich neben seiner Argumente auch der Stilmittel, wie sie im Kapitel zur Analyse einer Rede dargestellt sind. Wenn Ihnen diese nicht sofort ins Auge fallen, suchen Sie gezielt nach den Ihnen bekannten Stilmitteln (Checkliste im Kopf) und markieren Sie sie im Text (vgl. Kapitel zu *political speech,* S. 92).

Im Einzelnen finden wir in diesem Text:

Zeile	Text	Stilmittel
1, 2	What sort of ...	exclamatory "what"
1	strange	derogatory choice of words
2, 3, 19, 29, 30, 31	undead, threaten, ghastly ritual, scare out of their wits, blackmail, menace	word field of horror (choice of words)
5	very worst	superlative
7	pitted	metaphor
11, 12	"soul cakes", praying	contrast to word field of horror (choice of words)
24–25	frail and are frightened	alliteration
27	Why ...	(rhetorical) question
29	fair game	pun
34–36	"trying to repel" vs "allow ourselves to be shrouded"	antithesis
36	shroud	metaphor
40	pock-marked	metaphor
37–39	from fashion to TV, where we drink our coffee or even our government's foreign policy	enumeration
45	"oh-my-God" culture	derogatory choice of words
48, 49	self-obsession, "greed is good"[1]	derogatory choice of words
53	shallow	derogatory choice of words
56	aping	derogatory choice of words
59–62	German and French markets, Italian/Spanish restaurants vs American fast food	antithesis

Wenn Sie nun Ihren Text verfassen, ordnen Sie die Resultate wieder, anstatt textchronologisch vorzugehen. Auffällig ist die Wortwahl: Teils metaphorische, aber auch antithetische Strukturen fallen auf, was ja auch die inhaltlichen Kontraste Amerika/

1 Die Anspielung mit diesem Zitat auf den Film *Wall Street* und damit scharfe Kritik am amerikanischen Kapitalismus müssen Sie als Schüler nicht zwingend erkennen. Im Abitur wären dafür ggf. Zusatzpunkte zu erreichen.

England bzw. England/Deutschland widerspiegelt. Sinnvollerweise beginnt man mit dem vorherrschenden Stilmittel. Es folgen dann weitere Stilmittel, deren Funktion die Emphase, die besondere Betonung ist sowie die rhetorischen Fragen. Letztere haben wir in der Strukturanalyse schon erwähnt, sodass wir sie hier weglassen können.

TIPP zum Punktesammeln

Im Anforderungsbereich II ist Ihr Thema nicht Halloween, auch nicht *Americanization*. Es geht um Wörter, Ausdrücke und Sätze. Eine Formulierung wie „The author says that ..." führt in die falsche Richtung

Der Teil Ihrer zweiten Teilaufgabe, der sich mit der Stilanalyse befasst, könnte also wie folgt aussehen:

White's bias against American culture becomes even more obvious in the way he chooses his words. Derogatory words like "strange" – enhanced by an exlamatory "what" – (l. 1) and "shallow" (l. 53) and the reinforced superlative "very worst" (l. 5) are surpassed by a large number of words and expressions from the semantic field of "horror" ("undead", "threaten", "ghastly ritual", "scare out of their wits", "blackmail", "menace", ll. 2, 3, 19, 29, 30, 31), which on the one hand refer to the example of Halloween, and on the other hand are aimed at American society. In contrast to that stand the very positive words "soul cakes" and "praying" (ll. 11, 12), which refer to the harmless and peaceful origin of the "ghastly ritual" and also the expression "frail" and "frightened" (ll. 24-25) referring to its poor victims, a fact that is additionally stressed by alliteration. Moreover, their role of hunted victims is suggested by the use of the pun in the expression "fair game" (l. 29). Metaphors from the field of death and disease add to the gruesome tone of the text. The words "pitted" (l. 7) and "pock-marked" (l. 40) make the British mentality and the English language appear disfigured and distorted by the disease of Americanization. The metaphor "we ... allow ourselves to be shrouded" (ll. 35-36) compares British society to a dead body, which has given up its individual existence for the sake of Americanization.
The shallow nature of American culture is expressed by the term "'oh, my God' culture" (l. 45). It refers to the superficial enthusiasm for anything, uttered in a high-pitch female voice and getting on everybody's nerves, which we experience in American TV shows. White continues his derogatory choice of words with the terms "self-obsession" and "greed is good" (ll. 48, 49), the latter alluding to Gordon Gekko's speech in the 1987 film "Wall Street", and thus representing harsh criticism of the American capitalist system and greed-driven attitudes. Copying American culture is derided as "aping" (l. 56).
The writer also uses a number of emphatic means. The extent of Americanization in Britain is emphasized by enumeration. Contradictions (ll. 34-36) or pleasant contrast (ll. 58-62) are emphasized by antithesis.

Die Analyse des Cartoons verlangt nun die Interpretation der einzelnen Details. Grundsätzlich kann man sagen, dass jedes Detail eines Cartoons bedeutungstragend ist. Wie bei der Textanalyse sollten Sie sich Notizen auf Ihrem Konzeptpapier machen. Wir stellen die Detailanalyse in einer Tabelle dar.

Detail	Bedeutung
island	foreign country
palm trees, beach	idyll, beauty, paradise
invasion	Americanization
battle ships, logos of corporations	export by corporations
coke, windows,TVs	... of their products
TVs	... and their world view and culture
Disney characters – multiple Goofy – smiling Mickey Mouse	... by means of Hollywood culture, comic culture – stupid, brainless culture – superficial, hypocritical culture
natives, real people, individual faces, horrified	people, individual culture, unwilling to give it up

Die Analyse des Cartoons in ihrer zweiten Teilaufgabe könnte wie folgt aussehen:

The view presented in the cartoon coincides with White's view on Americanization.
The cartoon shows an island invaded by Disney characters who arrive on battleships and planes displaying the logos of prominent American corporations, namely Texaco, Shell, Nike, Motorola and McDonalds. They bombard the idyllic island, with its beautiful beach and palm trees, with American products like Microsoft Windows or Coca Cola. As a sign of their occupation, the invaders put up a flagpole flying the Windows flag. This alludes to the American landing on the Pacific island of Iwo Jima in World War II, which was one of the fiercest battles in the War in the Pacific[1]. Hence, globalization is here clearly presented as Americanization, the aggressive export of American products and of a culture which destroys local culture.
TV sets, which are dropped by Motorola bombers, not only represent American electronic products but also the forceful introduction of an American world-view by CNN or Fox, and by means of TV series and Hollywood films. The Disney characters in particular represent American comic book culture and Hollywood culture. Multiple Goofies, instructed by an angry Donald Duck, stress the shiftiness and stupidity of this culture. A smiling Mickey Mouse reveals superficiality and perhaps even hypocrisy.
The natives, on the other hand, are presented as people with individual faces. One of them has even been killed. Mickey Mouse in his Nike clothes and with an inviting gesture seems to promise them a good fortune, but their faces reveal fear and horror. In spite of its superficially promising attraction, Americanization is presented as not welcome in the world.

1 Die Anspielung auf das weltbekannte Foto der Besetzung von Iwo Jima, die in der Aufrichtung des Flaggenmastes zu finden ist, müssen Sie als Schüler nicht zwingend erkennen. Im Abitur wären dafür ggf. Zusatzpunkte zu erreichen.

Anforderungsbereich III *(Evaluation)*

3.1 Evaluate the view that local culture is "pitted" (l. 7) and "pock-marked" (l. 40) by American culture. Consider the cartoon, the text, and your own experience. *(Evaluation)*

Im Anforderungsbereich III wird von Ihnen eine Stellungnahme verlangt. Nachdem Sie sich intensiv mit der Textvorlage befasst haben, sollten Sie in der Lage sein, sich eine eigene Meinung zu bilden. Wichtig ist,

- dass Sie Ihre Stellungnahme auf den Ausgangstext, bzw. die Ausgangstexte beziehen,
- dass Sie Ihre eigenen Behauptungen mit Argumenten und Beispielen untermauern,
- dass Sie zu einer dezidierten persönlichen Stellungnahme gelangen, einer persönlichen Meinung, die sich aus Ihren Ausführungen ergibt.

Sammeln und ordnen Sie Ihre Gedanken auf Ihrem Konzeptblatt. Wählen Sie dazu eine Mindmap oder auch eine Liste.

Es geht um Kultur. Der Text hebt auf Unterhaltungskultur ab, was auch im Cartoon aufgegriffen wird. Stellen Sie Überlegungen an, was darüber hinaus die Kultur einer Gesellschaft ausmacht und inwieweit diese kulturellen Bereiche von der Amerikanisierung betroffen sind. Stellen Sie dem die Elemente der einheimischen beziehungsweise nicht-amerikanischen Kultur gegenüber. Wir stellen dies hier in einer Tabelle dar.

Cultural area	**Americanization**	**German/international culture**
music	English language pop music rap, etc.	British pop music German pop music German classical music
fashion	blue jeans, T-shirts, baseball caps brands: Nike, Calvin Klein, Hollister, Levis, … cosmetics	scarves, socks, other accessories
sports	basketball, American football, baseball, ice-hockey	football, handball, hockey, other world sports: e.g. rugby, cricket
food and drink	hamburgers, tex-mex, cocktails	Kebab (Döner), Currywurst, Pasta, home cooking
literature	*Hunger Games, Twilight*	German bestsellers
film and TV	high school soaps, *How I Met Your Mother, The Big Bang Theory*	German blockbusters

Entscheiden Sie dann für sich selbst, ob dies einer Dominanz der amerikanischen Kultur gleichkommt oder ob die einheimische beziehungsweise nicht-amerikanische Kultur der amerikanischen stark entgegensteht. In Ihrem Text sollten Sie dann die Ihre These unterstützenden Beispiele aussagekräftig darstellen, die Gegenbeispiele gegebenenfalls einräumen. Bereiche, die Ihre Meinung nicht belegen, müssen Sie nicht unbedingt ansprechen. Nehmen Sie anschließend auch Stellung zu der Kritik an dieser Kultur.

TIPP zum Punktesammeln

Beginnen Sie Ihre Stellungnahme nicht mit „In my opinion", „I think", etc.! Beziehen sie sich auf den Ausgangstext. Beziehen Sie sich vor allem nicht mit einem „this" oder „it" auf die Aufgabenstellung der Teilaufgabe! Ihre Gesamtaufgabe ist ein zusammenhängender Zieltext, der ohne Kenntnis der Formulierung der Teilaufgaben verständlich sein muss.

Ihre dritte Teilaufgabe könnte wie folgt aussehen:

Thus the cartoon supports White's view on American culture as being very dubious and shifty. White refers both to Halloween and to Hollywood entertainment culture, and although there may be lots of local film and TV productions in our country, there are still a large number of American TV soaps and crime series that take up a large part of TV time. In the cinema, there is no question that American films are dominant. Look at the all-time record holders "Titanic" and "Avatar" but also at the newest blockbusters like "Beauty and the Beast" or "La La Land". However, we can still see the success of German productions e. g. by Schweiger or Schweighöfer.

In other areas of culture, we find the same tendencies. Nobody would deny that American music is dominant at least as far as the popular sector is concerned. Much of the English language music is British, it is true, but still a large number of young people listen to rap, hip-hop, or black music.

In the field of fashion, jeans, T-shirts, sweatshirts, hoodies and baseball caps do not even have local counterparts. And we do not experience the introduction of traditional Asian or African clothes in the mainstream population either. There may be a German preference for scarves and other little accessories, but they remain what they are, just additional pieces.

In sports, we see a rising interest in American football and basketball. Yet football and handball are still the most popular sports here, but there are a lot more young people who are familiar with these American sports, even baseball, than there used to be.

As far as food and drink are concerned, we have seen the rise of the American fast food chains. And although Greek, Turkish and Italian food is still paramount, lots of Tex-Mex restaurants, which are American rather than really Mexican, have appeared in Germany and have become very popular among young people. 'Sausalitos' in many German cities, or 'Tijuana' not only in Aachen, are just two examples. Traditional German food has in many cases become restricted to homes and families.

As a conclusion, whether we condemn it like White and Singer, or welcome it, there is no doubt that global culture is not entirely, but largely American. It remains a matter of personal taste if you see it as foreign intrusion or rather an enrichment. Personally, I would say that as long as it does not replace or eliminate local culture completely, I would accept it as adding to the multiple options of our lifestyles.

Anforderungsbereich III *(Re-creation of text)*

3.2 Write a letter to the editor of the *Derby Telegraph* stating your personal view on the matter of globalization and Americanization with regard to White's article. *(Evaluation/re-creation of text)*

In diesem Fall ist die kreative Aufgabe der Stellungnahme inhaltlich sehr ähnlich. Indem Sie zu Whites Artikel Stellung nehmen, bewerten Sie die Frage nach der Amerikanisierung der europäischen Kulturen. Der große Unterschied zu 3.1 liegt in der Textform. Sie müssen einen Leserbrief schreiben, dessen Form wir im Kapitel Zieltextformate (s. S. 106) vorgestellt haben. Im argumentativen Teil wird sich dieser Leserbrief kaum von der Argumentation in Aufgabe 3.1 unterscheiden. Whites konkrete Beispiele (Halloween, Sprache, Reality TV) sollten mit Ihrem eigenen Land (i. d. R. Deutschland) abgeglichen werden. Wir werden uns in der Musterlösung auf den Anfang und das Ende beschränken.

TIPP zum Punktesammeln

Beachten Sie die formalen Aspeke eines *letter to the editor!* Beziehen Sie sich auf den Ausgangstext. Natürlich ist es bei der Wahl der kreativen Aufgabe nicht möglich, an die Lösung der vorhergehenden Aufgaben nahtlos anzuschließen.

Ihre dritte Teilaufgabe könnte wie folgt aussehen:

Sir,

I have read with interest Neil White's article on Halloween as the worst example of Americanization. Unfortunately, Mr White is wrong, when he says that the Germans just see Halloween as a reason for a cool party. Trick and treating has long been established in this country, too, and I hate it as much as Mr White does. To me it has always seemed like racketeering. I too see it as one of the worst examples of Americanization together with other influences. The German language, too, is "pocked-marked" by American English intruders and although there may be lots of local film and TV productions in our country, the vast number of American TV soaps and crime series still take up a large part of TV time.

… (see above)

Traditional German food has in many cases become restricted to homes and families. Thus, I would definitely agree with Mr White's view of Americanization, but I would like to emphasize that this is not just a British, but also a European, if not a global issue.
X. Y., Aachen, Germany

Klausurteil B: Sprachmittlung

Vergegenwärtigen Sie sich die Prinzipien der Sprachmittlung, wie wir sie auf Seite 102 dargestellt haben.
Für eine knappe, sachliche Wiedergabe gehen Sie wie bei einer Zusammenfassung vor, die wir an dieser Stelle nicht ein weiteres Mal ausführlich darlegen.

Adressatenorientierung

In Ihrer fiktiven Situation als Teilnehmer an einer Debatte in einer englischen Schule müssen Sie Ihr Statement adressatengerecht gestalten. Häufig müssen Begriffe oder Eigennamen, die es im Englischen so nicht gibt, erläutert werden. Dieser Text bezieht sich weniger auf Deutschland als auf Europa, deshalb finden wir solch typisch deutschen Begriffe wie im ersten Beispiel (Hartz IV, Aufstocker, siehe S. 115) hier nicht. In diesem Text sollte man sich aber überlegen, wie man mit der Erklärung der verschiedenen Identitäten umgeht. Die Erklärung der Autorin (Berlinerin, Atheistin, Schriftstellerin) zu übernehmen, wird in dem neuen Kontext merkwürdig erscheinen, denn Sie stellen die Autorin ja nicht explizit vor. Auch das Wort „Drehkreuz" in diesem übertragenen Sinne kann nicht einfach so wie im Deutschen benutzt werden.

Ihre vierte Teilaufgabe könnte wie folgt aussehen:

Unlike Americans, Russians or Africans, we Europeans do not have a common notion of identity. Instead of acknowledging one common European identity, Europeans have always confronted other nations, other cultures or non-Christian religions.
People complain a lot about Europe being just an economic union, yet they find it hard to define a European identity. Of course, European history has always been ambivalent. There has always been internal as well as external trade but also many wars. It is a region in the world where many countries share a relatively small geographical area. Today, Europe should really see itself as a crossroads between East and West.
Europe's self-image should be that of an international marketplace, a multi-ethnic place with cultural, linguistic, and economic ties with the rest of the world. A European is multicultural by birth. This does not mean that we have to give up our national identities. If we understand that transnational identity does not exclude national identity, we will overcome the fear that is being fuelled in many European countries and regions, especially if this notion includes non-European immigrants.
We have to establish a multidimensional notion of identity, which includes identity of origin, of sociocultural background and religion, as much as being part of a wider geographical area. In my case this would mean being German from the Rhineland, a Catholic high-school student and multicultural European. To sum up, European identity should be multilingual, multi-racial, and multicultural.

Aufgaben mit Bewertungskriterien

Themenfeld *Freedom and Justice – Myths and Realities*

Aufgabenbeispiel Abitur Englisch Grundkurs
Aufgabenart gemäß KLP: 1.1: Schreiben mit Leseverstehen integriert und Sprachmittlung isoliert
Bezug zu den Vorgaben: Amerikanischer Traum – Visionen und Lebenswirklichkeiten in den USA *Freedom and justice – myths and realities*
Auszug aus einem englischsprachigen Sachtext (413 W.) (Klausurteil A, Text 1) Auszug aus einem deutschsprachigen Sachtext (356 W.) (Klausurteil B, Text 2)
Quellenangaben: Text 1: Clinton, Hillary R., "Keynote": Rede vom 14.8.2014 http://www.newamerica.net/conference2014/keynote_by_the_honorable_hillary_rodham_clinton Text 2: Riedel, Donata: „Studie zur Chancengerechtigkeit: Sozialer Aufstieg in Deutschland bleibt die Ausnahme – OECD fürchtet Vergeudung von Talent", © Handelsblatt GmbH. Alle Rechte vorbehalten. 15.6.2018, https://www.handelsblatt.com/politik/deutschland/studie-zur-chancengerechtigkeit-sozialer-aufstieg-in-deutschland-bleibt-die-ausnahme-oecd-fuerchtet-vergeudung-von-talent/22690454.html?ticket=ST-7608828-73isM9rStOQV6VEN5bt7-ap5

Aufgabe

Klausurteil A: Leseverstehen/Schreiben (Text 1)

1. Sum up what, according to Hillary Clinton, are the basic values of America and what fault she finds with today's society. *(Comprehension)*

2. Examine the way Clinton proposes her view on America. In doing this, examine the structure of this excerpt as well as her stylistic strategies and devices. *(Analysis)*

3. Give your personal view on what Hillary Clinton calls the "hallmark of America" and on the chances of reversing the development she criticizes. *(Evaluation)*

Klausurteil B: Sprachmittlung (Text 2)

4. As a guest student at an American high school you are asked to give a talk on social mobility in Germany in your sociology class. Write the part of your talk that is based on the following article from Handelsblatt. *(Mediation)*

Text 1 "Keynote" *Hillary R. Clinton*

That's really how America is supposed to work. Each generation striving to create opportunity for the next, planting trees that we will not be sitting in the shade of, but expecting others who will follow to be able to; not expecting to be handed anything on a silver platter, but believing that all of us would be given a fair shot at success if we were willing to do the work that was required.

[...]

People everywhere told me that that is what they've always loved and admired about America. Our values of opportunity, freedom, equality. It's why so many people still look to us for leadership. It's why so many still risk so much to join our mosaic. [...]

We know that America is strongest when prosperity and common purpose are broadly shared. When all our people believe they have the opportunity, and in fact do, to participate fully in our economy and our democracy.

Now, the empirical evidence tells us that our society is healthiest and our economy grows fastest when people in the middle are working and thriving, and when people at the bottom believe that they can make their way into that broad-based middle. Now, this is not a new insight. It's time-tested wisdom. It's at the heart of what I believe is the basic bargain of America: No matter who you are or where you come from, if you work hard and play by the rules, you'll have the opportunity to build a good life for yourself and your family.

Now, unfortunately, it's no secret that for too many families in America today, that isn't the way it works anymore. Instead of getting ahead, they're finding it harder than ever to get their footing in our changing economy. The dream of upward mobility that made this country a model for the world feels further and further out of reach. And many Americans understandably feel frustrated – even angry.

The numbers are stark: More than four out of 10 children born into our lowest-income families never manage to climb out of relative poverty. Forget about getting rich. I'm just talking about getting into the middle class and staying there. That shouldn't be as hard as it is now. And what's more, an almost equal percentage of kids who are born into the most affluent families stay there for life, no matter what their effort. That is the opposite of the mobility we think of as a hallmark of America.

Text 2 Studie zur Chancengerechtigkeit: Sozialer Aufstieg in Deutschland bleibt die Ausnahme – OECD fürchtet Vergeudung von Talent

Donata Riedel

Für Kinder aus Arbeiterfamilien ist der soziale Aufstieg in Deutschland besonders schwer – ähnlich wie in den USA. Das hat Folgen für die Wirtschaft.

Berlin. „Der soziale Aufzug ist kaputt", schreiben die Ökonomen der Industrieländer-Organisation OECD. In einer neuen Studie vergleichen sie die soziale Mobilität in 30 Industrie- und Schwellenländern.

Die ist schwer eingeschränkt. In Deutschland kann es sechs Generationen dauern, bis die Nachkommen einer einkommensschwachen Familie das Durchschnittseinkommen erreichen, heißt es in der Studie. In Dänemark seien es nur zwei Generationen, in den übrigen skandinavischen Ländern drei Generationen. Nur in Schwellenländern wie China und Indien brauchen Menschen aus einkommensschwachen Familien noch länger – nämlich sieben bis acht Generationen.

Vergleicht man Väter und Söhne in Deutschland, dann gelingt nur neun Prozent der Söhne von Vätern mit geringem Einkommen der Aufstieg in die höchste Verdienstgruppe. Ganz anders sieht es für Kinder von Vätern mit hohem Verdienst aus: Die Hälfte von ihnen wird später einmal gut verdienen.

[...]

Ein gewisser Trost mag sein, dass es in anderen europäischen Ländern nicht besser aussieht, etwa in Frankreich und Großbritannien. Die Skandinavier allerdings haben es geschafft, Chancengerechtigkeit weitgehend herzustellen.

Die OECD-Ökonomen glauben, dass in Deutschland das Bildungssystem eine entscheidende Rolle für die fehlende soziale Mobilität spielt: Noch immer gebe es zu wenig Kitas und Ganztagsschulen, die Kindern aus sozial schwachen Familien mehr Bildung bieten könnten.

Die frühe Trennung nach der Grundschule in Gymnasien und andere Schulen verbaue zudem vielen Schülern die Chance auf Abitur und Universität.

Die OECD fürchtet, dass Deutschland damit Chancen verspielt und Talent verschwendet. Dies drücke auf die Produktivität der Wirtschaft insgesamt. Auch die Chance auf möglichst viele innovative Unternehmensgründer verspiele Deutschland so.

Die Ökonomen haben zudem die Aufstiegschancen innerhalb einer Generation verglichen, also die Frage gestellt, wie gut es gelingt, aus einem Niedriglohnjob in höhere Einkommenssphären aufzusteigen.

Auch diese Einkommensmobilität ist in Deutschland begrenzt. 58 Prozent der Geringverdiener bleiben für immer arm. Viele Teilzeitbeschäftigte blieben unter ihren Möglichkeiten, vor allem Frauen. [...]

Wer allerdings erst einmal einen Job mit hohem Einkommen erreicht hat, wird ihn kaum je verlieren: 74 Prozent aus dieser Gruppe steigen nicht wieder ab. Dies erhöhe die Gefahr, dass sich Vermögen in Händen weniger konzentrieren.

[...]

Bewertungskriterien

In diesem Kapitel finden Sie die Aspekte aufgelistet, die bei einer gelungenen Lösung von Ihnen erwartet werden. Sie sind für jede Teilaufgabe getrennt in einer Tabelle zusammengefasst. In der Spalte daneben sehen Sie jeweils die maximal zu erreichende Punktzahl.

Klausurteil A
Anforderungsbereich I

Der Prüfling

benennt den Grundsatz, dass eine Generation den Weg für die nächste bereitet.	2
benennt das Prinzip des Erfolgs durch harte Arbeit.	2
führt an, dass Amerika am stärksten ist, wenn Wohlstand geteilt und die Gesellschaft dem Gemeinwohl verpflichtet ist.	2
führt an, dass Chancengleichheit die Grundlage für gesellschaftliche und politische Teilhabe ist.	2
führt aus, dass viele Familien heute nicht mehr am Wohlstand teilhaben und keine Aufstiegschancen haben.	2
führt an, dass zahlreiche wohlhabende Amerikaner ohne jede Anstrengung wohlhabend bleiben.	2
	12

Anforderungsbereich II

Der Prüfling

erläutert die Argumentationsstruktur des Textes: Aufstieg und Arbeit als allgemeingültiger Wert – Bekräftigung und Einbettung in die Werte des *American Dream* – sozio-ökonomische Voraussetzungen (allgemein u. spezifisch) – Situation heute (allgemein – spezifisch)	6
erläutert die Metaphern (z. B. Z. 3–4, 6–7)	4
benennt die emphatischen Mittel, z. B. *antithesis,* (Z. 4, 6–7, 40–41) *alliteration,* (Z. 20, 33–34) *anaphora* (Z. 34–35)	4
benennt die statistischen Belege, die Clintons Kritik unterstreichen (Z. 48–57)	2
	16

Anforderungsbereich III

Der Prüfling

knüpft an den Ausgangstext an, indem er auf den Gleichheitsgrundsatz des *American Dream* verweist.	4

hinterfragt die allgemeine Gleichheit mit Blick auf die von Clinton genannten Probleme und erweitert sie um weitere benachteiligte Gruppen, z. B. Schwarze, Einwanderer, Homosexuelle, Frauen, etc.	5
führt die Problematik der schrumpfenden Mittelklasse aus mit Blick auf die Rolle der Großkonzerne und Superreichen, ggf. mit Blick auf die Globalisierung.	5
	14

Klausurteil B
Sprachmittlung

Der Prüfling gibt die wesentlichen Inhalte im Sinne der Aufgabenstellung sinngemäß zusammenfassend und adressatengerecht wieder.	18

Er stellt dar:
– die OECD-Studie der sozialen Mobilität in 30 Ländern,
– das schlechte Bild, das Deutschland demnach im Vergleich zu anderen Ländern abgibt (innerhalb der Generationen und über Generationen hinweg),
– die Zahlen, die dies dokumentieren,
– die Gründe, die im Bildungssystem zu finden seien,
  – zu wenig Betreuung,
  – zu frühe Differenzierung,
– die Folgen für die Wirtschaft,
  – Auswirkungen auf die Produktivität,
  – Vergeudung von Talenten,
  – Verspielen von Innovationspotential.	

Themenfeld *Tradition and Change in Politics – Monarchy and Modern Democracy*

Aufgabenbeispiel Abitur Englisch Leistungskurs
Aufgabenart gemäß KLP: 1.1: Schreiben mit Leseverstehen integriert und Sprachmittlung isoliert
Bezug zu den Vorgaben: Das Vereinigte Königreich im 21. Jahrhundert – Selbstverständnis zwischen Tradition und Wandel *Tradition and change in politics* *– monarchy and modern democracy*
Auszug aus einem deutschsprachigen Sach- und Gebrauchstext (317 W.) (Klausurteil B, Text 1) Auszug aus einem englischsprachigen literarischen Text (562 W.) (Klausurteil A, Text 2)
Quellenangaben: Text 1: Ira Schaible, et al., „Die Queen kommt: Was Deutschland für den Staatsbesuch vorbereitet“, 18.6.2015 © wgr/dpa Text 2: Peter Morgan, *The Audience*, London 2015 (Faber and Faber), S. 80–83

Aufgabe

Klausurteil B: Sprachmittlung

1. Your English friend's Mum writes you an enthusiastic text message, telling you that the Queen is going to be in Germany and she asks you what the Queen will be doing there. You write her an e-mail back summarizing the facts you get from this article from your local paper.
   Write this part of your e-mail.

Klausurteil A: Leseverstehen/Schreiben

2. Sum up what topics the Queen and the Prime Minister deal with in their audience. *(Comprehension)*

3. Examine the Queen's speech and behaviour with regard to her status as Head of State of the United Kingdom. *(Analysis)*

4.1. Against the backgrounds of your work in class and your own experience, evaluate the suitability of a monarch in a modern democracy. *(Evaluation)*

4.2 As a member of the debating club at your British host school you are asked to give a statement introducing an outsider's view on monarchy. Write your statement in favour of or against royalism. *(Evaluation/re-creation of text)*

Text 1 Die Queen kommt: Was Deutschland für den Staatsbesuch vorbereitet

Ira Schaible, Christina Sticht und Caroline Bock

Vor 50 Jahren kam die Queen zum ersten Mal nach Deutschland. Jetzt ist Elizabeth II. fast 90 Jahre alt. Bei ihrem fünften Staatsbesuch hat sie ein volles Programm – und einige Premieren.

[...]

Der Tross der Queen ist nach Angaben der britischen Botschaft kleiner als bei US-Präsident Barack Obama. Sie kommt mit einem gecharterten Flugzeug. Ihre Entourage besteht aus nur 15 Leuten [...].

Die Queen wohnt wie 2004 wieder im Hotel Adlon, direkt am Brandenburger Tor. Florist Mario Weidner plant den Blumenschmuck. Den bevorzuge die Queen „sehr dezent", verriet er. „Es darf kein Duft sein." Besonders gern habe die Monarchin Pastelltöne und Gelbtöne.

Am Mittwoch hat die Queen ein volles Programm: Nach dem Empfang bei Bundespräsident Joachim Gauck fährt sie im Regierungsviertel mit dem Boot über die Spree – Gelegenheit zum Winken. Dann trifft die Königin Bundeskanzlerin Angela Merkel (CDU) und legt anschließend an der Neuen Wache einen Kranz für die Opfer von Krieg und Gewaltherrschaft nieder.

[...]

Später besucht die Königin eine Vorlesung an der Technischen Universität, die „Queen's Lecture" mit dem Museumschef Neil MacGregor, der das British Museum in London leitet und bald für das Berliner Kulturzentrum Humboldtforum arbeiten wird. Was abends beim Staatsbankett in Schloss Bellevue serviert wird, blieb vorerst geheim.

Am Donnerstag geht es nach Frankfurt am Main – eine Premiere für die Königin. Das Protokoll der Stadt bereitet sich schon seit Monaten auf die rund drei Stunden vor, die die Queen zwischen Paulskirche und Rathaus Römer verbringen wird. Der Transport der Goldenen Bulle, die in einem Panzerschrank im Institut für Stadtgeschichte liegt, muss genau geplant werden. Die Queen will sich das Welterbe-Dokument bei ihrem Besuch in der ehemaligen Krönungsstadt in der Paulskirche ansehen.

Zu den wichtigsten Fragen gehört das Dreigänge-Menü im historischen Kaisersaal und die Liste der rund 120 Gäste. Darunter sind Familienmitglieder des Königshauses wie Heinrich Donatus von Hessen, ein Urenkel von Königin Victoria, der zugleich über das Haus Battenberg mit Prinz Philip verwandt ist. Regionale Küche habe sich die Queen gewünscht, heißt es bei der Stadt. Dabei ist in Frankfurt Grüne Soße Pflicht.

[...]

Annotations
Goldene Bulle: wichtigstes der „Grundgesetze" des Heiligen Römischen Reiches; regelte die Modalitäten der Wahl und der Krönung der römisch-deutschen Könige
Neue Wache: zentrale Gedenkstätte der Bundesrepublik Deutschland für die Opfer von Krieg und Gewaltherrschaft

Text 2 The Audience (extract) *Peter Morgan*

It's Spring 2015. The door opens and the Equerry comes in. The sound of a mobile telephone, with an 'All About That Bass' ringtone.

Equerry Mr Cameron, Ma'am.

David Cameron, forty-eight, enters, bows respectfully.

Cameron Your Majesty.

The 'All About That Bass' ringtone continues.

Elizabeth What's that?

Cameron Not me.

The Queen looks at the Equerry.

Equerry *(hands raised in innocence)* Nor me, Ma'am.

Elizabeth *(realising)* Oh, for heaven's sake.

The Queen moves with difficulty. Searches in her pockets. Finds the phone. Tries to turn it off.

Grandchildren.

Cameron May I, Ma'am?

He takes it and switches it off for her.

Elizabeth How did you do that?

Cameron The red button, here, Ma'am.

He presses the keyboard. The Queen squints.

Elizabeth There isn't a red button.

Cameron It disappears after you touch it.

The Queen stares. Bemused. Confounded.

Cameron *(indicates)* Nice.

Elizabeth What?

Cameron The new Samsung.

Elizabeth I begged them not to give me one, but then security persuaded me it doubled as a useful tracking device in case I try to escape. I expect you have one, too?

Cameron Four.

Elizabeth How awful. Anyway, we have more important things to discuss than this. Parliament has been dissolved. The campaigns are under way. The corridors of Whitehall are empty. Everyone's up and down the country shaking hands, knocking on doorsteps. Or am I being old-fashioned? Is it just the internet now?

Cameron No, we are indeed up and down the country. I was in Leeds, Hull and Scarborough yesterday. Cardiff, Swansea and Glamorgan the day before.

Elizabeth And amid all this electioneering you've still found time for a flying visit to Bonn. Or was it Bern?

Cameron Basle. *(Heart sinks.)* Yes.

Elizabeth I seem to have done nothing *but* welcome you back from European summits. How many have you been to over the past four years?

Cameron Lost count.

Elizabeth Me, too. So ... how did it all go? In a nutshell.

Cameron Well, the desire for the single currency to survive is still there among the core countries – just. But the green shoots of recovery people had hoped for post-austerity have simply not materialised, and now the very real possibility of the Greeks packing their bags and going their own way begs the question do the creditor states bail the Greeks out again, and risk disaster, or let them go and risk disaster? It wouldn't worry me so much if I got a deeper sense of hope, or a shared mission, or ideology –

Unseen by Cameron the queen has nodded off.

– among the rest of the member states. Or anyone doing it because they actually believe in it the way the post-war generation of politicians did. 'Never again.' It's hard to understand why we British have been so resistant to Europe historically.

Cameron notices the queen is asleep.

Mostly ... I'd say it's because we're an island, and not physically part of the continent. And that we still have too vivid a memory of the war –

The Queen sits up at mention of this.

– and struggle with the languages of the Europeans. Not to mention the fact that we –

The Queen shakes herself awake.

Elizabeth Tend not to like them very much ...

Cameron Quite. But don't you think it might also be the fact that in you –

Elizabeth Oh. My fault again is it?

Cameron – we have a head of state who has such strong emotional ties with the Commonwealth that it's impossible for us subjects to commit ourselves fully to any other union. That is, until you ...

Elizabeth Drop dead?

Annotations
audience *here:* weekly meeting of the Queen and the Prime Minister at Buckingham Palace
Equerry: personal attendant to the Royal household
'All About That Bass': 2014 best-selling pop song
Whitehall: London area where the government buildings are

Bewertungskriterien

Klausurteil B: Sprachmittlung

Der Prüfling gibt die wesentlichen Inhalte im Sinne der Aufgabenstellung sinngemäß zusammenfassend wieder.	18
Er fasst die Informationen zu Reise und Unterkunft zusammen.	
Er geht auf das Programm ein: – Berlin: Empfang, Spree, Kranzniederlegung, Universität, Bankett – Frankfurt: Paulskirche, Festbankett	
Er fügt für das Verstehen erforderliche Erläuterungen hinzu, z. B. hinsichtlich Adlon, Spree, Neue Wache, Schloss Bellevue, Goldene Bulle, Grüne Soße.	

Klausurteil A: Leseverstehen/Schreiben
Anforderungsbereich I (Teilaufgabe 2)

Der Prüfling

benennt das neue Smartphone und seine Funktion als Gesprächsgegenstand,	3
benennt den anstehenden Wahlkampf als weiteren Gesprächsgegenstand,	3
benennt den EU-Gipfel, von dem Cameron gerade zurückgekehrt ist, als Gesprächsgegenstand,	3
benennt die Problematik der Rolle der Queen in internationalen Beziehungen als Gesprächsgegenstand.	3
	12

Anforderungsbereich II

Der Prüfling

führt aus, wie der Umgang mit dem Handy die Queen als unbeholfene Großmutter erscheinen lässt.	4
benennt den hochaktuellen *bubble-gum-pop*-Klingelton als starken Kontrast zur tatsächlichen Haltung der Queen.	2
führt an, dass mit den Begriffen „escape“ und „tracking“ eine (selbst-)ironische Anspielung auf ihre eingeschränkte Freiheit als Head of State dargestellt wird.	2
führt ihre Zerstreutheit bzw. ihr Desinteresse am politischen Tagesgeschehen an (Bonn/Bern/Basel).	2
führt aus, wie ihr Desinteresse am internationalen Tagesgeschehen durch ihr Einschlafen deutlich wird.	4
führt aus, wie ihr konservatives, traditionelles, imperiales Denken in der Ablehnung der EU zugunsten des Commonwealth angedeutet wird.	2
	16

Anforderungsbereich III (Teilaufgabe 4.1)

Der Prüfling

knüpft an einen der Ausgangstexte an, indem er sich auf z. B. einen oder mehrere der angesprochenen Aspekte bezieht.	2
führt Argumente für das System der konstitutionellen Monarchie in GB an, z. B. – Wert der Tradition, – Identifikation, *Britishness,* – Verehrung der Royals,	4

– Stabilität, – Vorbildcharakter.	
führt Argumente gegen das System an, z. B. – Kosten, – Privilegien (Steuern), – Personenkult, – Nutzen.	4
gelangt zu einer verallgemeinernden Bewertung, indem er z. B. das System mit alternativen Systemen vergleicht, z. B. dem der Bundesrepublik oder dem der USA.	2
kommt zu einer dezidierten eigenen Meinung.	2
	14

Anforderungsbereich III (Teilaufgabe 4.2)

Der Prüfling

nimmt die situative Vorgabe auf, indem er z. B. sich auf die an ihn gerichtete Bitte bezieht oder einen aktuellen Bezug wählt.	2
unterzieht das Königtum einer genauen Betrachtung, indem er positive und negative Aspekte anführt, z. B. – Wert der Tradition, – Identifikation, *Britishness,* – Verehrung der Royals, – Stabilität, – Vorbildcharakter, oder – Kosten, – Privilegien (Steuern), – Personenkult, – Nutzen.	5
stellt das deutsche System dem gegenüber und führt entsprechend weitere positive oder negative Aspekte an, z. B. – demokratische Legitimation, – Abwählbarkeit bzw. Absetzbarkeit, aber auch Kosten und Sinnhaftigkeit.	5
formuliert eine dezidierte eigene Meinung zum Königtum oder auch allgemein zur Sinnhaftigkeit eines rein repräsentativen Staatsoberhauptes.	2
	14

Themenfeld *Visions of the Future*

Aufgabenbeispiel Abitur Englisch Leistungskurs
Aufgabenart gemäß KLP: 1.1: Schreiben mit Leseverstehen integriert und Sprachmittlung isoliert
Bezug zu den Vorgaben: Medien in ihrer Bedeutung für den Einzelnen und die Gesellschaft *Visions of the future – utopia and dystopia*
Englischsprachiger literarischen Text (235 W., Gedicht) (Klausurteil A, Text 1) Auszug aus einem deutschsprachigen Sach- und Gebrauchstext (443 W.) (Klausurteil B, Text 2)
Quellenangaben: Roger Mc Gough, "The Lake", Fundstelle: http://www.englishdaily626.com/poetry_corner.php?047 Schäfer, Christoph, „Müll zu trennen reicht nicht": © Alle Rechte vorbehalten. Frankfurter Allgemeine Zeitung GmbH, Frankfurt. Zur Verfügung gestellt vom Frankfurter Allgemeine Archiv http://www.faz.net/aktuell/wirtschaft/muell-zu-trennen-reicht-nicht-15376781.html#void

Aufgabe

Klausurteil A: Leseverstehen/Schreiben (Text 1)

1. Describe the physical and biological state of the lake in detail. *(Comprehension)*

2. Examine the way the speaker presents people and their environment and the results of pollution. In doing this, consider the speaker's choice of words and the syntax and imagery of the poem. *(Analysis)*

3. You have a choice here. Do either 3.1 or 3.2.

3.1 Evaluate the criticism inherent in the poem. Give arguments and examples to support or refute the author's negative view of the way people deal with their environment. *(Evaluation)*

OR

3.2 Imagine you are an environmentalist in the town where the lake is situated. Write an article for the local newspaper stating how bad the environmental situation has become. *(Re-creation of text)*

Klausurteil B: Sprachmittlung (Text 2)

4. While you are visiting your partner school in Ireland, you are praised for German awareness of environmental issues. Give a statement in class on the downsides of German rubbish production. Write your statement on the basis of the article from the "Frankfurter Allgemeine".

Text 1 The Lake *Roger McGough*

For years there have been no fish in the lake.
People hurrying through the park avoid it
like the plague. Birds steer clear
and the sedge of course has withered.
Trees lean away from it,
and at night it reflects, not the moon,
but the blackness of its own depths.
There are no fish in the lake.
But there is life there. There is life.

Underwater pigs glide between reefs of coral debris.
They love it here. They breed and multiply
in sties hollowed out of the mud
and lined with mattresses and bedsprings.
They live on dead fish and rotting things,
drowned pets, plastic and assorted excreta.
Rusty cans they like the best.
Holding them in webbed trotters
their teeth tear easily through the tin,
and poking in a snout, they noisily suck out
the putrid matter within.

There are no fish in the lake.
But there is life there. There is life.
For on certain evenings after dark
shoals of pigs surface
and look out at those houses near the park.
Where, in bathrooms,
children feed stale bread to plastic ducks,
and in attics,
toy yachts have long since run aground.
Where, in living-rooms,
anglers dangle their lines on patterned carpets,

and bemoan the fate of the ones that got away.
Down on the lake, piggy eyes glisten.
They have acquired a taste for flesh.
They are licking their lips. Listen ...

Annotations
sedge kind of grass growing in water; G.: Schilf
shoal G.: Schwarm

Text 2 Müll zu trennen reicht nicht *Christoph Schäfer*

Plastikmüll hat im Meer nichts verloren. Wenn in den Abendnachrichten Bilder gezeigt werden, wie in entfernten Weltgegenden Tausende Folien, Flaschen und Tüten auf der Wasseroberfläche treiben, ist die Empörung zu Recht groß. Glücklicherweise sind die deutschen Badeseen sauber. Das bestätigt die Deutschen darin, Klimaschützer und Recyclingmeister zu sein. Fast alle haben drei bis vier Mülltonnen vor dem Haus, um den Abfall zu trennen. Eine braune für den Bioabfall, eine blaue fürs Papier, die schwarze für den Restmüll und die gelbe für Metall und Kunststoff. Darüber hinaus gibt es Wertstoffhöfe und diverse Sammelbehälter für Elektroschrott, Altkleider und Schuhe. Gefühlt ist alles wunderbar in Ordnung.

Leider will sich eine Meldung der vergangenen Woche nicht ins harmonische Bild einfügen: Demnach droht Deutschland im Müll zu versinken, weil China unseren Plastikabfall nicht mehr haben will. Moment mal, denkt man da. Wieso exportiert Deutschland überhaupt Plastikmüll ins ferne China? Wer genauer nachliest, erfährt ganz Erstaunliches: Von den sechs Millionen Tonnen Plastikmüll, die hierzulande jedes Jahr anfallen, geht etwa ein Viertel ins Ausland. Etwa die Hälfte des exportierten Mülls landet im Reich der Mitte. Die Menge ist gigantisch: Allein im vorvergangenen Jahr kaufte China rund 750 000 Tonnen Plastikmüll aus Deutschland. Das entspricht mehr als 80 000 randvollen Müllwagen.

Was mit dem deutschen Müll in China passiert ist, will keiner so genau wissen. In die offiziellen Statistiken jedenfalls fließt das nach China verschiffte Plastik als erfolgreich recycelt ein. Dabei arbeitet laut Experten sogar die Müllverbrennung in Deutschland ökologischer als die chinesische Kunststoffverwertung. Aber weg ist weg, aus den Augen aus dem Sinn.

Müll trennen alleine reicht nicht

Bedauerlicherweise entpuppt sich die Vorstellung von den mülltrennenden Umweltchampions auch mit Blick auf andere Werte als Lüge. Der typische Bundesbürger hat laut EU-Statistikamt im vorvergangenen Jahr exakt 37,4 Kilo Plastikverpackungen als Abfall hinterlassen. Das ist dreimal mehr als ein Bulgare verursacht, und sogar sechs Kilo mehr als der durchschnittliche EU-Bürger ansammelt. Bei der Wiederverwertung sieht es besser aus, aber längst nicht vorbildlich. Das Recycling von Altpapier, Altglas, Weißblech und Aluminium klappt gut, die Aufbereitung von Kunststoffverpackungen hingegen unzureichend. Noch immer wird in Deutschland die Hälfte der Plastikabfälle verbrannt oder landet im Ausland. Tschechien und Bulgarien hingegen erreichen Aufbereitungsquoten von 62 Prozent. Immerhin ist Besserung in Sicht. Ende dieses Jahres tritt das neue Müllgesetz in Kraft, das steigende Recyclingquoten verlangt.

Doch auch damit wird längst nicht alles gut. Der bisherige Ablasshandel (Ich trenne meinen Müll, also darf ich sorgenlos einkaufen) greift zu kurz. Hersteller wie Konsumenten müssen umdenken. Um nur ein paar Beispiele zu nennen: Muss es wirklich sein, dass in eine große Gummibärchentüte Dutzende kleine Tütchen kommen? Muss jede einzelne Gurke im Supermarkt in Plastik verpackt werden? Müssen so viele Kaffee „to go“ sein?

[...]

Bewertungskriterien

Klausurteil A (70%): Schreiben mit Leseverstehen (integriert)

Anforderungsbereich I

Der Prüfling

beschreibt, das dunkle Aussehen der Oberfläche des Sees, in der sich nicht einmal der Mond spiegelt	2
führt an, dass keine Fische darin leben und selbst Riedgras verwelkt ist.	2
führt an, dass Tiere und Menschen gleichermaßen den See meiden,	2
beschreibt, was sich an Unrat in dem See befindet, z. B. – tote Haustiere – Plastik – Fäkalien – alte Matratzen – rostige Büchsen	4
beschreibt die mutierten Monsterschweine, die den See bewohnen	2
	12

Anforderungsbereich II

Der Prüfling

analysiert die Wortwahl des lyrischen Ich, die durchgehend Abscheu, Ekel, Fäulnis, Tod und Bedrohung suggeriert *(plague, blackness, sties, mud, dead, rotting, excreta, etc.)*	4
analysiert syntaktische Merkmale des Gedichtes, insbesondere – die sich wiederholenden Zeilen 8/9 und 21/22 und die Wiederholung – innerhalb der Zeilen, die Bedrohung suggeriert – die Auslassung in der letzten Zeile, die ebenfalls bedrohlich wirkt	4

erläutert die Symbolik der sich neigenden Bäume zur Illustration der Widerwärtigkeit und die Symbolik der Schweine, – als Indikator für den Verschmutzungsgrad (Schweinestall) – als Mutanten und damit Resultat der Veränderung der Natur durch den Menschen – als Bedrohung, die eines Tages über den See hinaus spürbar wird und dem Menschen selbst gefährlich wird	4
erläutert die Bedeutung des Verhaltens der Menschen sowie die Symbolik ihrer Gegenstände, die immer wieder Widernatürlichkeit, Unappetitlichkeit, Verfall und Künstlichkeit suggeriert und so auch den Verfall der Umwelt widerspiegelt, z. B. – altes Brot – Plastikenten im Badezimmer (statt Enten in der Natur) – vergessene Spielzeugyachten (nutzlos, kaputt, als Pendant zum See) – Angeln auf dem Teppich (statt in der Natur)	4
erfüllt ein weiteres aufgabenbezogenes Kriterium	(2)
	16

Anforderungsbereich III (Teilaufgabe 3.1)

Der Prüfling

nimmt einleitend Bezug auf die Intention des Gedichtes,	2
erläutert anhand von Beispielen den Zustand unserer Umwelt, der dem Gedicht Recht gibt oder führt an, dass allerdings auch viele Anstrengungen zum Schutz der Umwelt unternommen werden,	8
wägt die Punkte gegeneinander ab und kommt zu einer begründeten Schlussfolgerung,	4
erfüllt ein weiteres aufgabenbezogenenes Kriterium	(2)
	14

Anforderungsbereich III (Teilaufgabe 3.2)

Der Prüfling

wählt den Zustand des Sees als Aufhänger für seinen Artikel,	2
führt die Konsequenzen der Verschmutzung aus und/oder benennt und beschreibt weitere Bereiche, in denen Umweltschutz geboten ist,	6
benennt Lösungsvorschläge für das Problem des Sees und andere Probleme der Umweltverschmutzung,	4
appelliert an die Leser, mit zu einer Verbesserung beizutragen	2
erfüllt ein weiteres aufgabenbezogenes Kriterium	(2)
	14

Klausurteil B (30%): schriftliche Sprachmittlung D–E (isoliert)

1. Inhaltliche Leistung

	Anforderungen: Die Schülerin/Der Schüler gibt die wesentlichen Inhalte im Sinne der Aufgabenstellung sinngemäß zusammenfassend wieder:	**max. Punkt-zahl**
1	der scheinbar vorbildliche Umgang mit Plastikmüll in Deutschland	18
2	die Verschiffung ins Ausland	
3	das hohe Aufkommen trotz Recycling	
4	die Kritik an bestimmten Produkten *(coffee to go, Gummibärchen)*	

Themenfeld *The Impact of Shakespearean Drama on Young Audiences Today*

Aufgabenbeispiel Abitur Englisch Leistungskurs
Aufgabenart gemäß KLP: 1.1: Schreiben mit Leseverstehen integriert und Sprachmittlung isoliert
Bezug zu den Vorgaben: Literatur und Medien in ihrer Bedeutung für den Einzelnen und die Gesellschaft *The impact of Shakespearean drama on young audiences today: study of extracts and film scenes*
Auszug aus einem deutschsprachigen Sach- und Gebrauchstext (441 W.) (Klausurteil B, Text 1) Auszug aus einem englischsprachigen literarischen Text (365 W.) (Klausurteil A, Text 2)
Quellenangaben: Text 1: Frank Günther, „Sein oder Nichtsein?“, *Frankfurter Neue Presse* 19.04.2014, online http://www.fnp.de/nachrichten/kultur/Sein-oder-Nichtsein;art679,820195 Text 2: William Shakespeare, *The Taming of the Shrew*, Act V, Scene II

Aufgabe

Klausurteil B: Sprachmittlung

1. Your English teacher at your host school in England has asked you to give a talk in class on the relevance of Shakespeare in Germany. Write the part of your talk that deals with Frank Günter's view on Shakespeare's still being up-to-date. *(Mediation)*

Klausurteil A: Leseverstehen/Schreiben

2. Point out the view of a wife's duty as it is presented by Katherina. *(Comprehension)*

3. Explain the comparisons used in this monologue as well as their function. In doing this, also refer to the Elizabethan world picture. *(Analysis)*

4.1 Evaluate Katherina's speech from a 21st century point of view. *(Evaluation)*

4.2 After you have attended a performance of *The Taming of the Shrew*, write an article for an international online magazine with the title "The interest of young audiences in Shakespeare", in which you critically discuss the relevance of Shakespeare's plays for today's audiences. Refer to the excerpt from the play, Frank Günther's article, and other texts you have studied. *(Evaluation/re-creation of text)*

Text 1 Sein oder Nichtsein? *Frank Günther*

Nun feiern wir also Shakespeares 450. Geburtstag. Es gibt nur wenige Autoren der Weltliteratur, bei denen man auf eine vergleichbare Wirkungsgeschichte zurückblicken kann; Dante könnte man nennen, und Cervantes, auch wenn sein „Don Quichote" – trotz Windmühlen und Dulcinea – nicht Shakespeares breitgefächerte Wirkungsmacht erreichte. Shakespeare ist eine einzigartige literarische Ikone.

Wie es euch gefällt

Was sagt man über eine 400 Jahre alte Ikone? Über Shakespeare ist dieser Tage als bewunderndes Statement häufig zu lesen, er sei „auch heute noch aktuell". Das sagt sich so leicht dahin. Unklar ist, was es bedeuten soll. Es ist nämlich ein seltsam vergiftetes Lob. Im „auch-heute-noch" schwingt als Unterton ja mit, dass solche uralten Werke nach 400 Jahren eigentlich längst zum historischen Schutt gehören müssten. Aber nein, nicht bei Shakespeare – und dann folgt dieses Wörtchen „aktuell". Shakespeare ist auch heute noch aktuell! Also wichtig, relevant, bedeutsam für unsere heutigen Probleme, für dich und mich, hier und jetzt. Noch aktuell. Also morgen vielleicht schon nicht mehr?

Es ist gut gemeint, aber etwas glitschig, dieses schlagzeilenhascherische Adjektiv „aktuell". Wir gebrauchen es gewöhnlich im Kontext der „aktuellen Nachrichten", des „aktuellen Straßenzustandsberichts", der „aktuellen Herbstmode", der „aktuellen Frühjahrsfarben", der „aktuellen Looks", der „aktuellen Trends" – also für lauter entschieden flüchtige, nur für den konkreten Moment gültige Erscheinungen, zumeist in ranschmeißerischer Werbesprache formuliert. Was „aktuell" ist, ist schnellebig; es trägt sein baldiges Ende schon in sich, denn das Wörtlein „aktuell" signalisiert, dass es alsbald von noch „Aktuellerem" abgelöst werden wird. Was heute aktuell ist, ist schon morgen von gestern.

Was ihr wollt

Shakespeare, der „auch heute noch aktuell" sein soll, soll offenbar einen entscheidenden Beitrag zum heutigen Aktuellen leisten. Was aber sind unsere aktuellen Probleme zu Shakespeares Geburtstag? Die Euro-Krise. Die Griechenland-Krise. Die Energie-Krise. Die Ukraine-Krise. Die Migrationsproblematik. Der NSU-Skandal über Nazi-Umtriebe. Der NSA-Skandal über Geheimdienstumtriebe. Die Probleme mit Very Big Data. Die Frage der sozialen Gerechtigkeit. Die Quotenregelung für Frauen in Führungspositionen. Die EU-Regelung zu Energiesparbeschränkungen bei Staubsaugern und Kaffeemaschinen. Haben Shakespeares Werke uns dazu irgendetwas zu sagen? Nein, natürlich nicht. Die Rede vom „auch heute noch aktuellen" Shakespeare entpuppt sich schnell als hilflose Hohlfloskel. Seinem Werk ist mit solchen wohlfeilen Etiketten wohl nicht beizukommen.

[...]

Unter der „Aktualität" der Oberflächenzeitumstände, die von „verstaubten" Verhältnissen erzählen mag, brodelt sehr lebendig das Eigentliche, das Shakespeares Glanz ausmacht: die niemals an ein Ende kommende, niemals auserzählbare existenzielle menschliche Werdens- und Wandlungsmöglichkeit. So kommt es, dass wir durch Shakespeares paradoxe Erzählkunst uns selbst auch hinter der verblichenen Aktualität vergangener Weltverhältnisse wiedererkennen können. In seinen zahllosen Gestalten, in ihren Leiden und Freuden, ihren Gemeinheiten und Bösartigkeiten, ihren Irrtümern und Selbsttäuschungen, ihren Egoismen und ihrer Fähigkeit zu Güte, Liebe und Mitleid erscheinen wir uns selbst, nah und vertraut.

Text 2 The Taming of the Shrew (Act V, Scene 2) *William Shakespeare*

Katherina, who is the woman to be tamed in this comedy, speaks this monologue in the final scene.

Katherina
Fie, fie! unknit that threatening unkind brow,
And dart not scornful glances from those eyes,
To wound thy lord, thy king, thy governor:
It blots thy beauty as frosts do bite the meads,
Confounds thy fame as whirlwinds shake fair buds,
And in no sense is meet or amiable.
A woman moved is like a fountain troubled,
Muddy, ill-seeming, thick, bereft of beauty;
And while it is so, none so dry or thirsty
Will deign to sip or touch one drop of it.
Thy husband is thy lord, thy life, thy keeper,
Thy head, thy sovereign; one that cares for thee,
And for thy maintenance commits his body
To painful labour both by sea and land,
To watch the night in storms, the day in cold,
Whilst thou liest warm at home, secure and safe;
And craves no other tribute at thy hands
But love, fair looks and true obedience;
Too little payment for so great a debt.
Such duty as the subject owes the prince
Even such a woman oweth to her husband;
And when she is froward, peevish, sullen, sour,
And not obedient to his honest will,

What is she but a foul contending rebel
And graceless traitor to her loving lord?
I am ashamed that women are so simple
To offer war where they should kneel for peace;
Or seek for rule, supremacy and sway,
When they are bound to serve, love and obey.
Why are our bodies soft and weak and smooth,
Unapt to toil and trouble in the world,
But that our soft conditions and our hearts
Should well agree with our external parts?
Come, come, you froward and unable worms!
My mind hath been as big as one of yours,
My heart as great, my reason haply more,
To bandy word for word and frown for frown;
But now I see our lances are but straws,
Our strength as weak, our weakness past compare,
That seeming to be most which we indeed least are.
Then vail your stomachs, for it is no boot,
And place your hands below your husband's foot:
In token of which duty, if he please,
My hand is ready; may it do him ease.

Annotations
unknit your brows ≠ knit your brows; **blot:** stain; **meads:** meadows; **confounds thy fame:** destroys your reputation; **meet:** appropriate; **moved:** bad-tempered; **bereft:** robbed; **deign:** consent, want; **froward:** hardheaded; **big:** arrogant; **haply:** perhaps; **bandy:** hit back and forth (as at tennis); **vail:** lower; **stomach:** pride, temper; **no boot:** no use

Bewertungskriterien

Klausurteil B: Sprachmittlung

Der Prüfling gibt die wesentlichen Inhalte im Sinne der Aufgabenstellung sinngemäß zusammenfassend wieder.	18
Er führt an, dass Günther den Begriff aktuell ablehnt, da er Schnelllebiges und Vergängliches bezeichnet, z. B. Modetrends oder Verkehrshinweise.	
Er führt an, dass Shakespeare auch zu den aktuellen Problemen der Welt nichts Relevantes beitragen kann, z. B. zu internationalen Krisen, humanitären Belangen oder politischen Skandalen.	
Er führt an, dass es vielmehr Shakespeares Charaktere sind, in deren Facetten wir uns immer wieder wiedererkennen, selbst vor dem Hintergrund vergangener Weltbilder.	

Klausurteil A: Leseverstehen/Schreiben
Anforderungsbereich I (Teilaufgabe 2)

Der Prüfling

führt aus, dass die Frau freundlich zu sein hat, denn nur das macht sie liebenswert und attraktiv.	4
führt aus, dass sie ihrem Mann Liebe zu erweisen, zu gefallen, zu dienen und zu gehorchen hat, als eher noch zu geringe Gegenleistung für seine Sorge und die Strapazen und Entbehrungen, die er um ihretwillen auf sich nimmt.	4
führt aus, dass diese Rolle in den natürlichen körperlichen und charakterlichen Eigenschaften der Frau begründet liegt.	4
	12

Anforderungsbereich II (Teilaufgabe 3)

Der Prüfling

analysiert den zentralen Vergleich zwischen Ehe und Staatswesen, Untertan und König ("subject vs. lord", "sovereign", "prince"), und benennt weitere Vergleiche, die Hierarchie ausdrücken: "keeper", "head" und erläutert, dass der Souverän Sorge für seine Untertanen trägt, daher sind sie zu Dienst und Loyalität verpflichtet. So ist auch die Frau, die sich gegen den Ehemann auflehnt, gleichzusetzen mit dem Rebellen und dem Verräter, der sich gegen seinen König auflehnt.	4
benennt weitere Vergleiche (Störung der Natur: "frost/meads", "whirlwinds/buds", "fountain/mud") und ihre Funktion: Weibliches Missverhalten erscheint als Auflehnung gegen die gottgewollte Ordnung.	4
erkennt und benennt weitere Vergleiche, die Schwäche und Machtlosigkeit der Frau illustrieren: "unable worms", "lances are but straws".	4
erkennt die typisch elisabethanische Sichtweise der korrespondierenden Beziehung von – Mensch und Natur, – Mensch und Staatswesen, – Mikrokosmos und Makrokosmos.	4
	16

Anforderungsbereich III (Teilaufgabe 4.1)

Der Prüfling

nimmt Bezug auf die Ungleichheit der Geschlechter, wie Katherina sie propagiert.	2
äußert sich vor dem Hintergrund der modernen demokratischen, freiheitlichen, egalitären westlichen Weltanschauung kritisch zu diesem Frauenbild, z. B. mit Verweis auf – Menschenrechte, – Menschenwürde, – Frauenbewegung des 20. Jahrhunderts, – Veränderung der Familienstrukturen, – Veränderung in der Arbeitswelt.	5
weist hin auf immer noch bestehende Ungleichheit, z. B. – im Berufsleben, – in patriarchalischen Gesellschaftsformen, – in kriminellem Kontext (Gewalt gegen Frauen).	5
formuliert eine zusammenfassende, wertende persönliche Stellungnahme zur Rolle der Geschlechter.	2
	14

Anforderungsbereich III (Teilaufgabe 4.2)

Der Prüfling

nimmt einleitend Bezug auf die vorgegebene Situation und die Textpassage als Anlass seines Artikels.	1
äußert sich vor dem Hintergrund der modernen demokratischen, freiheitlichen, egalitären westlichen Weltanschauung kritisch zu dem dargestellten Frauenbild, z. B. mit Verweis auf – Menschenrechte – Menschenwürde – Frauenbewegung des 20. Jahrhunderts – Veränderung der Familienstrukturen – Veränderung in der Arbeitswelt; hinterfragt die Aktualität und Relevanz der Dramen Shakespeares und erweitert seine Argumentation um Beispiele aus anderen Dramen z. B. je nach Schwerpunkt hinsichtlich – Geschlechterrollen – Verhältnis der Generationen – Lehnstreue – Aberglaube – etc.	5
verweist auf die sprachlichen Schwierigkeiten des vorliegenden Textes sowie anderer Dramen.	2

stellt seinen Ausführungen Argumente entgegen, die die fortwährende Aktualität und Relevanz von Shakespeares Dramen unterstreichen. Dabei bezieht er sich z. B. auf – zeitlose Problematik wie Liebe, Zurückweisung, Eifersucht, Ehrgeiz, Neid etc., – unvermindertes Interesse an Theatervorstellungen, – Erfolge von Hollywood-Produktionen, – Adaption in modernen Werken, – zeitlose Kraft und Schönheit der Sprache.	4
formuliert eine zusammenfassende persönlich wertende Stellungnahme auf der Grundlage seiner Argumentation.	2
	14

Themenfeld *Studying and Working in a Globalized World*

Aufgabenbeispiel Abitur Englisch Grundkurs
Aufgabenart gemäß KLP: 1.1: Schreiben mit Leseverstehen integriert und Sprachmittlung isoliert
Bezug zu den Vorgaben: Lebensentwürfe, Studium, Ausbildung, Beruf international – Englisch als *lingua franca* *Studying and working in a globalized world*
Auszug aus einem englischsprachigen Sachtext (399 W.) (Klausurteil A, Text 2) Auszug aus einem deutschsprachigen Sachtext (302 W.) (Klausurteil B, Text 1)
Quellenangaben: Text 1: Miriam Olbrisch, „Glück- und Sinnsuche im Job. Die Andersmacher“, SPIEGEL ONLINE, Miriam Olbrisch, 12. Dezember 2013, 13:31 Uhr, http://www.spiegel.de/karriere/berufsstart/generation-y-und-die-arbeitswelt-die-andersmacher-a-931225.html Text 2: Tomas Chamorro-Premuzic, “Are millennials as bad as we think?” *The Guardian*, Friday 24 January 2014 15.59 GMT, last modified on Wednesday, 3 September 2014, 15.27 BST (online) https://www.theguardian.com/media-network/media-network-blog/2014/jan/24/millennials-generation-gap, Copyright Guardian News & Media Ltd 2019

Aufgabe

Klausurteil B: Sprachmittlung (Text 1)

1. As an introduction to a debate on the modern world of work at an international summer school the participants are asked to each give a short statement on the view of the young generation prevailing in their respective countries. Imagine you are a participant. Write the part of your statement which is based on the article from *Spiegel Online*.

Klausurteil A: Leseverstehen/Schreiben (Text 2)

2. Describe the millennial generation’s attitude towards work and leisure. *(Comprehension)*

3. Examine the way the author presents the millennials’ attitude and the way he puts forward his subjective view. In doing this, examine his choice of words and other stylistic devices and argumentative strategies. *(Analysis)*

4.1 Write a comment on the author's view of the young generation. In doing this, try to give an answer to the question asked in the title. *(Evaluation)*

4.2 As a member of the young generation you feel offended by the article and write an e-mail to the author. In doing this, try to refute his allegations. *(Evaluation/ re-creation of text)*

Text 1 **Glück- und Sinnsuche im Job** *Miriam Olbrisch*

[...]

Ein Café, gemütlich wie ein Wohnzimmer, an einem Samstagnachmittag in Köln: handgeschriebene Speisekarten, Kronleuchter an der Decke, die Torte kommt auf Goldrandtellerchen. Die Gäste: hauptsächlich junge Frauen mit grobgestricktem Schal und großer Brille. Sie hocken auf weißgestrichenen Flohmarkt-Stühlen, viel zu viele für den kleinen Raum.

Mittendrin: Nina Ebert, 29 Jahre alt und „eine richtige Kaffeetante", so nennt sie sich selbst. Kaffeetante ist Ninas Beruf. Bei Miss Päpki serviert sie Cappuccino, quatscht mit den Gästen, kassiert, organisiert. Vor allem aber backt sie Kuchen. Ihre Spezialitäten sind Schweizer Schokoladenkuchen und Brownie Cheesecake.

Nina ist unfassbar überqualifiziert für diesen Job. Sie hat Biologie studiert, ihren Master in der Tasche und müsste eigentlich, wenn alles so gelaufen wäre, wie Eltern oder Karriereberater das gern hätten, gerade an ihrer Doktorarbeit sitzen. Aber Nina hat sich anders entschieden. Vorletzten Sommer verabschiedete sie sich von Bienen, Genforschung und allem anderen, was die Biologie ihr noch bieten könnte.

„Ich habe Wissenschaftler gesehen, die ihr ganzes Leben im Labor verbringen, die für ihre Aufgabe brennen", erzählt Nina. „Ich konnte das nicht. Das war nicht meins." Stattdessen heuerte sie bei einer Freundin an, die in Köln das Miss Päpki aufgemacht hatte – und eine Konditorin und Kellnerin suchte. „Ich freue mich morgens auf die Arbeit", sagt Nina, die auch früher schon mit Leidenschaft Torten buk. „In der Forschung wäre ich nicht glücklich geworden."

„Typisch", sagen an dieser Stelle Soziologen, Personalchefs, Psychologen. Sie haben sich längst ein Bild von Menschen wie Nina gemacht, von diesen jungen Leuten, die derzeit auf dem Arbeitsmarkt ihr Glück suchen. Sie haben ihnen viele Namen verpasst: Digital Natives, Generation Praktikum, Millennials, Generation Y. Keine Altersklasse wird derzeit so fleißig erforscht wie Akademiker zwischen 25 und 35 Jahren. Und kaum einer Altersklasse werden so viele Etiketten angeheftet: Faulpelze, Weicheier, Traumtänzer, Dickköpfe, Selbstverwirklicher, Facebook-Junkies. Aber auch: Alleskönner, Multitasker, Weltverbesserer, Teamplayer.

Text 2 Are millennials as bad as we think? *Tomas Chamorro-Premuzic*

[...]

Ambitious but lazy: There is no clearer evidence for millennials' entitlement than the discrepancy between their ambitious aspirations and their lukewarm work ethic. Since much of Gen Y has been persuaded – first by overprotective parents, then by grade inflation and the unrealistic promises from universities – that their high expectations would eventually translate into actual achievements, it should come as no surprise that millennials are less interested in working hard to achieve them. Unfortunately, millennials have bought into the idea that the cause of success is high self-belief; not discipline, self-knowledge or humility. This keeps their hopes in their (self-perceived) talents intact, as if sooner or later their exceptional potential will be discovered, even if they don't devote much time to harnessing it.

Hyper-connected, but self-obsessed: Although the ubiquity of Facebook, Twitter and Instagram has led to the suggestion that millennials are incredibly sociable, the reverse is probably true. Millennials are hyper-connected, but they display little interest in others except as an audience. As the YouTube slogan suggests, their main ambition is to broadcast themselves, even if it requires collecting disposable friends and engaging in inappropriate self-disclosure with strangers.

Superficially, this phenomenon may be attributed to the social media revolution, but it's probably the other way around: the power of social media is just highlighting how vain we have become. Indeed, narcissism levels have risen steadily during the past few decades, making millennials more self-obsessed than their predecessors. For example, in the 1950s, 12% of high-school students perceived themselves as "an important person" – by the 1990s, 80% did. As Jean Twenge's seminal studies demonstrate, millennials are much more Gen Me than We. In the US, narcissism has increased at the rate of obesity and is the main explanation for the apparent extraversion of millennials – it's exhibitionism and attention-seeking, but camouflaged as sociability.

[...]

Nonconformist but materialistic: Although Gen Y is somewhat less materialistic than Gen X – at least in America, where levels of materialism seem to have peaked in the late 80s – they remain very interested in money, status and expensive things. However, this obsession with bling contrasts with their nonconformist nature. Indeed, Gen Y is more individualistic, rebellious and independent than past generations, except for their desire to fit in. As a result, millennials are trapped in a vicious circle: on one hand, they want to disrupt the system; on the other hand, they are more afraid of rejection.

Annotations
millennial generation/Gen Y generation born approximately between 1980 and 1999
seminal important, groundbreaking
narcissism tendency to admire oneself
bling *(informal)* expensive and flashy clothes or jewellery

Bewertungskriterien

Klausurteil B: Sprachmittlung

Der Prüfling gibt die wesentlichen Inhalte im Sinne der Aufgabenstellung sinngemäß zusammenfassend wieder:	18
Er stellt dar, welche Atmosphäre das Café kennzeichnet (Einrichtung, Gäste).	
Er fügt ggf. für das Verstehen erforderliche Erläuterungen hinzu, z. B. hinsichtlich Einrichtung oder Kleidung.	
Er stellt Nina Ebert vor (Diskrepanz zwischen Ausbildung und beruflicher Tätigkeit).	
Er benennt die von Soziologen behauptete typische Allgemeingültigkeit.	
Er fasst die kontrastierende Etikettierung der jungen Generation zusammen.	

Klausurteil A: Leseverstehen/Schreiben

Anforderungsbereich I

Der Prüfling

stellt die Diskrepanz zwischen dem Anspruch der *millenials* und ihrer Arbeitshaltung dar.	4
stellt den Kontrast zwischen der starken sozialen Vernetzung und der Ich-Bezogenheit der Generation dar.	4
stellt den Widerspruch zwischen ihrer non-konformistischen Haltung und ihren materialistischen Zielen dar.	4
	12

Anforderungsbereich II

Der Prüfling

beschreibt die Unterteilung des Textausschnittes in drei inhaltliche Abschnitte, die jeweils ein Paradox beschreiben, verweist auf antithetische Wortwahl der jeweiligen Überschriften sowie weitere antithetische Strukturen: "Ambitious but lazy" (Z. 2), "Hyper-connected, but self-obsessed" (Z. 22), "... attention-seeking, but camouflaged as ..." (Z. 50–51), "on the one hand, ... on the other hand" (Z. 64–66).	6
benennt die zahlreichen Wörter bzw. Ausdrücke mit negativer Konnotation, die eine herablassende Haltung des Autors widerspiegeln, z. B. "lukewarm", "overprotective", "grade inflation", "little interest", "disposable friends", "inappropriate", "vain", "narcissism", "obsessed", ("narcissism linked with obesity"), "exhibitionism", "attention-seeking", "obsession with bling".	4

benennt die zahlreichen Wörter, die auf einen falschen Anschein hinweisen und somit Falschheit und Täuschung suggerieren, z. B. “unrealistic”, “bought into”, “self-perceived”, “as if”, “suggestion, suggest”, “apparent”, “camouflaged”.	4
verweist auf statistische Angaben, die die Aussagen des Autors stützen. (Zeile 42, 44)	2
	16

Anforderungsbereich III (Teilaufgabe 4.1)

Der Prüfling

knüpft an den Ausgangstext an, indem er sich auf die Haltung des Autors bezieht.	2
bewertet jeden einzelnen in den Überschriften genannten Aspekt vor dem Hintergrund persönlicher Erfahrung oder mit Bezug auf Text 1.	6
stützt seine Argumente bzw. Gegenargumente mit Beispielen, z. B. – aus seinem persönlichen Umfeld, – bezüglich Innovation und Kreativität in Wirtschaft, Sport, Kunst, Musik, etc., – bezüglich der ethischen Fragwürdigkeit der Werte der Vorgängergenerationen, – mit Blick auf positive Konjunkturentwicklungen.	4
kommt zu einer dezidierten eigenen Meinung mit Bezug auf den Titel des Artikels	2
	14

Anforderungsbereich III (Teilaufgabe 4.2)

Der Prüfling

nimmt die situative Vorgabe auf, indem er sich auf den Artikel und insbesondere die subjektive Haltung des Autors bezieht.	2
drückt seine Empörung aus, indem er die Behauptungen des Autors kommentiert und durch Argumente und Beispiele widerlegt, z. B. – aus seinem persönlichen Umfeld, – bezüglich Innovation und Kreativität in Wirtschaft, Sport, Kunst, Musik, etc., – bezüglich der ethischen Fragwürdigkeit der Werte der Vorgängergenerationen, – mit Blick auf positive Konjunkturentwicklungen.	6
drückt seine Empörung aus, indem er sich auf die Diktion des Autors bezieht.	4
schließt seine E-Mail z. B. mit einer dezidierten Gegenthese oder mit einem Appell an journalistische Fairness.	2
	14

Original-Prüfungsaufgaben 2018 und 2019

GK Sachtext mit Beispiellösung und Bewertungskriterien

Quelle der Aufgabenstellung: Qualitäts- und UnterstützungsAgentur – Landesinstitut für Schule*

Aufgabe 1

Klausurteil A: Leseverstehen und Schreiben integriert

Aufgabenstellung:

1. Describe the situation Manny finds himself in, his plan and his motivation. *(Comprehension) (12 Punkte)*

2. Analyse the way Manny's situation is presented. Focus on point of view and use of language. *(Analysis) (16 Punkte)*

3. Choose **one** of the following tasks:

3.1 Comment on Manny's view of the United States. Refer to the text and work done in class. *(Evaluation: comment) (14 Punkte)*

3.2 Write a letter to Gary Paulsen, the author of the novel, in which you reflect on the effect the extract from his novel has on your view on Trump's plan to build a wall between the US and Mexico. Refer to the extract and work done in class. *(Evaluation: re-creation of text) (14 Punkte)*

Klausurteil B: Sprachmittlung isoliert

Aufgabenstellung:

4. Your American friend is doing a school project on *Underage Refugees in Europe* and has asked you for information.
Write him/her an email in which you summarize what D. Betzholz says about the situation of underage refugees in Germany and the problems they face. *(Mediation) (18 Punkte)*

* Die Beispiellösungen sind nicht amtliche Lösungen.

Materialgrundlage:

Klausurteil A:

Gary Paulsen, *The Crossing* (excerpt), Copyright © 1987 by Gary Paulsen. Reprinted by permission of Orchard Books, an imprint of Scholastic Inc., S. 3–9

Wortzahl: 419

Klausurteil B:

Dennis Betzholz, „Die Tragödie der Kinder-Flüchtlinge", in: *Welt*, 20. April 2015, https://www.welt.de/vermischtes/article139802318/Die-Tragoedie-der-Kinder-Fluechtlinge.html (Zugriff : 09.05.2017)

Wortzahl: 319

Zugelassene Hilfsmittel:

- Ein- und zweisprachiges Wörterbuch
- Herkunftssprachliches Wörterbuch für Schülerinnen und Schüler, deren Herkunftssprache nicht Deutsch ist
- Wörterbuch zur deutschen Rechtschreibung

Wichtigste Bezüge zum Kernlehrplan und zu den Vorgaben 2018

1. Inhaltsfelder und inhaltliche Schwerpunkte
Klausurteil A:
- Amerikanischer Traum – Visionen und Lebenswirklichkeiten in den USA
  Freedom and justice: myths and realities

Klausurteil B:
Globale Herausforderungen und Zukunftsvisionen
- Chancen und Risiken der Globalisierung
  Globalization and global challenges: Lifestyles and communication

2. Medien/Materialien
Klausurteil A:
- Narrative Texte: 20th-/21st-century novel

Klausurteil B:
- Sach- und Gebrauchstexte

Klausurteil A

The Crossing *Gary Paulsen*

This is the beginning of the novel.

Manny Bustos awakened when the sun cooked the cardboard over his head and heated the box he was sleeping in until even a lizard could not have taken it, and he knew, suddenly, that it was time. This was the day. He would make the crossing today.

Juárez, Mexico, was never quiet. As a border town it was made of noise – noise that filled all the hours of the day – but the noises changed, and he listened to them now without thinking.

Honking horns, the market starting to fill with people trying to get fresh goat cheese or the thick coffee, people yelling insults and curses at each other – a hum of noise. Mornings were the best time, not a good time – there were no good times for him – but the best. He lived on the street, moving, always moving because he was fourteen and had red hair and large brown eyes with long lashes, and there was danger if he did not move – danger from the men who would take him and sell him to those who wanted to buy fourteen-year-old street boys with red hair and long eyelashes.

So now he rolled out when the sun warmed the cardboard of his lean-to, wiped his mouth with a finger, and stood to begin moving for the day. Another day in Juárez. But this time it was different. [...] This day he would cross to the north to the United States and find work, become a man, make money, and wear a leather belt with a large buckle and a straw hat with a feathered hatband.

Hunger was instant, had never gone. He went to bed hungry, slept hungry, awakened hungry [...].

"Later in this day I will be leaving," he said, lowering his voice as he thought a man would speak. "It is time for me to be crossing to the north and finding work."

[Old Maria] studied him through the screen. A dozen flies worked to get in, making a high buzzing sound that somehow matched the talking sounds of the café in front. "You are too young to make the crossing."

Manny shrugged. "It is not age. I am ready to make the crossing and so it is time. Age does not matter." "But you are small." "I am not so small." He bridled. "I have strength and I am fast and I know how to work hard. That is all that is required to cross to the north. They only wish you to work hard."

She sighed.

Annotations
27 **lean-to** – *here:* improvised shelter
43 **Old Maria** – a woman making and selling tortillas in a simple place to eat
44 **screen** – *here:* transparent curtain used to protect against heat or insects

Beispiellösung

Aufgabe 1 – 3.1

In the extract (pp. 3–9) from the very beginning of the novel "The Crossing" by Gary Paulsen, published in 1987, the reader is introduced to Manny Bustos, a 14-year-old homeless teenager living in the Mexican town of Juárez and dreaming of a new and better life in the USA. His current situation is anything but safe and stable: he sleeps on the streets, is always hungry and, with his prominent features (red hair and large brown eyes), fears that he may be abducted, sold and sexually abused. So he is always on the move and never stays long in one part of the city.

One morning Manny wakes up and feels that this is the day that he will cross the border to the USA. He plans to make the crossing, find work and make a living.

When he reveals his plans to Old Maria, a woman making and selling tortillas in a simple place to eat, she tells him that he is too young and too small to cross the border. Manny replies that age and size are irrelevant, as he already has the strength, perseverance and ability to work hard, which are all that is needed to succeed in the USA.

Aufgabe 2

As the opening sentences of the extract show, the reader is immediately confronted with Manny's situation without any kind of introduction (ll. 1-6).

The story is told by a limited third person narrator from Manny's point of view. Consequently the reader gets an insight into the boy's thoughts, feelings and plans for the future: "This day he would cross to the north to the United States and find work, become a man, make money, and wear a leather belt with a large buckle and a straw hat with a feathered hatband." (ll. 30-35).

The way his dreams are depicted shows that he is still a child: his dreams of wearing a particular sort of belt and hat would not usually be enough motivation for an adult to make the illegal and highly dangerous crossing from Mexico to the USA. That he is still a child and underestimates the danger of crossing the border is also shown by the fact that he "[…] [lowers] his voice as he [thinks] a man would speak" (ll. 40-41) when he talks to Old Maria about his plans.

In this extract the focus is mainly on Manny's thoughts and feelings. The use of a stream of consciousness technique enables the reader to see and experience the world through Manny's eyes. This is highlighted by the fact that direct speech is only used when Manny reveals his plans to Old Maria (ll. 39–56). Moreover, the language used throughout the extract is easy to understand and emphasizes that the story is told from the point of view of a homeless teenager.

In order to clarify how complicated, dangerous and poor Manny's life on the street is, certain aspects of his daily struggle are elaborated upon, such as his constant hunger, which "[…] was instant, had never gone. He went to bed hungry, slept hungry, awakened hungry […]" (ll. 36-38); or the fact that there are "[…] no good times for him" (ll. 17-18). The detailed description of Manny's personal situation (ll. 1-6) and street life in Juarez (ll. 7-16) immediately evokes vivid images in the reader's mind.

The simple sentence structure, often marked by parallelism and repetition, helps to describe both the desolate situation Manny is in and also his determination to cross the border and start a better life in the USA.

Aufgabe 3.1

Manny's view of the USA is an entirely positive one and he is convinced that he will be able to lead a successful life there. His view is based on to the belief that any can fulfill their dreams in the USA as long as they work hard enough and keep their mind set on their goals. This concept is often compared to that of a person developing from "dishwasher to millionaire", and in the past there actually were people who fitted that vision. Consequently, many generations of immigrants were attracted by the seemingly unlimited opportunities offered by the USA. The right to pursue one's own notion of happiness as long as it does not interfere with that of others is also included in the American Declaration of Independence. For Manny, making his dreams come true also means that he will "[...] wear a leather belt with a large buckle and a straw hat with a feathered hatband." (ll. 33-35), as he regards these two items as the symbols of success for a Mexican man who has crossed the border and made it in the USA. His vision of his future life in the USA neglects the fact that he might not manage to cross the border and that, even if he makes the crossing, he will not be welcomed in the USA with open arms. His positive picture of the USA is most likely based on hearsay and pictures. One has to keep in mind that he is only 14 and does not seem to have much to lose in Juárez, where he is homeless and continually exposed to all the hardships of life on the streets (ll. 1-6, ll. 18-25).
While Manny is certain that he possesses all that is necessary to change his life for the better – "[...] [to] have strength and [to be] fast and [...] know how to work hard [...]" (ll. 52-56) – Old Maria, who has far more experience in life, is not euphoric about his plans to leave Juarez (ll. 47-48, l. 57).
Even at the time when Gary Paulsen's novel was first published (1987), laws and regulations concerning illegal immigration to the USA were tough. Today, illegal immigrants from South American countries like Mexico still cannot apply for well-paid jobs, as they live in constant fear of being exposed and sent back to their country of origin. Most of the jobs they can take are restricted to domestic work (housekeeping, gardening etc.) or working in agriculture (e.g. as fruit pickers). In many cases these jobs are only temporary and not well paid, which means that illegal immigrants and their families often have to move – e.g. travelling from one fruit farm to the next. This means that their children are often uprooted and do not get a proper education, as they cannot attend school regularly. So they too will only get low-paid jobs in future – jobs for which not much skill or training is needed. This creates a vicious circle that is not easy to escape from.
Former US presidents have granted amnesties in the past, giving illegal immigrants permission to stay and work in the USA, but the current US president Donald Trump has announced plans to tighten the grip on illegal immigrants. He even wants to build a wall separating Mexico from the USA, for which he expects Mexico to pay.
Since the extract from "The Crossing" analysed in this exam is taken from the beginning of the novel, it is unclear whether Manny will succeed and manage to turn his dreams from fiction into reality. As the title of the novel suggests, the actual crossing of the border seems to play a vital role in the novel. One can only hope that Manny is successful.

Aufgabe 3.2

Dear Mr. Paulsen,

I read the beginning (pp. 3–9) of your novel "The Crossing" with interest and I have to say that I really enjoyed it. Right from the very first sentence you caught my attention and I immediately felt with Manny Bustos.

I am a secondary school student from Germany and in my English course we have dealt with the concept of the American Dream, its history, and its relevance for today. When we talked about the key concepts of the American Dream, we also discussed everyone's right to pursue their own dreams and visions. Manny Bustos' determination to lead a better life in the USA reminded me of what we talked about in class.

As a homeless boy, Manny does not seem to have that much to lose by leaving Juárez, and for him the USA is the "promised land". Because of his lack of alternatives and his youth, he is convinced that once he has crossed the border, everything will change for the better. While reading about Manny's thoughts and feelings, I could not help asking myself what Manny would do if your novel was not set in 1987 but in 2018. US president Donald Trump most certainly would not welcome Manny with open arms and honour his determination to work hard and would not grant him US citizenship. Trump's plans to build a wall between the USA and Mexico have been eyed with suspicion by people all around the globe. Especially since he plans to make Mexico pay for the cost of building the wall.

Trump's determination to put a stop to illegal immigration has even resulted in temporarily separating families caught in the attempt to cross the border. Children, even babies and toddlers, were taken away from their parents or guardians and sent to orphanages or foster families. In doing this, Trump wanted to set an example and threaten anyone planning to enter the USA illegally.

In my opinion, all the harsh criticism Trump faced for this action was entirely justified: wilfully separating families is barbaric and traumatizing for children and adults alike.

Learning about Manny's life and all the hardship he has to endure on the streets has given all these numerous illegal immigrants, especially the children, a human face. Your portrayal of Manny has also helped me to get a deeper insight into the hardship people like Manny hope to escape from and the dreams they wish to pursue. I am looking forward to reading the rest of the novel and I can only hope that many other readers will feel the same.

Maybe this will help open the eyes of those who still regard every immigrant as a threat to the USA but completely ignore the problems and dangers these immigrants wish to escape from.

Yours sincerely,
M. Miller

Vorgaben für die Bewertung der Schülerleistungen

Aufgabe 1 *(Comprehension)*

Es können maximal 12 Punkte erreicht werden. Um die maximale Punktzahl zu erreichen, werden folgende inhaltliche Aspekte erwartet:

- Beschreibung der schwierigen Lebensumstände in der mexikanischen Stadt an der Grenze zur USA: Obdachlosigkeit, auf sich allein gestellt sein, Hunger, Gefahren wie Missbrauch oder Verschleppung *(6 Punkte erreichbar);*

- Darstellung von Mannys Plan und Motivation, an diesem Tag die Grenze zur USA zu überqueren, seinen Wunsch nach Arbeit und Geld, sein Glaube an die eigene Stärke, sein Streben nach Sicherheit und einem besseren Leben *(6 Punkte erreichbar).*

Aufgabe 2 *(Analysis)*

Es können maximal 16 Punkte erreicht werden. Um die maximale Punktzahl zu erreichen, werden folgende inhaltliche Aspekte erwartet:

- Ausarbeitung, wie beim Leser Empathie erzeugt wird für Mannys aussichtslose Situation in Juárez und für seinen naiven Plan auszuwandern, dabei Blick auf die durch Mannys Wahrnehmungen und Überlegungen gesteuerte Erzählperspektive und auf die intensivierenden sprachlichen Mittel *(4 Punkte erreichbar);*
- Analyse der Art und Weise, wie durch die Verwendung eines *third-person narrators* mit einem *limited point of view* für Mannys aussichtslos wirkenden Plan Mitgefühl erzeugt wird, z. B. durch die detaillierte Beschreibung der Umgebung und Mannys Äußerem, die eindringliche Darstellung von Manny innerem Zustand und die Kontrastierung seines kindlichen Optimismus mit den berechtigten Sorgen Marias *(6 Punkte erreichbar);*
- Erläuterung, wie die Darstellung von Mannys trostlosen Lebensbedingungen und seines Plans durch sprachlich stilistische Mittel betont wird, z. B. mithilfe der Verwendung einer einfachen, durch parallele Strukturen gekennzeichneten Syntax, durch die bildhafte Ausdrucksweise und durch Aufzählungen und Wiederholungen *(6 Punkte erreichbar).*

Aufgabe 3.1 *(Evaluation: comment)*

Es können maximal 14 Punkte erreicht werden. Um die maximale Punktzahl zu erreichen, werden folgende inhaltliche Aspekte erwartet:

- Untersuchung – ausgehend vom Textauszug und unter Rückgriff auf im Unterricht erworbenes Wissen – inwiefern Mannys Vorstellung von den USA geprägt ist durch einen bedingungslosen Glauben an den amerikanischen Mythos des Erfolgs, dabei Bezug auf relevante zentrale Ideen des amerikanischen Traums und auf Mannys stereotypes Verständnis dieser Ideen *(6 Punkte erreichbar);*
- kritisch-wertende Stellungnahme zur Realisierbarkeit von Mannys Traum, z. B. mit Bezug auf Mannys Lebenssituation, insbesondere sein Alter, seinen Bildungsstand, seine Sprachkenntnisse und seinen familiären Hintergrund, auf die Vision und die Realität des American Dream und auf aktuelle wirtschaftliche, soziale und politische Entwicklungen *(6 Punkte erreichbar);*
- eine begründete und nachvollziehbare persönliche Einschätzung *(2 Punkte erreichbar).*

Aufgabe 3.2 *(Evaluation: re-creation of text)*

Es können maximal 14 Punkte erreicht werden. Um die maximale Punktzahl zu erreichen, werden folgende inhaltliche Aspekte erwartet:

- Abfassung eines situations- und adressatengerechten Briefs an den Autor Gary

Paulsen, der den Schreibanlass und die Intention des Briefs erläutert und Bezug nimmt zum Textauszug und zur aktuellen politischen Situation in den USA *(4 Punkte erreichbar);*

- kritisch-wertende Beleuchtung (ausgehend von der eigenen Lesart des Textausschnitts und mit Rückgriff auf im Unterricht erworbenenen Wissens) der möglichen Konsequenzen eines Mauerbaus, z. B. für Mexikaner wie Manny und ihre beruflichen, gesellschaftlichen und persönlichen Zukunftschancen, für die wirtschaftliche und soziale Zukunft der USA, für das Selbstverständnis der USA als Einwanderungsland und für die Rolle von Vorurteilen in selektiver Immigration *(6 Punkte erreichbar);*
- Abschluss auf der Basis der eigenen Ausführungen, z. B. mit einer pointierten Zusammenfassung der eigenen Position, mit einem Blick auf mögliche Zukunftsperspektiven und mit einem Appell an den Autor *(4 Punkte erreichbar).*

Klausurteil B

Die Tragödie der Kinder-Flüchtlinge *Dennis Betzholz*

Noch 2010 nahmen deutsche Kommunen 2822 minderjährige Flüchtlinge in Obhut, die ohne Begleitung aufgegriffen wurden. 2013 waren es bereits 6584 – eine Steigerung von rund 133 Prozent.

Ulrike Schwarz, Referentin beim „Bundesfachverband Unbegleitete Minderjährige Flüchtlinge“ in Berlin, kennt die Schicksale hinter den Zahlen. „Entweder werden die Kinder auf der Flucht von ihren Eltern getrennt“, sagt Schwarz. „Oder die Familie kratzt ihre Ersparnisse zusammen und schickt sie ganz bewusst alleine los, damit wenigstens die Töchter und Söhne aus dem Krisengebiet rauskommen und die Chance auf eine bessere Zukunft haben.“ Schlepper, gefälschte Papiere, die Fahrt übers Mittelmeer kosten viel Geld – von Afghanistan nach Italien bis zu 10.000 Euro pro Person.

Kinder, Jugendliche allein auf dem weiten Weg nach Europa. „UMF“, unbegleitete minderjährige Flüchtlinge, werden sie genannt. Schätzungsweise rund 18.000 leben derzeit in Deutschland; zwei Drittel sind Jungen. Die meisten von ihnen kommen aus Afghanistan, Syrien, Somalia und Eritrea. [...]

Franz Joseph Freisleder weiß, was passieren kann, wenn die, die aus dem Krieg kommen, keinen Frieden finden. Er ist Ärztlicher Direktor des Heckscher-Klinikums für Kinder- und Jugendpsychiatrie in München und Oberbayern, der größten Einrichtung dieser Art in Deutschland. Zu ihm bringen Polizisten und Sozialarbeiter Jugendliche aus den umliegenden Flüchtlingsunterkünften, die auffällig werden oder die sie nicht mehr unter Kontrolle haben. Seit Januar nahm Freisleder bereits 30 unbegleitete minderjährige Flüchtlinge auf seiner Station in München auf. So viele wie im gesamten Jahr 2012. Für dieses Jahr rechnet er mit mindestens 120 Fällen. Jugendliche, die aggressiv werden, um sich schlagen oder in Angstzustände verfallen. [...]

„Sie haben ein Maß an Gewalt erlebt, das wir uns nicht vorstellen können.“ Auf der Flucht hätten sie gelernt, dass nur die Starken durchkommen, erklärt der Arzt. Da sei es nicht verwunderlich, dass sich Aggressionen aufstauten. „In denen brodelt es", sagt Freisleder. Es käme jedoch nur selten vor, dass Jugendliche wegen gewalttätigen Ausfällen zu ihm in die Klinik kämen. Die meisten seien depressiv und selbstmordgefährdet. Viele sorgten sich sehr um ihre Familien.

Beispiellösung

Aufgabe 4

Dear Archie,

Thank you for your email. I did some research about the situation of Underage Refugees in Europe and came across an interesting article that might help you with your school project. In his article "Die Tragödie der Kinder-Flüchtlinge" the author, Dennis Betzholz, focuses on the situation of underage refugees in Germany. The number of underage refugees travelling without any adult accompanying him or her rose by 133 per cent between 2010 and 2013. Most of these 18,000 children are boys from Afghanistan, Syria, Somalia or Eritrea. There are several reasons why children travel on their own: they have either been separated from their parents or guardian at some point on their refugee journey, or the families have saved all their money (up to €10,000) to send their sons or daughters ahead, hoping that at least they will have the chance of a better life.

The number of children seeking medical help because of their traumatic experiences is also increasing. The violence these children have experienced often results in depression, suicidal tendencies, constant fear for the wellbeing of their families back home, and violent outbursts, although those do not occur that often.

I hope this information will help you with your project and that you will send me your presentation when it is finished. Please do not hesitate to contact me again if you have any more questions.

Bye,
Betty

Vorgaben für die Bewertung der Schülerleistungen

Aufgabe 4 *(Mediation)*

Es können maximal 18 Punkte erreicht werden. Um die maximale Punktzahl zu erreichen, werden folgende inhaltliche Aspekte erwartet:

- Verfassen einer situations- und adressatengerechten E-Mail, in der
  - die Situation unbegleiteter minderjähriger Flüchtlinge in Deutschland zusammengefasst wird, mit Verweis insbesondere auf die rapide steigenden Zahlen, auf die Tatsache, dass die meisten männlich sind, auf die Vielzahl der Herkunftsländer und die Motivation der Familien
  - die Probleme dargestellt werden, insbesondere die Angst der Flüchtlinge, die Agression aufgrund von Gewalterfahrungen und die Niedergeschlagenheit und Suizidgefahr

- die Ursachen dieser Probleme beschrieben werden, insbesondere negative Erlebnisse in den Heimatländern und auf der Flucht, das Gefühl, dass es nur die Stärksten schaffen können und der fehlende Kontakt zur und die Sorge um die Familien.

LK mit Beispiellösungen

Aufgabe 1

Klausurteil A: Leseverstehen und Schreiben integriert

Aufgabenstellung:

1. Describe the family's situation and Ajay's thoughts and feelings as presented in this extract. *(Comprehension) (12 Punkte)*

2. Analyse the way the situation and Ajay's state of mind are presented. Focus on point of view, setting and use of language. *(Analysis) (16 Punkte)*

3. Choose **one** of the following tasks:

3.1 Discuss Ajay's mother's statement that she is "going for Birju and Ajay" (l. 67). In doing so, refer to work done in class on postcolonial India and the *American Dream*. *(Evaluation: comment) (14 Punkte)*

3.2 Ajay and Birju spend the night at the grandparents' house. The next morning Ajay overhears a conversation between his grandparents in which they talk about their hopes and fears for the family's future.
Write a continuation of the given extract.
(Evaluation: re-creation of text) (14 Punkte)

Klausurteil B: Sprachmittlung isoliert

Aufgabenstellung:

4. Together with students from your American partner school, you are working on the issue of *Cultural Identity in a Globalized World*.
Write a report for the project's website in which you outline the German concept of "Heimat" and its development as presented in Christina Berndt's article.
(Mediation) (18 Punkte)

Materialgrundlage:

Klausurteil A:

Akhil Sharma, *Family Life*, London: Faber & Faber Limited 2015, S. 14–16

Wortzahl: 560

Klausurteil B:

Christina Berndt, „Im Wohlfühl-Ort", in: *Süddeutsche Zeitung*, 30. Dezember 2010 http://www.sueddeutsche.de/wissen/gemischte-gefuehle-heimatgefuehl-im-wohlfuehlort-1.1041384 (Zugriff : 20.04.2017)

Wortzahl: 427

Zugelassene Hilfsmittel:

- Ein- und zweisprachiges Wörterbuch
- Herkunftssprachliches Wörterbuch für Schülerinnen und Schüler, deren Herkunftssprache nicht Deutsch ist
- Wörterbuch zur deutschen Rechtschreibung

Wichtigste Bezüge zum Kernlehrplan und zu den Vorgaben 2018

1. Inhaltsfelder und inhaltliche Schwerpunkte

Klausurteil A:

Globale Herausforderungen und Zukunftsvisionen

- Chancen und Risiken der Globalisierung
  India: from postcolonial experience to rising nation

Politische, soziale und kulturelle Wirklichkeiten und ihre historischen Hintergründe

- Postkolonialismus – Lebenswirklichkeiten in einem weiteren anglophonen Kulturraum

Klausurteil B:

Globale Herausforderungen und Zukunftsvisionen

- Chancen und Risiken der Globalisierung

Alltagswirklichkeiten und Zukunftsperspektiven junger Erwachsener

- Lebensentwürfe, Studium, Ausbildung, Beruf international – Englisch als *lingua franca*
  Studying and working in a globalized world

2. Medien/Materialien

Klausurteil A:

- Literarischer Text

Klausurteil B:

- Sach- und Gebrauchstext

Klausurteil A

Family Life *Akhil Sharma*

The novel is set in 1970s Delhi. Eight-year-old Ajay and his older brother Birju are visiting their grandparents.

She shook us awake while it was still dark. We went out onto the roof and bathed using a bucket and a mug. It was strange to bathe with the moon above us. And when the horizon began to brighten that first light felt rare and precious. And then, a little later, as the sky brightened, we walked down the street toward the bus stand. Birju walked beside my mother and I walked in the shadow of the boundary walls. In the shade, the dust was heavier and things smelled different, as if a fragment of the night lingered.

Everything about where my grandparents lived was pleasingly miniature. Their lane was so narrow I could reach out and touch the houses on both sides. In the morning, when we arrived, the gutters ran with soapy water and the lane smelled of soap and also of hot oil and dough from the parathas being fried.

My grandfather, seeing us, straightened up from sweeping his small whitewashed courtyard. "Who are these two princes? Are they saints who have come to bless my house?" He wore white pajamas and a homemade sleeveless undershirt with long shoulder straps. I hurried forward [...] to show that I was good and knew to display respect, touched his feet.

"We have gotten our airplane tickets, nanaji," Birju said.

Hearing this, I wished I had said it so that then I would be the one bringing the news.

"I'm not letting both of you go. One of you I will keep."

"We'll miss you," Birju said, reaching down to touch our grandfather's feet. He had long, bony arms.

"I will miss you, too," I murmured, again feeling jealous that Birju had said something that made him look good.

There were small rooms on two sides of the courtyard. These were cool, shadowy places. They smelled of mothballs, and this was pleasant because it suggested closed trunks and things that would be revealed when the seasons changed.

Around eleven that morning, I fell asleep on a cot in one of the rooms. When I woke, Birju was lying next to me, smelling of the coconut oil that my mother put into his hair because of his dandruff. My mother and grandmother were sitting on the floor near the courtyard. They were talking in whispers and making seemi, rubbing wads of dough between their fingers so that the dough became thin as a thread, then pinching off small pieces so that these fell on the towels spread in their taps. The seemi looked like fingernail clippings.

"You don't speak English," my grandmother whispered.

"I will learn."

"You're almost forty."

"I'm going for Birju and Ajay."

"Isn't it better for them to be here with their whole family?"

"Their father is there."

"Here you have a job."

"What is here? Thieves? That Indira woman will eat us."

I lay on my side and watched and listened. Usually, naps left me melancholy. Lying there, I began to think that when I was in America, I wouldn't be able to see my grandparents every Sunday. Till then, I had not fully understood that going to America meant leaving India. [...]

The melancholy wouldn't go away. I couldn't quite believe that when I left India, my grandparents' house would continue to exist, that the gutters along the sides of the lane would still run with soapy water.

Annotations
21 **paratha** – flat bread
32 **nanaji** – grandfather
57 **seemi** – small pieces of dough
72 **Indira** – Indira Gandhi, Prime Minister of India at the time

Beispiellösung

Aufgabe 1

The excerpt from Akhil Sharma's novel "Family Life" (2015) deals with eight-year-old Ajay and his brother Birju, who are visiting their grandparents before they emigrate to America with their mother. Their father is already in America.
They leave home early in the morning to take a bus to their grandparents' village. Ajay is pleased with the view of the village with its narrow lanes and tiny houses and the smell from people's cooking and washing.
The grandfather greets the two boys happily but Ajay feels jealous of his brother because it is he who does the talking and thus seems to make a better impression on their grandfather. Later in the morning, Ajay overhears a conversation between his mother and his grandmother. The old woman is sceptical about their emigration. At that moment, Ajay realizes that going to America means leaving India forever. The thought of having to leave his grandparents and not being able to see them regularly any more and of the house and the village being there without him leaves him melancholy.

Aufgabe 2

Ajay's state of mind is first and foremost conveyed to the reader by the use of the first-person point of view. The first-person pronoun is used throughout the text, thus the subjective, limited view of the narrator is apparent. In some cases, the narrator directly refers to and reflects on his feelings (l. 3 "strange", l. 42 "jealous", l. 75, 81 "melancholy"). Mostly it is the narrator's sensory perception of the situation that reveals his state of mind. He mentions the "strange" feeling, when he bathes with the moon above him (l. 4), he perceives the first light as "rare and precious" (l. 6), and he describes how he can enjoy the cool shade in the shadow of the walls, referring to the smells and the touch of dust, which remind him of the pleasant coolness of the night (ll. 10-13). The image "as if a fragment of the night lingered" extends the overall pleasant atmosphere, even though the bright light of day has arrived, which might otherwise be associated with unpleasant heat and dust.

His visual and olfactory perception on arriving at the grandparents' village also contributes to the pleasant atmosphere, which in turn reveals the narrator's state of mind. The village is "pleasingly miniature" (l. 15) and not threatening and overwhelming like the big city. Houses do not tower above him but can be touched on both sides. Cleanliness is suggested as "the gutters ran with soapy water" and by the grandfather's "sweeping the small whitewashed courtyard" and his "white pyjamas" too. Smells from people's cooking add to the pleasant, homely atmosphere (ll. 18-26).
In lines 45 to 46, it is again the shade and the coolness that are perceived as pleasant. Even the smell of mothballs, which in other contexts might have negative connotations, is perceived as positive from the child's point of view, because "it suggested closed trunks and things that would be revealed when the season changed" (l. 47-49).
Scents again play a role when the narrator awakens next to his brother, who smells of coconut oil (l. 53). The familiar smell, associated with his mother, because she always puts it in Birju's hair, adds to the narrator's pleasant feeling of homeliness, just as much as the whispering of his mother and grandmother (l. 57) as they work preparing the family food. The situation is emphasised by the narrator's careful observation and detailed description (ll. 57-62) and the simile in line 62 ("The seemi looked like fingernail clippings.").
The narrator's reflection on his melancholy is apparent in lines 74 to 86. We get an insight into the child's thoughts and feelings as he begins to understand the impact of his emigration to America. These are conveyed to the reader by means of reported thoughts, a device already used in lines 33 to 35 and 48 to 49.

Aufgabe 3.1

This melancholy and the narrator's apparent love of his home and India give way to some critical thoughts on his mother's emigration plans.
As the father is already in the United States, it seems obvious that the family should follow. We do not learn much about the family's reasons for leaving India, but we do learn (ll. 72-73) that the mother is not happy with Indira Gandhi's politics. Apparently, there are high taxes which do not leave a lot of money in a worker's pocket. Poverty – as always – seems to be the main reason for emigration. India is known for its poverty, for the huge gap between rich and poor, for its giant slums and overpopulation. Today, India's economy has experienced a boom, globalisation has brought large investments, slums have been turned into shiny business centres, but the majority of the population cannot participate in this accumulation of wealth. There is still immense social inequality, a hierarchy that is still solidly in place. However, this story is set in the seventies, long before the boom started. The mother does not seem to be educated. She does not speak English, so she has had no access to higher or even secondary education in India. Although the local languages are still used there remains the practical problem of teaching, lecturing and educational literature being predominantly in English. The mother does have a job, but apparently it does not earn her enough money to give her a satisfactory life in India. She wants to have a better life for herself and especially for her children.
There is shiny America luring, with its promises of golden opportunity. The American Dream, which many people still believe in, promises equal chances to everybody. It promises that anybody who is prepared to work hard will be able to climb the ladder of success, to find

their way "from rags to riches". From this excerpt we do not know how successful the father has become in the U.S., but we can infer from the conversation between the two women that his success cannot have been so immense. "Their father is there" (l. 70) is the only argument the boys' mother can put forward. If her husband was an IT-specialist earning 200,000 dollars in Silicon Valley – or whatever was the equivalent in the 1970s – she would certainly have mentioned it and her emigration would not have been an issue anyway. But what awaits her in America is probably the fate of all poor immigrants who do not even speak the language: bad housing conditions, no social security, hard work and low pay, racism and prejudice. As the story is set in Indira Gandhi's times, in the 1970s, the recession had not yet hit America, jobs in production had not yet gone overseas, but it was hard to become successful as an immigrant, especially if you were not white. With the quality of schools depending on the wealth of the surrounding area, it will also be hard for Ajay and Birju to succeed in America. They, too, do not speak the language, so they will have a hard time catching up at school. As the excerpt shows, the children are deeply attached to their home and their family. Psychologically, a change would not be beneficial to them, considering what may await them in the U.S. They will lose their cultural identity, their feeling of belonging. They will not be able to speak their mother tongue anymore except at home. Cultural and family bonds will be severed. Perhaps an education in India, already at that time a slowly rising nation, would do the boys more good.

Aufgabe 3.2

The thought haunted me throughout the day. It was difficult to enjoy grandmother's seemi or the parathas. I would probably never taste them again. I chewed them a thousand times but still I was hardly able to swallow. I was tired when I finally went to bed at night and dreamt of some strange new country of which I only knew the name. I woke to the clanking of buckets being emptied into the gutters. I also heard my grandparents' voices, muffled through the thin walls of the house, but I still understood what they were saying.

"We shouldn't worry too much, they'll be all right."

"How do you know? She is almost 40. She will never learn the language perfectly. She will always be a stranger and she will have a hard time finding a job."

"America has always been a country of immigrants. All the people in America are immigrants. America holds opportunities for all of them. You have to work hard and you will make it. Everybody knows that."

"And the boys, how will they cope? They must learn the language, go to school there. They will have to catch up with those who were born there. There is a lot of competition."

"The boys are young. They will grow up in America, adapt to the culture, learn the language easily. They are clever, too."

"But America is also racist. Coloured people have fewer rights, maybe not in theory, but in practice. White people get all the good positions. Look at all the protest in America. And that Martin Luther King was shot not long ago."

"They are good people. Ajay and Birju are good boys. They will learn quickly and people will like them."

"They will be there without their family. I mean apart from their mother and father. They won't have any support. We won't be there for them. And none of their aunties will be there.

There is only one auntie in San Francisco, but this is far from where they are going."
"Immigrants will stick together. There will be other people from India, so they will be able to form communities."
"And what about us? We are old. We won't be around much longer. We will never see them again. It will break my heart."
My grandmother's words made the impact of my mother's decision so much clearer to me than it had been before. The pain in my stomach became even worse. My eyes filled with tears. I felt this deep attachment to my grandfather, who had always been so kind to us and so proud of us. He had said he would not let both of us go. Here I am, I am the one who should stay, I don't want to leave. I am Indian. This is where I belong.

Vorgaben für die Bewertung der Schülerleistungen

Aufgabe 1 *(Comprehension)*

Es können maximal 12 Punkte erreicht werden. Um die maximale Punktzahl zu erreichen, werden folgende inhaltliche Aspekte erwartet:

- Nennung des Anlasses und der Ausgangslage des Familientreffens: jeden Sonntag Besuch der Kinder und ihrer Mutter bei den Großeltern, Nachricht vom Erhalt der Flugtickets, geplante Auswanderung der Mutter und der Kinder nach Amerika, Vater bereits in den USA *(6 Punkte erreichbar);*
- Beschreibung von Ajays Gedanken und Gefühlen, insbesondere seine Eifersucht auf Birju und der Wunsch, dem Großvater zu gefallen, seine Wertschätzung der Umgebung, das Bewusstwerden der Konsequenzen der Auswanderung und seine Schwermut *(6 Punkte erreichbar).*

Aufgabe 2 *(Analysis)*

Es können maximal 16 Punkte erreicht werden. Um die maximale Punktzahl zu erreichen, werden folgende inhaltliche Aspekte erwartet:

- Herausarbeitung, wie die besondere Bedeutung des Besuchs und Ajays Gemütszustand durch erzählerische Mittel entfaltet werden, insbesondere die subjektive Wahrnehmung des Erzählers, die Wirkung der unterschiedlich angelegten *settings* und die wirkungsvolle sprachliche Gestaltung *(4 Punkte erreichbar);*
- Analyse der Art und Weise, wie die Erzählperspektive des Ich-Erzählers Einblick in Ajays Gefühle und Gedanken ermöglicht, z. B. durch die Beschreibung intensiver Sinneseindrücke, durch die durchgängige Kommentierung der Beobachtungen und Gefühle und die explizite Reflexion seines melancholischen Gefühlszustands *(4 Punkte erreichbar);*
- Analyse der Art und Weise, wie die Wirkung der ausführlichen Momentaufnahmen der jeweiligen *settings* Ajays Gefühl von Geborgenheit widerspiegeln, z. B. durch den Wechsel von Enge und Weite, durch den Gegensatz zwischen Licht und Schatten, durch die Wirkung der Kühle *(4 Punkte erreichbar);*
- Herausarbeitung, wie Ajays Erleben des Besuchs mit sprachlichen Mitteln effektvoll gezeichnet wird, z. B. durch den Einsatz von Adjektiven, die Gefühle betonen, durch den effektvollen Gebrauch des Konjunktivs, durch den Satzbau, der das kindliche Empfinden spiegelt *(4 Punkte erreichbar).*

Aufgabe 3.1 ***(Evaluation: comment)***

Es können maximal 14 Punkte erreicht werden. Um die maximale Punktzahl zu erreichen, werden folgende inhaltliche Aspekte erwartet:

- kritisch-wertende Bezugnahme auf die Entscheidung der Mutter, mit den Kindern zum Vater nach Amerika auszuwandern, z. B. im Hinblick auf ihre persönliche Ausgangslage und die daraus resultierende Familiensituation *(4 Punkte erreichbar);*
- eine Erörterung möglicher Gründe für die Auswanderung unter Rückgriff auf im Unterricht erworbenes Wissen zur sozialen, kulturellen und ökonomischen Wirklichkeit Indiens sowie zum American Dream, z. B. in Bezug auf die Armutsproblematik, auf die gesellschaftlichen Normen und Traditionen in Indien, auf die Gleichberechtigung und gesellschaftliche Teilhabe in den USA und die individuellen Entwicklungsmöglichkeiten in einer offenen Gesellschaft *(4 Punkte erreichbar);*
- ein Erörterung möglicher Gründe gegen die Auswanderung unter Rückgriff auf im Unterricht erworbenes Wissen zur sozialen, kulturellen und ökonomischen Wirklichkeit Indiens sowie zum American Dream, z. B. in Bezug auf die Trennung von Familie und Heimat, auf den Verlust kultureller Identität, auf die gesellschaftliche Realität der USA und die Grenzen des American Dream *(4 Punkte erreichbar);*
- Ausformulierung ein Fazits, das die Äußerung der Mutter vor dem Hintergrund des Diskutierten schlüssig bewertet *(2 Punkte erreichbar).*

Aufgabe 3.2 ***(Evaluation: re-creation of text)***

Es können maximal 14 Punkte erreicht werden. Um die maximale Punktzahl zu erreichen, werden folgende inhaltliche Aspekte erwartet:

- Verfassen eines Textes, der die vorgegebene Situation weiterführt, indem die Rollenvergaben genau beachtet und schlüssig umgesetzt werden *(2 Punkte erreichbar);*
- Entwicklung eines hoffnungsvollen Blicks der Großeltern auf die Zukunft, z. B. einer optimistischer Sicht der Integrationskraft der USA für Einwanderer, die Erwähnung des Vertrauens in die auswandernde Familie, den Glauben an deren Erfolg und eine bessere Zukunft *(4 Punkte erreichbar);*
- Darstellung der Sorgen und Ängste der Großeltern in Bezug auf die Entwicklung der Familiensituation, z. B. die Schwierigkeiten, sich in den USA zurechtzufinden, auf den Verlust von Zuwendung und Unterstützung durch die Familie und die mögliche Entfremdung und das Zerbrechen der Familie *(4 Punkte erreichbar);*
- Darstellung von Ajays Gefühlen und Gedanken angesichts des Gesprächs seiner Großeltern, z. B. seiner emotionalen Bindung an die Großeltern, des entstehenden Zwiespalts zwischen Heimatverlust und unbestimmten Gefühlen des Aufbruchs *(4 Punkte erreichbar).*

Klausurteil B

Im Wohlfühl-Ort *Christina Berndt*

Ganz offensichtlich erlebt der Begriff „Heimat“ eine Renaissance. 88 Prozent der Bundesbürger stuften ihn einer Umfrage der Hamburger Sozialbehörde zufolge als „wichtig“ oder „sehr wichtig“ ein, nur zwei Prozent sagte er gar nichts. Dabei scheint der Begriff mit höherem Alter wichtiger zu werden. Aber auch junge Leute fühlen sich heute wieder stärker heimatverbunden als Ende des vergangenen Jahrtausends. Sie finden es schick, Jägermeister im Schrebergarten zu trinken, Volkslieder beim Bergwandern zu singen und in Dirndl oder Lederhose aufs Oktoberfest zu gehen. Und Deutschland-Wimpel am Auto sind während sportlicher Großereignisse schon fast ein Muss geworden. Auf der Suche nach dem schönsten deutschen Wort landete „Heimat“ im Jahr 2004 auf einem der Spitzenplätze. Nur noch sieben Prozent der Deutschen verbinden mit diesem Begriff vor allem Enge oder Spießigkeit.

Was vor kurzem noch als abstoßend kitschig galt, scheint nun zum Zielort einer allgemeinen Sehnsucht nach bleibenden Werten zu werden. Globalisierung und Finanzkrise haben die Menschen in ihrem bisherigen Streben nach Ferne und Weite, in ihrer Sehnsucht nach fremden Ländern und Kulturen so stark verunsichert, dass sie ihr Heil wieder in der Welt der Traditionen suchen, wie Volksmusik, Luis Trenker und eigene Kinder sie verkörpern. Heimatliebe gelte wieder als „unpolitisches, kommerzfreies und tief menschliches Bedürfnis“, sagt die Berliner Autorin Verena Schmitt-Roschmann, die vor kurzem ein Buch mit dem Titel „Heimat – Neuentdeckung eines verpönten Gefühls“ verfasst hat. Sogar die großen Globalisierer haben diesen Trend erkannt und besinnen sich aufs Regionale, wie der Historiker Heinz Schilling betont, der bis vor kurzem an der Humboldt-Universität Berlin gelehrt hat. Bei McDonald's gibt es auf dem Burger neben Rinderhack deshalb auch mittlerweile Nürnberger Bratwürste.

„Heimat ist heute eine Sehnsuchtslandschaft der Gefühle“, sagt Schilling. Dabei sei das Gefühlige zu dem Begriff erst spät gekommen. Bis ins 19. Jahrhundert hinein sei Heimat ein juristischer Begriff gewesen. Wer einer Heimatscholle zuzuordnen war, der besaß Bürgerrechte. Es ging also nicht um Emotionen, sondern um Ansprüche.

Heute ist nicht einmal mehr klar, wo die Heimat eigentlich liegt. Sie kann ein ganzes Land sein, aber auch eine Gegend oder ein kleines Dörfchen, das schon mit dem Nachbardörfchen in Feindschaft lebt. [...]

Doch bei allem Positiven, das der Mensch des beginnenden 21. Jahrhunderts der Heimat abgewinnen kann: Es bleibt auch die andere, die dunkle Seite des Heimatgefühls, das verklärt, verkitscht und von Ideologen missbraucht wurde. Es gibt kaum ein Wort, das so zwischen Intimität und Weltpolitik zerrissen wird. Während Heimat vielen Geborgenheit vermittelt, erleben andere sie als finsteres Verlies, aus dem es kein Entkommen gibt. Und wieder andere spüren Heimat vor allem dann, wenn sie fehlt, und kranken unheilbar am Verlust dieses Wohlfühl-Ortes. [...]

Anmerkung:
32/33 **Luis Trenker** – südtiroler Schauspieler, Schriftsteller und Bergsteiger (1892-1990)

Beispiellösung

Aufgabe 4

"Heimat", a typical German concept

The term "Heimat", roughly translated as "home", is rather an emotional concept than a geographical one. Heimat can be the entire country but also a small village. In the past, Heimat was just a legal term: somebody who was assigned to a place could enjoy civil rights. The emotional side of the concept was added in the 19th century. Today, the term is experiencing a renaissance: 88% of Germans see "Heimat" as important or very important. Even young people are more closely attached to where they come from than at the end of the 20th century. Typical traditions and pastimes, which would once have been considered bourgeois or narrow-minded, repulsive or kitschy, have become popular, even with the young. Globalisation and financial crisis have made people insecure, so they are seeking refuge in homely traditions and family. The love of your home and traditional culture is seen as a deeply human, unpolitical and uncommercial need. Even global corporations have recognized the trend, e.g. McDonald's offering German sausages on their burgers.
Still, we must not forget the darker side of the word Heimat. The concept has in the past been romanticised, glorified, kitschified, abused by ideologists. There is hardly a word which is so torn between intimacy and world politics. Whereas many experience Heimat as a place giving security, others see it as a dark dungeon from which there is no escape. Others feel the need for Heimat most strongly when it is gone and they suffer from this loss.

Vorgaben für die Bewertung der Schülerleistungen

Aufgabe 4 *(Mediation)*

Es können maximal 18 Punkte erreicht werden. Um die maximale Punktzahl zu erreichen, werden folgende inhaltliche Aspekte erwartet:

- Verfassen eines situations- und adressatengerechten Berichtes, in dem
  - die die Bedeutung des Begriffs Heimat für die Deutschen zusammengefasst wird, insbesondere die Aufwertung des Begriffs, die neue Beliebtheit des Begriffs auch bei der jüngeren Generation;
- der Bedeutungswandel und die Ambivalenz des Heimatkonzepts laut Berndt dargestellt wird, z. B.
  - die Entwicklung vom Rechtsbegriff hin zum individuellen Konzept,
  - Heimat als emotional verortet statt lokal verankert,
  - der Widerspruch zwischen Geborgenheitsgefühl und Einengung,
  - die ideologische Konnotation des Begriffs;
- die Gründe erläutert werden, die laut Berndt zur veränderten Bedeutung und Popularität des Begriffs Heimat geführt haben:
  - das Bedürfnis nach Orientierung in einer globalisierten Welt,
  - der Wunsch nach Stabilität,
  - die Suche nach Geborgenheit *(18 Punkte erreichbar).*

LK mit Beispiellösungen

Aufgabe 2

Klausurteil A: Leseverstehen und Schreiben integriert

Aufgabenstellung:

1. Point out the challenges first-generation students face at US elite colleges and universities as well as the measures taken to support them according to Laura Pappano. *(Comprehension) (12 Punkte)*

2. Analyse Pappano's intention and the way she uses communicative strategies as well as language to make her point. *(Analysis) (16 Punkte)*

3. Choose **one** of the following tasks:

3.1 "*No one expects us – people like us – to be here*" (ll. 80-81). Evaluate this statement against the background of the *American Dream*. Refer to the text as well as work done in class. *(Evaluation: comment) (14 Punkte)*

3.2 The United Nations organizes an annual conference for Youth Leaders aged 16-24+ on *Pathways to Education in a Globalized World*. You have been invited to participate. With reference to the given text and from your personal knowledge write a speech commenting on ways of dealing with the problem of social exclusion in educational contexts. *(Evaluation: re-creation of text) (14 Punkte)*

Klausurteil B: Sprachmittlung isoliert

Aufgabenstellung:

4. In your senior year you participate in an international project on *After school – what next?* in which you compare career options worldwide.
Based on Heimann's article write a report for the project's website in which you outline how the German concept of "Duales Studium" works. *(Mediation) (18 Punkte)*

Materialgrundlage:

Klausurteil A:

http://www.nytimes.com/2015/04/12/education/edlife/first-generation-students-unite.html (Zugriff: 01.04.2017)

Wortzahl: 533

Klausurteil B:

Klaus Heimann, „Drei Monate Uni, drei Monate Büro“, ©Klaus Heimann für *ZEIT ONLINE* (www.zeit.de) vom: 29.11.2013, „Drei Monate Uni, drei Monate Büro“ http://www.zeit.de/studium/hochschule/2013-11/duales-studium-ueberblick?print (Zugriff 01.04.2017)

Wortzahl: 415

Zugelassene Hilfsmittel:

- Ein- und zweisprachiges Wörterbuch
- Herkunftssprachliches Wörterbuch für Schülerinnen und Schüler, deren Herkunftssprache nicht Deutsch ist
- Wörterbuch zur deutschen Rechtschreibung

Wichtigste Bezüge zum Kernlehrplan und zu den Vorgaben 2018

1. Inhaltsfelder und inhaltliche Schwerpunkte

Klausurteil A:

Globale Herausforderungen und Zukunftsvisionen

- Chancen und Risiken der Globalisierung
  Studying and working in a globalized world

Politische, soziale und kulturelle Wirklichkeiten und ihre historischen Hintergründe

- Amerikanischer Traum – Visionen und Lebenswirklichkeiten in den USA
  Freedom and justice: myths and realities

Klausurteil B:

Globale Herausforderungen und Zukunftsvisionen

- Chancen und Risiken der Globalisierung
  Studying and working in a globalized world

2. Medien/Materialien

Klausurteil A und B:

- Sach- und Gebrauchstext

Klausurteil A

First-Generation Students Unite *Laura Pappano*

Ana Barros grew up in a two-family house built by Habitat for Humanity, hard by the boarded-up buildings and vacant lots of Newark. Neither parent attended college, but she was a star student. With a 2200 on her SATs, she expected to fit in at Harvard.

Yet here she was at a lecture for a sociology course called, paradoxically, "Poverty in America," as a classmate opened her laptop and planned a multicountry spring break trip to Europe. (Ms. Barros can't afford textbooks; she borrows from the library.) On the sidewalks of Cambridge, students brush past her in their $700 Canada Goose parkas and $1,000 Moncler puffer jackets. (Ms. Barros saved up for two years for good boots.) On an elite campus, income inequality can be in your face.

A professor once described how hardships become inscribed on one's body, and Ms. Barros thought of her father, a janitor at a home for troubled boys, and the wrinkles carved in his face from worrying about money and her mother's health. Majoring in sociology, she says, "has made me hyperaware of class differences here."

Weary of trying to pass as middle class, Ms. Barros decided to "come out," borrowing the phrase from the gay community. She joined and now leads the two-year-old Harvard College First Generation Student Union, which has 300 on its email list. "This is a movement," she said. "We are not ashamed of taking on this identity." [...]

One of the hard things about being a low-income student, Mr. Jack said, is the breezy talk that unfolds when students describe "going to Martha's Vineyard or the Hamptons because that's where someone's graduation party was." Or when they recount vacations and travel. That makes spring break difficult, which is why he considers it a victory that, after being pressed, administrators kept two dining halls open last month, for the first time, in recognition that not all students can leave.

Administrators are still figuring out how to help.

Public four-year colleges and universities educate large numbers of first-generation students (1.7 million versus 623,000 at private nonprofits), though their graduation track records are mixed. Some, like the University of Kentucky and the University of Cincinnati, offer residence halls with special programming.

Elites are trying to catch up. Campuses have designated first-gen administrators, bolstered mentoring programs and added articles about socioeconomics to faculty readings on diversity. Some are careful in assigning roommates. "In a double, we would not put a student not on aid with a student on full aid," said Thomas Dingman, dean of freshmen at Harvard. [...]

First-generation students live in a parallel universe on campus. They cannot text parents for help with paper topics or insights on choosing a major. They rarely see them. "Every time there is a parents' weekend it's painful," Mr. Contreras said. "It's another reminder mine can't afford to be here with me on this journey."

But more than any single challenge,

first-generation students describe the pressure of something less firm to the grasp: the constant and steady weight of assumptions.

"We are at some of the wealthiest institutions in the world," said Mr. Stewart, whose family relies on public assistance. "No one expects us – people like us – to be here."

Annotations

2	**Habitat for Humanity** – a nonprofit initiative which builds affordable housing for families in need
4	**Newark** – *here:* a city in the New York metropolitan area
6	**SATs** – (Scholastic Assessment Test) a college admission test in the USA
6	**Harvard** – one of the world's most prestigious universities situated in the USA
13	**Cambridge** – a city in Massachusetts, USA, where Harvard University is located
14	**Canada Goose, Moncler** – expensive premium brands
36	**Mr. Jack** – a Ph.D. candidate at Harvard who studies low-income students and their paths to college
38	**Martha's Vineyard or the Hamptons** – very expensive US holiday destinations
53	**graduation track records** – statistics showing the number of students graduating from a particular university or college
65	**dean of freshmen** – person responsible for advising all first-year students

Beispiellösung

Aufgabe 1

The text "First-Generation Students Unite" by Laura Pappano from the New York Times of 8 April 2015 deals with the challenges first-generation students, i.e. students whose parents have not had a university education, are confronted with. In general, first-generation students come from low-income families and have to cope with the class differences which become apparent especially at elite colleges. The ratio of first-generation students at state colleges and elite private colleges is about three to one.

Pappano illustrates how inequality shows in things like books, clothes, and holidays. While many first-generation students cannot afford textbooks, new shoes or even a trip home, others use laptops, wear expensive clothes and go on expensive trips. So the poorer students inevitably inhabit a parallel universe on campus. They do not feel they belong, they are not integrated. Parents cannot afford to come and see them, and they are not able to help them in academic matters. The worst thing first-generation students sense is that they are just not expected to be there.

Colleges, however, are introducing measures to alleviate the situation. Dining halls are open during the spring break, residence halls with special programming are offered. There are first-gen administrators, mentoring programmes, faculty readings on diversity, and careful matching of roommates. At Harvard there is also a first-generation union as a representative body.

Aufgabe 2

Pappano's article is meant to make readers aware of the challenges first-gen students have to face. She cites case studies like Ana Barros (ll. 1-4) or Mr Jack (l. 36), Mr Contreras (l. 71), or Mr Stewart (l. 79) to evoke the readers' empathy. Especially Ms. Barros's case is presented very drastically. The harsh contrast between her and middle-class students is emphasised by means of striking examples: "multicountry spring break trips to Europe" booked on a laptop are contrasted with "books from the library" (ll. 10-13), "$700 Canada Goose parkas" and "$1000 Moncler puffer jackets" are contrasted with the fact that

Ms Barros had to "save up for two years for good boots" (ll. 14-17). Irony is made use of when she mentions the lecture on "Poverty in America" in this context.
Contrasts are also apparent in the language Pappano uses. "Habitat for Humanity" (also ironic in this case) "boarded-up buildings" and "vacant lots" (ll. 2-3) contrast harshly in their connotations with "the sidewalks of Cambridge". Informal language contrasts with her generally formal diction when she mentions how students "brush past" (13-14), and inequality can be "in your face" (l. 18), or when she mentions the "breezy" talk of the rich (l. 37). All these contrasts serve to underline the gap between rich and poor students.
The description of Ms. Barros's father, who is marked by his hard life and the worries about his wife, also arouses empathy in the reader. Again, Pappano's choice of words is rather drastic when she writes that "hardships become inscribed on one's body" and describes the wrinkles "carved" in her father's face (ll. 19-23).
It is also bitterly ironic when we learn that it is considered "a victory that, after being pressed, administrators kept two dining halls open" for the spring break (ll. 43-44). It becomes so obvious that poverty is not even considered an issue on campus.
The first-gen student union and movement, as Ms. Barros calls it, is linked to the gay community through Ms. Barros's use of the term "come out" and the author's subsequent explanation (ll. 28-29). This makes the reader associate the situation of first-gen students with the situation homosexuals once found themselves in: a rejected, outlawed minority, a fringe group, but also a group starting to take up an identity and show pride in themselves.
Facts and figures are used to emphasise the points Pappano wants to make. In lines 5 to 6 she emphasises Ana's brilliant exam, and in lines 32 and 51 to 52 she emphasises the poor representation of first-gens at elite universities. Her enumeration of facts (ll. 54-65) is to make the reader understand the perspective of the colleges. Also in this case, a quotation is used to give the reader a deeper understanding (ll. 62-64).
Quotations fom Anna Barros (and the other first-gen students mentioned above) make Pappano's text credible and authentic. The use of Ms. Barros's own words in particular creates empathy, and so do the views of Mr. Jack (ll. 35-40) and Mr. Contreras (ll. 70-73). But it is the quotation from Mr. Stewart (ll. 78-81) with which Pappano hammers her point home. In the prominent position of the final sentence in the text, not only the contrast between rich and poor, between them and us, between the "wealthiest institutions" and "us" is emphasised again, but also the prevailing contempt for the poor, for "people like us".

Aufgabe 3.1

Mr Stewart says, "No one expects us … to be here." The division, even the spatial division between the classes becomes all too obvious at America's elite universities. Middle-class students are so far removed from poverty and hardship that they are not even aware of the problems other people have. In their suburban neighbourhoods they have no experience of material need and social contempt whatsoever. Why would "people like them" all of a sudden appear at their college? Thus, they may not even be aware that they cast them out, deprive them of overall participation in university life.
It shows how closely connected wealth and education still are. Even though there are scholarships, the problems pointed out in the text still prevail. No matter how intelligent you are, if you are born poor, you are very likely to stay poor.

This is in complete opposition to the idea of the American Dream. It is true, the Dream does not say that all people are equal, but – as the Declaration of Independence says – all people are created equal and have the same rights. But the concept of the American Dream that anybody who works hard enough can climb the ladder of success seems to me very dubious in the light of Pappano's article. The path from rags to riches is not open to everybody anymore – even if it was ever open at all. From the beginning, rich children have a better start, growing up with parents who can afford to spend time with them, who can afford educational activities, who are educated themselves and thus provide books, serious talk and free-time activities that train children's brains rather than numb them.
Poor parents all too often have little time for their children, trying to make ends meet, working in two or three jobs, and they very often do not have the education to know about what is good for their children's mental development.
America does not do much to change this. State schools do not really provide excellent education, high school life is marked rather by internal and external competition. What counts is the success of the sports teams and who is most popular in school. Private preparatory schools – on the other hand – mostly provide an excellent education. Parents and alumni ensure that there is excellent equipment, but of course, here again, access is limited to the rich.
With the present administration, things will only get worse. President Trump as one of the ultra-rich people in the US anyway has no understanding of the needs of the poor, let alone any sense of solidarity, which is a foreign term to him. The gap between rich and poor will only widen with the renaissance of self-centredness and selfishness that the US currently stands for.
Looking at Mr. Stewart's quotation "No one expects us – people like us – to be here" against the background of the American Dream, which promises "life, liberty and the pursuit of happiness" to all Americans, we sense that the American Dream has gone utterly wrong.

Aufgabe 3.2

Dear Fellow Youth Leaders,
I have been given the chance of talking to you on the issue of social exclusion in educational contexts. I will try to give you a European point of view, although you should be aware that – with the variety of European educational systems and the many differences between the European nations – my view will be largely German, because this is the country I'm most familiar with.
A New York Times article caught my attention: it deals with first-generation students at elite colleges, especially at Harvard. I realized that no matter how smart you are, no matter how many scholarships you win, your education will largely depend on where you come from. If you are completely foreign to a middle-class lifestyle, you will be excluded from college life. You can't be part of the crowd. You may say this will not impede your learning. Maybe, but your career opportunities also largely depend on your family background. Many are digitally illiterate, nor can they expect academic support from their parents, and finding a job will be a lot easier if you – or your parents – know the right people, too. The US education system is simply unfair.

The same applies to schools: rich people send their children to expensive prep schools, the poor have to put up with state schools, where the quality of education will also depend on the wealth of the area where they live.
We may conclude that the binary system of state and private schools and colleges is to blame for the unfairness of the education system. Yet, as the NYT article mentioned above shows, it is not only a matter of getting to these institutions, it is also a matter of being able to make the most of it.
In Germany there is basically no such system. (There are private colleges, but they do not play an important role.) Elite universities like Aachen University, which is excellent in sciences and engineering, are state universities and free for everybody. Schools are basically all free, charging fees is not allowed, not even for those which are not run by the state but by the church or a religious organization. This is a model which I personally prefer to the US one, because at least students from all walks of life can attend these institutions, they do not have to bear the "weight of assumptions", as the article words it.
Still, surveys have found that even – or even especially – in Germany your education and career largely depend on your parents' income. And this particularly affects people from immigrant families. Simple minds among politicians and journalists cry discrimination at school, but the reasons are manifold and more complex. No matter what school you are at, no matter how committed your teachers are, if your education does not start before school, you've had it. Primary school teachers report about pupils who have never had a pen or pencil in their hands, pupils who don't speak the language of the country, pupils who have never been read to from a book. For them it will be too late when they start at the age of six. At the other end of the scale there are those who have learned to read just like they learned to speak because they've grown up with books and newspapers. These students will take the lead and will remain the dominant group. This is where the problem lies. We cannot leave education simply to schools. That is too easy. Education must start in the families. Kindergarten must be compulsory. We need assistance for low-income families who have to work so hard that they cannot care enough for their children. And this is not just a matter of giving them money. They need advice. Compulsory visits to the doctor for physical examination are the norm anyway, but at the same time parents should be advised by experienced counsellers about education. Parents must be informed about the dangers of TV and other media and they should be made aware of the importance of mental input, which will help the brain develop rather than let it wither. Parental education is more important than ever, also regarding attitudes. Immigrants from different cultures may not be aware of western values like women's rights or gender equality, and may thus convey their archaic views to their offspring. Perhaps the state should stop paying child benefits and put the money directly into assistance that helps a child's development and education: Free compulsory seminars on children's education, free kindergarten, free sports clubs, free music schools, free theatres, free school books, free outdoor activities, free transport – you name it.
This still does not solve the problem of poor students being excluded at elite campuses, which the NYT article describes. I fear there is no solution. As long as there are people with money and people without, there will be segregation in all areas of life, and college is one of them.

Vorgaben für die Bewertung der Schülerleistungen

Aufgabe 1 *(Comprehension)*

Es können maximal 12 Punkte erreicht werden. Um die maximale Punktzahl zu erreichen, werden folgende inhaltliche Aspekte erwartet:

- Erläuterung des Begriffs „first-generation students“: Kinder, die als erste ihrer Familie studieren und aus bildungsfernen und sozial schwachen Familien kommen *(2 Punkte erreichbar);*
- Beschreibung der Herausforderungen, denen sich *first-generation students* an elitären amerikanischen Universitäten stellen müssen, insbesondere das mangelnde Zugehörigkeitsgefühl und Identitätskonflike, die schwache Repräsentation und Ignoranz der anderen und die Benachteiligung aufgrund ihres familiären Hintergrunds *(6 Punkte erreichbar);*
- Nennung der Unterstützungsmaßnahmen, insbesondere die Interessenvertretung durch die *First-Generation Student Union,* die zielgruppenspezifischen curricularen und organisatorischen Angebote einiger Universitäten *(4 Punkte erreichbar).*

Aufgabe 2 *(Analysis)*

Es können maximal 16 Punkte erreicht werden. Um die maximale Punktzahl zu erreichen, werden folgende inhaltliche Aspekte erwartet:

- Herausarbeitung, dass Pappano ihre Leser für die Herausforderungen der *first-generation students* sensibilisieren und ein tieferes Verständnis für ihre Probleme erreichen möchte, und zwar durch eine anschauliche Darstellung des Themas und durch eine die Aussageabsicht unterstützende sprachliche Gestaltung *(4 Punkte erreichbar);*
- Untersuchung der Art und Weise, wie Pappano mittels kommunikativer Strategien Betroffenheit für die Situation der *first-generation students* auszulösen versucht, z. B. durch Zitate und an den Leser adressierte pointierte Einschübe, durch Einblicke in verschiedene Perspektiven, durch stark kontrastierende Beispiele zum Aufzeigen der sozialen Kluft zwischen den Studentengruppen und durch Zahlen und Fakten, die die Argumentation untermauern *(6 Punkte erreichbar);*
- Analyse der sprachlichen Mittel und deren Einsatz zur Verdeutlichung des sozioökonomischen Kontrasts zwischen den Studentengruppen, z. B. die anschauliche Sprache, der Wechsel zwischen formellem und informellem Sprachgebrauch und wertende Begriffe *(6 Punkte erreichbar).*

Teilaufgabe 3.1 *(Evaluation: comment)*

Es können maximal 14 Punkte erreicht werden. Um die maximale Punktzahl zu erreichen, werden folgende inhaltliche Aspekte erwartet:

- kritisch-wertendes Aufgreifen der im Zitat zum Ausdruck kommenden Randstellung der *first-generation students* an Eliteuniversitäten, z. B. mit Blick auf den Mangel an Problembewusstsein und Unterstützung im universitären Umfeld, auf den Zusammenhang zwischen sozialer Herkunft und akademischer Bildung und auf Stereorypisierung *(6 Punkte erreichbar);*

- Erörterung des Zitats unter Rückgriff auf im Unterricht erworbenes Wissen zu Chancen und Grenzen des American Dream, z. B. mit Bezug auf Möglichkeiten der Selbstverwirklichung, auf Fragen sozialer Gerechtigkeit und Mobilität und auf aktuelle sozio-ökonomische Entwicklungen *(6 Punkte erreichbar);*
- Formulierung eines Fazits, in dem das Zitat vor dem Hintergrund des Amerikanischen Traums zusammenfassend bewertet wird *(2 Punkte erreichbar).*

Teilaufgabe 3.2 *(Evaluation: re-creation of text)*

Es können maximal 14 Punkte erreicht werden. Um die maximale Punktzahl zu erreichen, werden folgende inhaltliche Aspekte erwartet:

- Verfassen eines situations- und adressatengerechten Redebeitrags, in dem die vorgegebenen Rahmenbedingungen berücksichtigt und die Intention und Vorgehensweise aufzeigt werden *(2 Punkte erreichbar);*
- Begründung der Aktualität und Relevanz des Themas im globalen Kontext als Ausgangspunkt für die Rede (unter Rückgriff auf den Text), z. B. angesichts von Bildung als Menschenrecht, von ungleicher Verteilung von Bildungschancen und von gesellschaftlicher und ökonomischer Bedeutung von Bildung *(4 Punkte erreichbar);*
- Entwicklung von eigenen Ideen, wie sozialer Ausgrenzung im Bildungsbereich begegnet werden kann, z. B. durch Schärfung des öffentlichen Problembewusstseins, durch finanzielle Förderung von Bildungseinrichtungen, durch pädagogische Unterstützung betroffener Jugendlicher und durch die Verbesserung der Qualität von Bildungsangeboten *(6 Punkte erreichbar);*
- Abschluss der Rede (auf der Basis der vorangegangenen Ausführungen), z. B. mit einer pointierten Zusammenfassung, einer eigenständigen Schlussfolgerung oder mit einem persönlichen Appell *(2 Punkte erreichbar).*

Klausurteil B

Drei Monate Uni, drei Monate Büro

Klaus Heimann

Seit Christian Schumann studiert, kann er kostenlos Bahn fahren. Er gehört zur kleinen, aber wachsenden Gruppe dual Studierender und kombiniert Betriebswirtschaftslehre mit einer Berufsausbildung bei der Deutschen Bahn. 2012 hat er mit dem Unternehmen einen Studienvertrag abgeschlossen. Drei Monate ist er im Betrieb, dann drei an der Hochschule. Die Hälfte des sechssemestrigen Studiums hat Schumann bereits hinter sich. Am Ende steht der Bachelor-Abschluss.

Duale Studiengänge sind begehrt. Laut Sabine Behrenbeck, Leiterin der Abteilung Tertiäre Bildung beim Wissenschaftsrat, würde ein Drittel der Studienanfänger gerne im Doppelpack studieren. Aktuell sind es gerade einmal 3,4 Prozent. Der Grund: Dual studieren kann nur, wer einen Betrieb gefunden hat und die Plätze in den Unternehmen sind begrenzt. Aufgrund der hohen Nachfrage erwarten Experten, dass künftig mehr Betriebe dieses Studienformat anbieten werden.

910 duale Studiengänge gibt es an Fachhochschulen, dualen Hochschulen und

Berufsakademien in Deutschland. Universitäten halten sich bei diesem Studienformat eher zurück. [...]

Beim dualen Studium gibt es eine „große Vielfalt an Formaten und Strukturen", schreibt der Wissenschaftsrat in einem gerade verabschiedeten Positionspapier. Die Räte hätten gerne mehr Klarheit. Für Laura Gersch, die den Ausschuss beim Wissenschaftsrat betreut, ist die Herausforderung bei dualen Studiengängen die Qualitätssicherung: „Es geht um den Erhalt von Wissenschaftlichkeit, gelungenes Praxislernen, die inhaltliche Verzahnung der Lerninhalte und um eine vernünftige Betreuung der Studenten im Betrieb und an der Hochschule." [...]

Gerade Kinder aus Nicht-Akademikerfamilien interessieren sich für ein duales Studium. Das hat Sirikit Krone, Wissenschaftlerin am Institut für Arbeit und Qualifikation in Essen, in einer Untersuchung herausgefunden. Die Wissenschaftlerin hat auch nach Gründen für die Entscheidung zum dualen Studium gefragt. Zwei Vorteile dominieren: die Beschäftigungssicherheit nach Studienende und das Gehalt während des Studiums.

Die Bezahlung variiert von Betrieb zu Betrieb. Laut Bernd Kassebaum von der IG Metall sind die Vergütungen meist gestaffelt: „Im ersten Jahr werden im Schnitt 900 Euro gezahlt. Das steigert sich dann bis auf 1.200 Euro im dritten Jahr." Damit orientieren sich die Betriebe weitgehend an den Tarifverträgen für Ausbildungsvergütungen. „Eine einheitliche Festlegung gibt es allerdings nicht", sagt Kassebaum. Allemal sind die Beträge höher als der Bafög-Satz. Ein Kostenfaktor für Studenten können allerdings die Studiengebühren der privaten Hochschulen sein. Die meisten Betriebe übernehmen sie, aber nicht alle.

Als Gegenleistung zum Gehalt verlangen die Betriebe, dass Bachelor-Absolventen ihren ersten Arbeitsvertrag mit dem Ausbildungsunternehmen abschließen. Die Mindestdauer des Vertrages beträgt meist ein Drittel der Studienzeit, bei sechs Semestern Bachelorstudium also ein Jahr. Für Schumann ist das kein Nachteil. Er findet es gut, zu wissen, dass sein erster Arbeitsplatz in der Personalabteilung der Konzernleitung in Berlin sein wird.

Anmerkungen:
12 **Bachelor-Abschluss** – der erste Hochschulabschluss im Rahmen des mehrstufigen Bachelor-Master-Systems
27 **Berufsakademien** – Studieneinrichtungen, die ein Studium mit starkem Praxisbezug anbieten
57 **IG Metall** – die größte deutsche Einzelgewerkschaft
65 **Bafög** – (Bundesausbildungsförderungsgesetz) regelt die staatliche Unterstützung von Schülern und Studenten während der Ausbildung

Beispiellösung

Aufgabe 4

"Duales Studium"

In Germany there is the concept of "Duales Studium" meaning "dual or twin-track study". It is called dual because a student attends a course of study at university and at the same time undergoes job training in a company. For example, a student spends three months at university and then three months at the company. A course of study lasts six semesters and leads to a Bachelor's degree. After their degree, students are expected, or even obliged, to work for the company for a certain period of time.

Dual courses of study are in demand. A third of all beginners would like to take such a course but only 3.4% actually do so, because there are not many companies offering places, though it is expected that more places will be offered in the future due to the high demand. The challenge is the combination of academic and practical learning, which is why traditional universities seem rather reluctant to offer these courses. It is rather the universities of applied sciences and similar institutions that offer them. Nevertheless, there are already 910 different courses of this sort nationwide. They vary a lot in their structure and organisation, there is a need for more clarity here.

It is especially first-gen students who are interested in dual courses of study due to the money they earn during their studies and the guaranteed job afterwards. Payment varies from company to company. Some students may have to pay fees for private universities but some companies pay the university fees, too.

Vorgaben für die Bewertung der Schülerleistungen

Aufgabe 4 *(Mediation)*

Es können maximal 18 Punkte erreicht werden. Um die maximale Punktzahl zu erreichen, werden folgende inhaltliche Aspekte erwartet:

- Verfassen eines situations- und adressatengerechten Berichts, in dem Folgendes beschrieben bzw. dargestellt wird:
  - die Organisation des dualen Studiums in Deutschland mit der Kombination von Studium und bezahlter Berufsausbildung, einem sechssemestrige Studium mit einem Bachelor-Abschluss und einem Anschlussvertrag im Ausbildungsbetrieb;
  - die Vorteile des Studiums, insbesondere die Verknüpfung von Theorie und Praxis, dem Gehalt während des Studiums, die sichere berufliche Einstiegsperspektive und die Öffnung von akademischer Ausbildung auch für sozial Benachteiligte;
  - die Herausforderungen, wie z. B. die begrenzte Anzahl an Ausbildungsplätzen, die Schwierigkeit der Orientierung angesichts der Vielfalt dualer Studiengänge und die ggf. selbst zu zahlenden Studiengebühren an privaten Hochschulen *(18 Punkte erreichbar)*.

Die sprachliche Leistung im Abitur

Der Stellenwert der sprachlichen Leistung

Bei der Bewertung der Abiturprüfung können 150 Punkte vergeben werden. Davon fallen 90 Punkte für die sprachliche und 60 Punkte für die inhaltliche Leistung an. Über das Fachwissen zu den lehrplanrelevanten Inhalten hinaus ist also die sprachliche Leistung im Englischen für ein gutes Ergebnis in der Abiturprüfung von grundlegender Bedeutung. Natürlich bedingen sich die beiden Teilbereiche gegenseitig: Ohne stichhaltigen Inhalt kann nicht die volle Punktzahl im Bereich Sprache erreicht werden und umgekehrt.
Die Entwicklung der englischen Sprachkompetenz ist ein komplexer Prozess, der sich über viele Jahre hinweg bis zum Abitur hin entwickelt. Es ist an dieser Stelle nicht möglich, eine umfassende Revision der sprachlichen Grundlagen anzubieten, aber Sie finden hier Hinweise auf die wichtigsten Aspekte, die Sie zum Zeitpunkt des Abiturs beherrschen sollten. Bei Bedarf können Sie dann das eine oder andere Kapitel mit Hilfe eines grammatikorientieren Buches wiederholen.

TIPP zur individuellen Wiederholung der Grammatik

Wenn Sie das Gefühl haben, in wichtigen Bereichen der Grammatik noch Defizite zu haben, analysieren Sie gezielt Ihre persönlichen Schwachpunkte aus den Klausuren und wiederholen Sie selbstständig die entsprechenden Kapitel anhand einer Grammatik oder eines Übungsbuches auf Sprachniveau B2 des Gemeinsamen Europäischen Referenzrahmens.
Klassische Fehlerquellen sind zum Beispiel *if*-Sätze, Passivkonstruktionen, die Wahl der richtigen Zeitform oder Präpositionen nach bestimmten Verben.

Die Leistungskriterien

Eigene Fehlerschwerpunkte erkennen

Um eigene Fehlerschwerpunkte zu erkennen, ist es empfehlenswert, die Darstellungsleistung in eigenen Klausuren genau zu analysieren.

- Lesen Sie Ihre eigenen Klausuren inklusive der Randbemerkungen und Kommentare Ihres Englischlehrers erneut durch und halten Sie auf einem separaten Blatt fest, welche Teilbereiche besonders „fehleranfällig“ sind.
- Wenn Ihre Klausuren mittels eines Korrekturrasters bewertet worden sind, studieren Sie dieses in Hinblick auf die Darstellungsleistung genau: In welchen Teilbereichen haben Sie besonders wenige Punkte erhalten? Lesen Sie nun Ihre Klausuren in Hinblick auf diese Teilbereiche erneut durch. Halten Sie schriftlich fest, wo Ihre individuellen Fehlerschwerpunkte liegen.

Wenn Sie die eigenen Fehlerschwerpunkte identifiziert haben, sollten Sie diese beim Anfertigen – und anschließendem Korrekturlesen – schriftlicher Hausaufgaben und Klausuren besonders im Blick haben.
Defizite im Bereich der Grundgrammatik können Sie mit entsprechenden Übungsbüchern aufarbeiten. Auch hier gilt: Üben Sie konsequent über einen längeren Zeitraum hinweg und trainieren Sie immer wieder das Verfassen schriftlicher Texte, indem Sie z. B. im Unterricht angefertigte Stichpunkte ausformulieren.
In den meisten Wörterbüchern finden Sie Zusammenstellungen der unregelmäßigen Verben und der wichtigsten ***phrasal verbs.*** Es empfiehlt sich, diese vor Klausuren zu wiederholen.

Die Vorgehensweise in Klausuren und in der schriftlichen Abiturprüfung

Um in Klausuren und in der schriftlichen Abiturprüfung ein möglichst gutes Ergebnis zu erzielen, ist es unerlässlich, eine sinnvolle und gut strukturierte Vorarbeit zu leisten.
Lassen Sie sich nicht von Mitschülern irritieren und aus der Ruhe bringen, die nach kürzester Bearbeitungszeit und ohne das Anfertigen von Notizen sofort anfangen zu schreiben!
Je intensiver Sie sich mit der Aufgabenstellung und dem Ausgangstext auseinandersetzen und entsprechende Notizen anfertigen, desto einfacher wird es Ihnen fallen, die Aufgabenstellungen in zusammenhängenden Texten zu bearbeiten.

Die Bearbeitung in folgenden Schritten hat sich bewährt:

1. Lesen Sie zunächst die Aufgabenstellung und den Ausgangstext ein erstes Mal durch. Achten Sie hierbei auch auf eventuelle Erläuterungen, die dem Ausgangstext vorangestellt sind. Diese sind meist kursiv gedruckt und enthalten wichtige Zusatzinformationen, die Ihnen die Bearbeitung der Aufgaben erleichtern. Beim ersten Lesen sollten Sie auch Wörter unterstreichen, deren Bedeutung Sie nicht kennen und auch nicht aus dem Kontext erschließen können.

2. Schlagen Sie nun die Wörter nach, die Sie beim ersten Lesen nicht verstehen bzw. erschließen konnten, und die für das Textverständnis von Bedeutung sind. Oft lassen sich unbekannte Wörter aus dem Zusammenhang bzw. mit Rückgriff auf andere Sprachen erschließen.

3. Bevor Sie den Text nun erneut lesen, sollten Sie die Aufgabenstellungen einer genauen Betrachtung unterziehen. Achten Sie auf die verwendeten Operatoren – diese „verraten" Ihnen, was genau Ihre Aufgabe ist bzw. welche Aspekte sie untersuchen sollen. Auch im Abitur werden Sie die „Dreiteilung" in „Comprehension",

„Analysis“ und „Evaluation: Comment/re-creation of text“ vorfinden. Beachten Sie: Bei der Bearbeitung der „Comprehension“-Aufgabe sollen – im Gegensatz zur „Analysis“-Aufgabe – keine Zitate und Textverweise verwendet werden!

4. Lesen Sie nun den Ausgangstext erneut und nehmen Sie zunächst (farbige) Markierungen und Randbemerkungen für die Bearbeitung der ersten Aufgabe vor. Auf einem separaten Blatt sollten Sie darüber hinaus Stichpunkte anfertigen, die Ihnen die anschließende Bearbeitung der jeweiligen Aufgabenstellung erleichtern. Bevor Sie die Stichpunkte ausformulieren, empfiehlt es sich, diese in eine sinnvolle Reihenfolge zu bringen, etwa durch Nummerierung. Denken Sie daran, Ihre Ausführungen zur ersten Aufgabe mit einem entsprechenden Einleitungssatz (Nennung von Autor, Titel, Textsorte, Erscheinungsdatum, Quelle und Thema) zu beginnen. Anschließend wenden Sie diese Verfahrensweise auf die Aufgaben 2 und 3 an. Für die Aufgaben 2 und 3 ist es nicht notwendig, den Einleitungssatz der ersten Aufgabe zu wiederholen – Ihr Leser weiß ja nun, welcher Ausgangstext Ihren Ausführungen zugrunde liegt! Es ist allerdings notwendig, kurz darzulegen, welche Aspekte nachfolgend untersucht bzw. bearbeitet werden.

5. Nachdem Sie alle Aufgaben bearbeitet haben, sollten Sie ausreichend Zeit (ca. 20 Minuten) einplanen, um Ihre Klausur Korrektur zu lesen. Achten Sie auf Ihre individuellen Fehlerschwerpunkte!

In der schriftlichen Abiturprüfung haben Sie im Fach Englisch im Grund- und im Leistungskurs die Auswahl zwischen jeweils zwei Klausurvorschlägen.
Hierbei handelt es sich stets um einen literarischen Text und einen Sach- oder Gebrauchstext – möglicherweise in Kombination mit einem Cartoon, einer Grafik oder einer Statistik.

Sie haben 30 Minuten Zeit, sich mit beiden Themenvorschlägen zu befassen und einen der beiden zur Bearbeitung auswählen. Der nicht gewählte Vorschlag verbleibt bei Ihnen. Theoretisch könnten Sie sich nach zwei Stunden noch umentscheiden. TUN SIE DIES JA NICHT! Wenn Sie sich entschieden haben, legen Sie den Vorschlag weit weg, am besten auf den Boden, um Verwechslungen zu vermeiden!
Anschließend dürfen Sie sofort mit der Bearbeitung des von Ihnen gewählten Vorschlags beginnen, d.h. Sie müssen nicht das Ende der dreißigminütigen Auswahlzeit abwarten.

Nur ein- und zweisprachige Wörterbücher und der Duden (für die Sprachmittlung) sind in der Klausur als Hilfsmittel zugelassen.
Bislang bezieht sich dies jedoch ausschließlich auf Wörterbücher in Printform. Elektronische Wörterbücher sind also im Abitur nicht erlaubt.

Kommunikative Textgestaltung

Aufgabenbezug, Textformate, Textaufbau, Ökonomie, Belegtechnik

Aufgabenbezug

Hier wird bewertet, ob der von Ihnen verfasste Text konsequent an der jeweiligen Aufgabenstellung ausgerichtet ist.
Dies hört sich recht banal an, doch aufgrund des im Unterricht erworbenen Vorwissens zu einem bestimmten Themenbereich ist in Klausuren die Versuchung oft groß, eben dieses Wissen in seiner Gesamtheit abzubilden und sich damit zu verzetteln.
Achten Sie also genau darauf, was von Ihnen verlangt wird. Auch hier hilft Ihnen das Anfertigen von Stichpunkten zu den verschiedenen Aufgaben dabei, Ihre Gedanken zu bündeln und nicht den Überblick zu verlieren.
Die im Abitur gestellten Aufgaben enthalten stets die vom Schulministerium aufgelisteten Operatoren, die Sie auch auf S. 14 in diesem Buch finden.
Den verschiedenen Anforderungsbereichen („Comprehension", „Analysis" und „Evaluation") sind unterschiedliche Operatoren zugeordnet, deren Bedeutung klar definiert ist.
Vor Bearbeitung der konkreten Aufgaben empfiehlt es sich, die Aufgabenstellung genau in den Blick zu nehmen. Es ist hilfreich, wenn Sie die verwendeten Operatoren farbig markieren und dann für sich die folgenden Fragen beantworten:

- Welche Operatoren werden verwendet?
- Was wird konkret von mir erwartet?
- In Hinblick auf welche inhaltlichen Schwerpunkte soll ich bei der Aufgabe „Comprehension" den Text wiedergeben? Welche Gestaltungsmerkmale/stilistischen Mittel innerhalb des Textes soll ich bei Bearbeitung der Aufgabe zur „Analysis" näher untersuchen?
- Welches Zieltextformat wird bei der Aufgabe „Evaluation/re-creation of text" verlangt?

Textformate

TIPP zum Punktesammeln

Beim Verfassen der Zieltexte sollten Sie stets darauf achten, welche Textsorte Sie produzieren sollen. Eine Übersicht über die verschiedenen Zieltextformate, die in Klausuren von Ihnen verlangt werden können, finden Sie ab Seite 104 in diesem Buch.
Denken Sie daran, bei den oben genannten Teilaufgaben keine ***short forms*** wie *don't, isn't* oder Ähnliches zu verwenden.

Nachfolgend finden Sie eine allgemeine **Übersicht** über die Konventionen der verschiedenen Zieltextformate innerhalb der Schreibaufgabe:

Comprehension:

Beginnen Sie Ihre Ausführungen mit einem **Einleitungssatz** (Autor, Titel, Textsorte, Publikation, Ort und Jahr der Erscheinung). Sollte es sich bei dem Ihnen vorliegenden Text um einen Textauszug handeln oder sollte der Text an eine ganz bestimmte Zielgruppe gerichtet sein, dann merken Sie dies ebenfalls im Einleitungssatz an.
Zitate und Textverweise sind bei Teilaufgabe 1 **nicht angebracht.**

Analysis:

Während bei Aufgabe 1 eine erste inhaltliche Annäherung an den Text erfolgen soll, wird bei der zweiten Aufgabe **eine detaillierte Analyse des Ausgangstextes** unter Beachtung der in der Aufgabenstellung genannten Gesichtspunkte und **mit Rückgriff auf Zitate** beziehungsweise **Textverweise** verlangt.
Die Bearbeitung der zweiten Teilaufgabe sollte in einem **sachlich-neutralen Stil** erfolgen. Eine Darstellung der eigenen Meinung beziehungsweise eine Wertung erfolgen also nicht.
Zu den verschiedenen Herangehensweisen an die Analyse von literarischen Texten sowie von Sach- und Gebrauchstexten sei auf das entsprechende Kapitel in diesem Buch verwiesen (S. 79).

Evaluation:

Bei der dritten Aufgabe („evaluation") haben Sie die Wahl zwischen zwei unterschiedlichen Aufgabentypen: der Kommentierung eines entsprechenden Sachverhalts („comment") und einer kreativen Schreibaufgabe („re-creation of text").

Comment:

Hier sind Sie aufgefordert, Ihrer **eigene Meinung** zu einem beziehungsweise **Ihre subjektive Sicht auf einen bestimmten Sachverhalt** zu erörtern und begründen.

Achten Sie darauf, Ihre Argumentation **logisch** zu entwickeln und die einzelnen Argumente sinnvoll aneinander anzuschließen.
Ihre Ausführungen sollten mit einem **abschließenden Fazit** enden.

Re-creation of text:

Sollte es bei der kreativen Aufgabe durch die Vorgabe der anzufertigenden Textsorte (z. B. Dialog, Blog-Eintrag, E-Mail, innerer Monolog) nicht zwangsläufig gefordert sein, sollten Sie beim Verfassen Ihres Zieltextes auch bei Aufgabe 3.2 (bzw. 4.2) auf die Verwendung umgangssprachlicher Formulierungen, Slang und Kurzformen *(can't, wouldn't, doesn't* usw.) unbedingt verzichten.
Achten Sie auch stets darauf, an wen Ihr Zieltext gerichtet sein soll. Bei Verfassen eines *speech script* ist es zum Beispiel mit Blick auf das Vorwissen und den Erfahrungsschatz des Adressaten ein großer Unterschied, ob Sie sich an eine Gruppe von

High School-Absolventen oder eine Versammlung von Managern richten. Dies sollten Sie durch die Verwendung passender sprachlicher Mittel kennzeichnen.

Textaufbau

Der von Ihnen verfasste Text soll für die Leserinnen und Leser leicht lesbar sein – und das nicht nur mit Hinblick auf das Schriftbild und die formale Gestaltung.
Mit „Textaufbau“ ist vielmehr gemeint, dass ein für die Leserinnen und Leser leicht erkennbarer „roter Faden“ durch Ihren Text führt und der von Ihnen verfasste Text klar und sachgerecht strukturiert ist.
Damit ist gemeint, dass Sie Ihren Text in klar erkennbare Abschnitte gliedern, die auch inhaltliche Sinneinheiten ergeben. Leiten Sie neue Gedanken durch die Verwendung von ***signal words*** (etwa *First ..., Second ..., Third, ...)* ein. Diese ermöglichen Ihnen die sinnvolle Gliederung Ihres Textes und strukturieren diesen auch für die Leserinnen und Leser in klare Einheiten.
Denken Sie daran, Ihre Argumentation logisch aufzubauen und vermeiden Sie Gedankensprünge, die den Leserinnen und Lesern das Textverständnis erschweren.
Durch Verwendung geeigneter Konnektoren gelingt es Ihnen, Ihre Argumente und Beobachtungen sinnvoll verknüpfen, sodass Ihre Leserinnen und Leser Ihren Ausführungen leicht folgen können.

Nachfolgend eine Übersicht über die wichtigsten Konnektoren:

Reihung von Argumenten

and	und
first(ly), ... second(ly), ... third(ly),	erstens, zweitens, drittens
furthermore,	außerdem, darüber hinaus
in addition to	zusätzlich zu
moreover,	ferner, überdies
not only ... but also	nicht nur ... sondern auch
as well as	sowie
finally,	schließlich

Gegensatz

but	aber, sondern
although	obwohl
however,	jedoch
despite the fact that	trotz der Tatsache, dass
in spite of	trotz
nevertheless, nonetheless,	nichtsdestotrotz
even so,	selbst dann

on the contrary	im Gegensatz dazu
on the one hand, ... on the other hand,	einerseits ... andererseits
unlike	anders als
whereas	während/wogegen/indessen
while/whilst	während (dagegen)
yet	dennoch

Bedingung

if	falls, wenn
unless	wenn nicht
otherwise	ansonsten

Folge

because	weil
since	da
so	daher
consequently,	folglich
as a result,	demzufolge
therefore,	daher, deshalb
due to	infolge
accordingly,	daher
that is why	deshalb

Vergleich

like	wie
in comparison with	im Vergleich zu
similarly,	ähnlich
equally,	gleichermaßen

Autorenintention

An mehreren Stellen in Ihrer Abiturklausur werden Sie Ihre eigenen Aussagen in Relation zur Autorenmeinung setzen müssen. Dafür empfiehlt es sich, eine Reihe von sprachlichen Ausdrücken parat zu haben, z. B.:

He/She points out/argues that ...	Er weist darauf hin/argumentiert, dass ...
He implies/claims/states that ...	Er behauptet, dass ...
He/She believes/suggests ...	Er/Sie glaubt/schlägt vor ...

He/She emphasizes ...	Er/Sie legt sein/ihr Hauptaugenmerk auf ...
His/Her idea was to ...	Er/Sie wollte ...
He/She writes with the intention of (+ gerund) ...	Er/Sie schreibt mit der Absicht ...
His/Her aim is to ...	Sein/Ihr Ziel ist es ...
His/Her attitude towards ...	Seine/Ihre Einstellung gegenüber ...
When he/she says/writes ... he/she means that ...	Wenn er/sie sagt/schreibt ..., meint er/sie ...
According to the author ...	Dem Autor/der Autorin zufolge ...

Ökonomie

TIPP zum Punktesammeln

Vorweg: Der Umfang des von Ihnen verfassten Zieltextes ist nicht zwangsläufig ausschlaggebend für die Qualität Ihrer Klausur. Bearbeiten Sie die Ihnen gestellten Aufgaben zielgerichtet und hinreichend ausführlich, aber vermeiden Sie inhaltliche Doppelungen. Anstatt einen Sachverhalt zu wiederholen, sollten Sie auf bereits erfolgte Erläuterungen zurückverweisen.
Verwenden Sie konkrete Beispiele, um komplexe Sachverhalte zu illustrieren.

Belegetechnik

Um Ihre Aussagen zu belegen, fügen Sie geeignete Zitate aus dem Originaltext in Ihre Antworten ein. Setzen Sie diese in englische Anführungszeichen – diese beginnen oben und enden oben. Da es sich in der Abiturklausur um einen relativ kurzen Ausgangstext handelt, genügt als Quellenangabe die Angabe der Zeilennummer in Klammern direkt hinter dem Zitat.

Beispiel zu Shakespeare, *Romeo and Juliet:*

In his speech Prince Escalus speaks about the Montagues and the Capulets as "enemies to peace" (l. 1) and finishes by even menacing them with "pain of death" (l. 23).
Verwenden Sie nicht das ganze Zitat, können Sie die ausgelassenen Passagen mit eckigen Klammern kennzeichnen. Genauso können Sie ein Bezugswort in eckigen Klammern einfügen, wenn dies aufgrund der Satzkonstruktion notwendig ist.
Die wörtliche Übernahme von Formulierungen aus dem Ausgangstext bzw. einem anderen Text ohne entsprechende Kennzeichnung ist nicht zulässig und wird negativ bewertet.
Da mit Zitaten Aussagen belegt oder gefestigt werden, stehen sie normalerweise nach der entsprechenden Behauptung. Diese sollten Sie zunächst mit eigenen Worten paraphrasieren. Nehmen Sie dabei Ihr einsprachiges Wörterbuch zur Hilfe, um nach Synonymen zu suchen.

Ausdrucksvermögen/Verfügbarkeit sprachlicher Mittel

Eigenständigkeit, allgemeiner und thematischer Wortschatz, Textbesprechungs- und Textproduktionswortschatz, Satzbau

Eigenständigkeit

Es wird in Klausuren von Ihnen erwartet, dass Sie einen eigenständigen Text formulieren und sich vom Ausgangstext lösen. Sie sollen also nicht Formulierungen aus dem Ausgangstext in Ihren Text übernehmen, ohne diese kenntlich zu machen.
Selbstverständlich können und sollen Sie aus dem Ausgangstext zitieren, um eigene Gedanken zu stützen. Allerdings müssen Sie Zitate auch immer als solche kennzeichnen, damit die Eigenständigkeit Ihrer Leistung zu erkennen ist.
Die Vorgaben des Ministeriums weisen aber auch darauf hin, dass „ein punktuell das Sprachmaterial des Ausgangstextes kreativ verarbeitendes Vorgehen (...) durchaus erwünscht (ist)." Dies ist insbesondere beim Aufgabentyp 3.2 (bzw. 4.2) der Fall.

Allgemeiner und thematischer Wortschatz

Es wird erwartet, dass Sie sich sachlich und stilistisch angemessen ausdrücken (Beachten Sie das jeweilige Zieltextformat!). In diesem Buch finden Sie eine Vielzahl von Wortlisten, die Ihnen dabei helfen können, Ihren thematischen Wortschatz zu den einzelnen Unterrichtsinhalten zu festigen und zu erweitern.
Auch Wortwiederholungen sollten Sie vermeiden. Nachfolgend finden Sie eine Übersicht über Synonyme für häufig verwendete Wörter und Begriffe. Diese ermöglichen Ihnen, sich variantenreich auszudrücken und einen abwechslungsreich formulierten Text zu verfassen.

to say (im Sinne von „sagen"/„ausdrücken")

state, remark, announce, affirm, assert, maintain, declare, express, put into words, tell, phrase, communicate, make known, convey, reveal, disclose, indicate, suggest

to see (im Sinne von „erkennen"/„verstehen")

grasp, get, comprehend, follow, take in, know, realize, discover, learn

to think (im Sinne von „denken"/„meinen")

believe, suppose, expect, imagine, surmise, conjecture, guess, consider

to understand

comprehend, apprehend, grasp, see, take in, recognize, think, believe, conclude

because/because of

because: since, as, in view of the fact that, owing to the fact that, seeing that because of: on account of, as a result of, owing to, by reason of, as a consequence of, thanks to, by virtue of

many

numerous, a large/great number of, great quantities, multiple, various, several, frequent

few

not many, a small number, one or two, a handful

in addition to (im Sinne von „zusätzlich")

additionally, besides, as well (as)

furthermore (im Sinne von „außerdem")

moreover, further, additionally, on top of that, also, as well

Vermeiden Sie auch sogenannte ***false friends.*** Als *false friends* werden Wörter und Begriffe bezeichnet, von denen man annimmt, dass sie in Mutter- und Fremdsprache die gleiche Bedeutung haben, weil sie sich im Schriftbild oder in der Aussprache ähneln beziehungsweise ein identisches Schriftbild oder eine identische Aussprache besitzen. Ein bekanntes Beispiel ist das im Deutschen für Mobiltelefone verwendete Wort „handy", welches im Englisch zwar existiert, aber im Englischen unter anderem „geschickt" und „praktisch" bedeutet.

Hier finden Sie eine Übersicht über häufig miteinander verwechselte *false friends:*

deutsch	**englisch**	***false friend***
bekommen	to get	nicht: become
die Kritik	criticism	nicht: critic – der Kritiker
die Politik	politics	nicht: policy – persönliche Strategie – außer in Begriffen wie „foreign policy" = Außenpolitik
sensibel	sensitive	nicht: sensible – vernünftig

meinen/ glauben	to think	nicht: mean – bedeuten (oder Adj. = gemein)
aktuell	current	nicht: actually – in der Tat
also	so	nicht: also – auch
brav	honest, good	nicht: brave – mutig, tapfer
Chef	boss	nicht chef – der Küchenchef
engagiert	committed	nicht: engaged – verlobt; besetzt
eventuell	possibly	nicht: eventually – schließlich
Handy	mobile phone (AE: cell phone)	nicht: handy – handlich, praktisch
Konfession	denomination	nicht: confession – die Beichte
Konkurrenz	competition	nicht concurrence – Zusammentreffen
konsequent	consistent	nicht: consequently – folglich
Lager	warehouse	nicht: department store – Warenhaus
mobben	to bully	nicht: mob – das gemeine Volk
Mörder	murderer	nicht: murder – der Mord
prägnant	concise	nicht: pregnant – schwanger
prinzipiell	fundamentally, basically, in/on principle	nicht: principally – hauptsächlich
Prospekt	brochure, leaflet	nicht: prospect(s) – die Zukunftsaussichten
Protokoll	minutes	nicht: protocol – die Etikette (außer bei EDV)
Publikum	audience	nicht: public – die Öffentlichkeit
rentabel	profitable	nicht: rentable – zu mieten
Rückseite	back	nicht: backside – Hinterteil
spenden	to donate	nicht: to spend – ausgeben

Textbesprechungs- und Textproduktionswortschatz

Selbstverständlich ist es von großer Bedeutung, dass Sie nicht nur die entsprechenden Zieltextformate erstellen, sondern dass Sie dabei auch die entsprechenden sprachlichen Mittel verwenden.
Nachfolgend erhalten Sie einen ersten Überblick darüber, welche Art von Vokabular bei den Teilaufgaben 1, 2 und 3 des Klausurenteils A von Ihnen erwartet wird.

Teilaufgabe 1: Um diese Aufgabe erfolgreich bearbeiten zu können, sollten Sie über Vokabular zur Wiedergabe und Zusammenfassung von Inhalten verfügen.

Teilaufgabe 2: Grundsätzlich ist die Analyse eines Ausgangstextes (dies können auch Filmausschnitte, Karikaturen, Grafiken usw. sein) Gegenstand der zweiten Teilaufgabe. Vokabellisten, die Ihnen die Analyse von Texten erleichtern können, finden Sie im Kapitel „Methoden der Textarbeit“ (S. 79) in diesem Buch.

Teilaufgabe 3.1: Zur Bearbeitung dieser Teilaufgabe ist vor allen Dingen Vokabelmaterial zur eigenen Meinungsäußerung und Bewertung von Sachverhalten erforderlich. Wichtige Redewendungen sind in der nachfolgenden Übersicht enthalten.

Teilaufgabe 3.2: Bei dieser Teilaufgabe müssen Sie darauf achten, welches Zieltextformat von Ihnen verlangt wird, und das von Ihnen verwendete Vokabular entsprechend anpassen. Die verschiedenen Zieltextformate werden Ihnen auf den Seiten 104–113 genauer vorgestellt.

Eine Sicherheit ausdrücken

The fact is that ...	Es ist eine Tatsache, dass ...
It cannot be denied that ...	Man kann nicht leugnen, dass ...
It goes without saying that ...	Selbstredend ...
Undoubtedly, ...	Zweifellos (am Satzanfang) ...
I am convinced that ...	Ich bin überzeugt davon, dass ...
It is indisputable/obvious that ... There is no doubt that ...	Es ist unbestreitbar/offensichtlich/ kein Zweifel, dass ...
It is inevitable that ...	Es ist unvermeidbar, dass ...

Eine Vermutung ausdrücken

Apparently, ...	Anscheinend (am Satzanfang) ...
They will probably ...	Sie werden wahrscheinlich ...
It seems highly likely that ...	Es scheint äußerst wahrscheinlich, dass ...

It may be the case that ...	Es kann sein, dass ...

Einen Zweifel ausdrücken

It is doubtful whether ...	Es ist zweifelhaft, ob ...
I wonder if ...	Ich frage mich, ob ...
There is no proof/evidence that ...	Es gibt keine Beweise, dass ...

Einen Sachverhalt betonen

In order to stress that ...	Um hervorzuheben, dass ...
to emphasize	betonen
I would like to make it clear that ...	Ich möchte klarstellen, dass ...

Eine Meinung ausdrücken

In my opinion/To my mind/From my point of view	Meiner Meinung nach
My thoughts on the subject are ...	Meine Meinung zu diesem Thema ist ...
Personally, I think/My personal view is that ...	Ich persönlich denke, dass ...
As far as I am concerned ...	Was mich angeht ...
From my point of view	Aus meiner Sicht
I assume	Ich vermute
I am (not) convinced that ...	Ich bin (nicht) überzeugt davon, dass ...
I can't help thinking that ...	Ich kann nicht umhin zu denken, dass ...
I get the impression that ...	Ich habe den Eindruck, dass ...
I am afraid that ...	Ich fürchte, dass (abschwächend) ...
Honestly, ... To be honest, ...	Ehrlich gesagt ...
I can't judge ...	Ich kann ... nicht beurteilen
I am in no position to say ...	Es steht mir nicht zu, mich zu ... zu äußern.

Einen Widerspruch einräumen

in contrast to	im Gegensatz zu
On the contrary, ...	Ganz im Gegenteil (am Satzanfang)
whereas	während (dagegen)
I strongly object to ...	Ich spreche mich deutlich gegen ... aus

One could argue that ... but ...	Man könnte argumentieren, dass ... , aber ...
Although it is true that ... it would be wrong to claim that ...	Obwohl es wahr ist, dass ..., wäre es falsch zu behaupten, dass ...

Zustimmung ausdrücken

Fortunately, ...	Glücklicherweise (am Satzanfang)
I entirely agree with/I share the opinion that ...	Ich stimme vollkommen mit ... überein
I support his view.	Ich unterstütze seine Meinung.
I share her views.	Ich teile ihre Meinung.
I am of the same opinion (as) ...	Ich bin der gleichen Meinung (wie) ...
I approve of his/her opinion.	Ich bin mit seiner/ihrer Meinung einverstanden.
I take your point about ...	Ich akzeptiere Ihre Meinung über ...
I am in favour of ...	Ich bin für ...
He rightly mentions that ...	Zu Recht betont er, dass ...
I won't object to ...	Ich widerspreche ... nicht.
It cannot be justified that ...	Es gibt keine Rechtfertigung für ...
Nobody would disagree with that statement.	Niemand würde dieser Behauptung widersprechen.
This statement is very convincing.	Diese Aussage ist sehr überzeugend.
I have to admit that the author ...	Ich muss zugeben, dass der Autor/die Autorin ...

Ablehnung ausdrücken

It is only partly true that ...	Es entspricht nur teilweise der Wahrheit, dass ...
I disagree completely with ...	Ich muss widersprechen ...
I see things differently.	Ich sehe den Sachverhalt anders.
I (must) have to disagree on this matter.	Ich bin in dieser Angelegenheit anderer Meinung.
One cannot possibly accept that ...	Man kann unmöglich akzeptieren, dass ...
I must object to	Ich muss ... widersprechen.
I have to criticize strongly that	Ich muss scharf kritisieren, dass ...
I doubt whether	Ich bezweifle, dass ...
This statement entirely contradicts ...	Diese Behauptung widerspricht ganz und gar ...

However, ...	jedoch (am Satzanfang)
It is not as simple as it seems.	Es ist nicht so einfach wie es scheint.
Unlike the author, I think ...	Abweichend vom Autor/der Autorin glaube ich ...
I cannot share the author's view on ...	Ich kann die Meinung des Autors/der Autorin über ... nicht teilen.

Einen Grund angeben

As/Since	Da/Weil (am Satzanfang)
In view of the fact that ...	Angesichts der Tatsache, dass ...
The reason for this development lies in ...	Der Grund für diese Entwicklung liegt bei ...
This causes confusion.	Das sorgt für Verwirrung.
That is why	Aus diesem Grund
Given that ...	In Anbetracht der Tatsache, dass ...
therefore	deshalb
That was caused by ...	Das wurde verursacht durch ...
For this reason/purpose	Aus diesem Grund

Eine Folge darstellen

Consequently, ... /As a consequence,	Folglich (am Satzanfang)
In view of this statement	In Anbetracht dieser Behauptung
in order to	um zu
as a result of	als Folge von

Vergleiche anstellen

to be comparable	vergleichbar sein
compared to/in comparison with	im Vergleich zu
to be different from	sich unterscheiden von
differentiate between (A and B)	(A von B) unterscheiden
to be considerably better than	wesentlich besser sein als
get more and more difficult	immer schwieriger werden
Nowadays, it is less and less common	Heutzutage ist es immer weniger üblich
superior/inferior to	überlegen/unterlegen
The former ... the latter	Der erstere ... der letztere
They have little in common.	Sie haben wenig gemeinsam.
They are equal in price.	Sie haben den gleichen Preis.

Beispiele anführen

For example/For instance	Zum Beispiel
Let me give you an example.	Lassen Sie mich ein Beispiel anführen.
such as	wie (zum Beispiel)
Look at ...	Sehen wir uns einmal ... an.

Conclusion

To sum up, ...	Zusammenfassend kann man sagen ...
I come to the conclusion that ...	Ich komme zu der Schlussfolgerung, dass ...
In short, ...	Kurz gesagt
To put it all in a nutshell ...	Um es auf einen Nenner zu bringen
I can support the author's view on ...	Ich kann die Ansicht des Autors/der Autorin über ... unterstützen
To summarize, ...	Um das zusammenzufassen ...
All in all, I believe that ...	Insgesamt glaube ich ...

Satzbau

Ein abwechslungsreicher und klarer Satzbau erleichtert Ihren Leserinnen und Lesern die Lesbarkeit Ihres Textes.

TIPP zum Punktesammeln

Versuchen Sie nicht krampfhaft, mehrere Gedanken in einen Satz zu packen. Bedenken Sie: Überlange Sätze sind fehleranfälliger als mehrere kurze, prägnante und sinnvoll miteinander verbundene Sätze.

Machen Sie sich gegebenenfalls noch einmal mit den grammatischen Eigenschaften von z. B. Aktiv- und Passivkonstruktionen sowie Gerundial-, Partizipial und Infinitivkonstruktionen vertraut.

Sprachliche Richtigkeit

Wortschatz und Grammatik

Zu den Bereichen Wortschatz und Grammatik ist an anderer Stelle in diesem Buch schon einiges gesagt worden. Der Übersicht des Ministeriums auf der nächsten Seite können Sie entnehmen, wie die für diese Kriterien maximal erreichbaren Punkte aufgeteilt sind.

Orthografie

Beim Verfassen eines Klausurtextes passiert es schnell, dass sich Rechtschreibfehler einschleichen.
Daher ist es wichtig, dass Sie zum Korrekturlesen Ihres Textes genug Zeit einplanen. Achten Sie insbesondere auf Wörter, deren Aussprache oder Schreibweise zwar ähnlich oder sogar identisch ist, deren Bedeutung aber eine vollkommen andere ist, beispielsweise„sale“ (Verkauf) und „sail“ (das Segel, segeln).

Orientierungsangaben des Ministeriums für den Bereich Sprachrichtigkeit

Punkte	Wortschatz	Grammatik	Orthographie
volle Punktzahl ↕ keine Punkte	• Der Wortgebrauch (Struktur – und Inhaltswörter) ist fast über den gesamten Text hinweg korrekt. • Vereinzelt ist eine falsche Wortwahl feststellbar. Abschnitte bzw. Textpassagen sind weitgehend frei von lexikalischen Verstößen. • Einzelne Sätze sind frei von lexikalischen Verstößen. Fehler beim Wortgebrauch beeinträchtigen z. T. das Lesen und Verstehen. • In nahezu jedem Satz sind Schwächen im korrekten Gebrauch der Wörter feststellbar. Die Mängel im Wortgebrauch erschweren das Lesen und Textverständnis erheblich und verursachen Missverständnisse.	• Der Text ist weitgehend frei von Verstößen gegen Regeln der Grammatik. Wenn Grammatikfehler auftreten, betreffen sie den komplexen Satz und sind ein Zeichen dafür, dass die Schülerin/der Schüler Risiken beim Verfassen des Textes eingeht, um sich dem Leser differenziert mitzuteilen. • Es sind vereinzelt Verstöße gegen die Regeln der Grammatik feststellbar. Jedoch sind Abschnitte bzw. Textpassagen weitgehend frei von Grammatikfehlern. Das Lesen des Textes wird durch die auftretenden Grammatikfehler nicht erschwert. • Einzelne Sätze sind frei von Verstößen gegen grundlegende Regeln der Grammatik. Grammatikfehler beeinträchtigen z. T. das Lesen und Verstehen. • In nahezu jedem Satz ist wenigstens ein Verstoß gegen die grundlegenden Regeln der Grammatik feststellbar. Diese erschweren das Lesen erheblich und verursachen Missverständnisse.	• Der Text ist weitgehend frei von Verstößen gegen orthographische Normen. Wenn vereinzelt Orthographiefehler auftreten, haben sie den Charakter von Flüchtigkeitsfehlern, d. h. sie deuten nicht auf Unkenntnis von Regeln hin. • Es sind zwar durchaus Orthographiefehler feststellbar, jedoch sind Abschnitte bzw. Textpassagen weitgehend ohne Verstoß gegen orthographische Normen. Das Lesen des Textes wird durch die auftretenden Orthographiefehler nicht wesentlich beeinträchtigt. • Einzelne Sätze sind frei von Verstößen gegen orthographische Normen, Orthographiefehler beeinträchtigen z. T. das Lesen und Verstehen. • In nahezu jedem Satz ist wenigstens ein Verstoß gegen die Regeln der Orthographie feststellbar. Die Orthographiefehler erschweren das Lesen erheblich und verursachen Missverständnisse.

Quelle: https://www.standardsicherung.schulministerium.nrw.de/cms/zentralabitur-gost/faecher/getfile.php?file=4307)

Stichwortverzeichnis

Quellenverzeichnis

Textquellen:

- “Correspondences”, http://academic.brooklyn.cuny.edu/english/melani/cs6/ren.html (S. 56)
- „Orientierungsangaben zur Sprachrichtigkeit“: www.schulministerium.nrw.de unter dem Link „Standardsicherung“ (S. 219)
- „Themenfelder des Kernlehrplans“ (Vorgaben Abitur 2018): www.schulministerium.nrw.de unter dem Link „Standardsicherung“ (vollständige Übersicht); https://www.standardsicherung.schulministerium.nrw.de/cms/zentralabitur-gost/faecher/getfile.php?file=4586 (S. 9)
- Berndt, Christina: „Im Wohlfühl-Ort“, in: Süddeutsche Zeitung, 30. Dezember 2010; http://www.sueddeutsche.de/wissen/gemischte-gefuehle-heimatgefuehl-im-wohlfuehlort-1.1041384 (Zugriff : 20.04.2017) (S. 189)
- Betzholz, Dennis: „Die Tragödie der Kinder-Flüchtlinge“, in: Welt, 20. April 2015, https://www.welt.de/vermischtes/article139802318/Die-Tragoedie-der-Kinder-Fluechtlinge.html (Zugriff : 09.05.2017) (S. 179)
- Chamorro-Premuzic, Tomas: “Are millennials as bad as we think?”, *The Guardian,* Friday 24 January 2014 15.59 GMT Last modified on Wednesday 3 September 2014 15.27 BST (online); https://www.theguardian.com/media-network/media-network-blog/2014/jan/24/millennials-generation-gap, Copyright Guardian News & Media Ltd 2019
- Clinton, Hillary: “Keynote Address”: Rede vom 14.08.2014, http://www.newamerica.net/conference2014/keynote_by_the_honorable_hillary_rodham_clinton (S. 144)
- Dückers, Tanja: „Von Geburt an Multikulturalist“, Die Zeit Online, 6.2.2015 http://www.zeit.de/gesellschaft/zeitgeschehen/2015-02/europa-identitaet-migration-einwanderung/komplettansicht (zuletzt abgerufen: 26.4.2019) (S. 130)
- Grundsätze für die Bewertung (Notenfindung) von der Website des Schulministeriums (Bildungsserver NRW), Standardsicherung, z. B. in: „Unterlagen für die Lehrkraft“ (S. 17)
- Günther, Frank: „Sein oder Nichtsein?“, *Frankfurter Neue Presse* 19.04.2014, online; http://www.fnp.de/nachrichten/kultur/Sein-oder-Nichtsein;art679,820195 (S. 161)
- Heimann, Klaus: „Drei Monate Uni, drei Monate Büro“, ©Klaus Heimann für ZEIT ONLINE (www.zeit.de) vom: 29.11.2013, „Drei Monate Uni, drei Monate Büro“ http://www.zeit.de/studium/hochschule/2013-11/duales-studium-ueberblick?print (Zugriff 01.04.2017) (S. 199)
- McGough, Roger: “The Lake”, *Selected Poems,* London: Penguin 2006 (S. 155)
- Morgan, Peter: *The Audience,* London 2015 (Faber and Faber), S. 80-83 (S. 150)
- Oetker, Alexander: „Das hässliche Gesicht der Zuwanderung – Slums mitten in deutschen Großstädten“, rtlNEXT.de 12.02.2014, https://rtlnext.rtl.de/cms/das-haessliche-gesicht-der-zuwanderung-slums-mitten-in-deutschen-grossstaedten-1799988.html (S. 115)

- Olbrisch, Miriam: „Glück- und Sinnsuche im Job. Die Andersmacher", SPIEGEL ONLINE, 12. Dezember 2013, 13:31 Uhr http://www.spiegel.de/karriere/berufsstart/generation-y-und-die-arbeitswelt-die-andersmacher-a-931225.html (S.168)
- Pappano, Laura: "First-Generation Students Unite": from The New York Times, 2015-04-12© 2015 The New York Times. All rights reserved. Used by permission and protected by the Copyright Laws of the United States. The printing, copying, redistribution, or retransmission of this content without express written permission is prohibited. http://www.nytimes.com/2015/04/12/education/edlife/first-generation-students-unite.html (Zugriff: 01.04.2017) (S. 193)
- Paulsen, Gary: *The Crossing* (excerpt), Copyright © 1987 by Gary Paulsen. Reprinted by permission of Orchard Books, an imprint of Scholastic Inc., S. 3–9 (S. 174)
- Riedel, Donata: „Studie zur Chancengerechtigkeit: Sozialer Aufstieg in Deutschland bleibt die Ausnahme – OECD fürchtet Vergeudung von Talent", © Handelsblatt GmbH. Alle Rechte vorbehalten. 15.6.2018, https://www.handelsblatt.com/politik/deutschland/studie-zur-chancengerechtigkeit-sozialer-aufstieg-in-deutschland-bleibt-die-ausnahme-oecd-fuerchtet-vergeudung-von-talent/22690454.html?ticket=ST-7608828-73isM9rStOQV6VEN5bt7-ap5 (S. 145)
- Schäfer, Christoph: „Müll zu trennen reicht nicht": © Alle Rechte vorbehalten. Frankfurter Allgemeine Zeitung GmbH, Frankfurt. Zur Verfügung gestellt vom Frankfurter Allgemeine Archiv; http://www.faz.net/aktuell/wirtschaft/muell-zu-trennen-reicht-nicht-15376781.html#void (aktualisiert am 07.01.2018) (S. 156)
- Schaible, Ira, et al.: „Die Queen kommt: Was Deutschland für den Staatsbesuch vorbereitet", 18.6.2015, © wgr/dpa (S. 149)
- Shakespeare, William: *The Taming of the Shrew,* Act V, Scene 2 (S. 162)
- Sharma, Akhil: *Family Life,* London: Faber & Faber Limited 2015, S. 14–16 (S. 183)
- Swarup, Vikas: *Q&A: Slumdog Millionaire,* Random House UK 2005, S. 156–157 (S. 116)
- White, Neil: "Trick or treat? The worst example of Americanisation in modern society", *Derby Telegraph,* November 03, 2014 (S. 129)

Bildquelle:

- Singer, Andy: Cartoon "Globalization" (S. 130)